# CHARLES DICKENS

*Places and Objects of Interest*

# CHARLES DICKENS

*Places and Objects of Interest*

Paul Kendall

**f**

FRONTLINE
BOOKS

**Charles Dickens: Places and Objects of Interest**

This edition published in 2021 by Frontline Books,
An imprint of Pen & Sword Books Ltd,
Yorkshire - Philadelphia

Copyright © Paul Kendall, 2021

The right of Paul Kendall to be identified as the author of this work has been asserted by him in accordance with the Copyright, Designs and Patents Act 1988.

ISBN 978 1 39909 136 7

All rights reserved. No part of this publication may be reproduced, stored in or introduced into a retrieval system, or transmitted, in any form, or by any means (electronic, mechanical, photocopying, recording or otherwise) without the prior written permission of the publisher. Any person who does any unauthorized act in relation to this publication may be liable to criminal prosecution and civil claims for damages.

CIP data records for this title are available from the British Library

Pen & Sword Books Limited incorporates the imprints of Atlas, Archaeology, Aviation, Discovery, Family History, Fiction, History, Maritime, Military, Military Classics, Politics, Select, Transport, True Crime, Air World, Frontline Publishing, Leo Cooper, Remember When, Seaforth Publishing, The Praetorian Press, Wharncliffe Local History, Wharncliffe Transport, Wharncliffe True Crime and White Owl.

PEN & SWORD BOOKS LTD
47 Church Street, Barnsley, South Yorkshire, S70 2AS, England
E-mail: enquiries@pen-and-sword.co.uk
Website: www.pen-and-sword.co.uk

Or
PEN AND SWORD BOOKS
1950 Lawrence Rd, Havertown, PA 19083, USA
E-mail: Uspen-and-sword@casematepublishers.com

For more information on our books, please visit www.frontline-books.com, email info@frontline-books.com or write to us at the above address.

Printed and bound in India by Replika Press Pvt. Ltd.

Typeset in 10/14pt Adobe Caslon by SJmagic DESIGN SERVICES, India.

# Contents

Introduction ..................................................................................................................8
Acknowledgements ......................................................................................................10

1   No. 1 Mile End Terrace, Portsmouth ..................................................................11
2   No. 22 Cleveland Street, London ........................................................................13
3   Navy Pay Office, Chatham Royal Naval Dockyard.............................................15
4   No. 11 Ordnance Terrace, Chatham ...................................................................17
5   Window of the Little Attic from No. 16 Bayham Street, London .....................19
6   Marshalsea Prison Wall, Southwark, London.....................................................21
7   Warren's Blacking Factory Bottle ........................................................................24
8   The Sign of the Dog's Head in the Pot ...............................................................26
9   Ellis & Blackmore Offices, No. 1 Raymond Buildings, Gray's Inn, London .................28
10  The House of Commons ....................................................................................31
11  *Sketches by Boz*..................................................................................................33
12  Dickens' Memorial and Plaque, Furnival's Inn, London ...................................35
13  Manuscript of *The Pickwick Papers* and Dickens' Quill ....................................37
14  Characters from *The Pickwick Papers* ...............................................................40
15  The Royal Victoria & Bull Hotel, Rochester ......................................................42
16  Charles Dickens' Honeymoon Cottage, Chalk ..................................................44
17  No. 48 Doughty Street, London ........................................................................46
18  Frontispiece of *Oliver Twist* ...............................................................................49
19  Characters from *Oliver Twist* .............................................................................51
20  Cleveland Street Workhouse, London ...............................................................54
21  Jacob's Island......................................................................................................56
22  No. 14 Market Place, Barnard Castle .................................................................58
23  Bowes Academy, Yorkshire .................................................................................60
24  Characters from *Nicholas Nickleby* ...................................................................62
25  Royal Albion Hotel, Broadstairs ........................................................................64
26  Sculptured Panel Commemorating Dickens, Marylebone, London ..................66
27  The Old Curiosity Shop, London ......................................................................69
28  Characters from *The Old Curiosity Shop*...........................................................71

| | | |
|---|---|---|
| 29 | Butler's Wharf | 74 |
| 30 | Statue of Dickens and Little Nell | 76 |
| 31 | Lawn House, Broadstairs | 78 |
| 32 | *Barnaby Rudge* | 80 |
| 33 | Dickens' Pet Raven named Grip | 82 |
| 34 | Bust of Charles Dickens | 84 |
| 35 | *American Notes* | 86 |
| 36 | *Martin Chuzzlewit* | 88 |
| 37 | *A Christmas Carol* | 91 |
| 38 | Palazzo Peschiere, Genoa | 94 |
| 39 | John Forster's Home – 58 Lincoln's Inn Fields, London | 96 |
| 40 | Rosemont Villa, Lausanne, Switzerland | 99 |
| 41 | No. 48 Rue de Courcelles, Paris | 101 |
| 42 | Characters from *Dombey & Son* | 103 |
| 43 | *Children's New Testament* | 105 |
| 44 | Theatre Royal Haymarket, London | 107 |
| 45 | Gates of Winterbourne, Bonchurch, Isle of Wight | 109 |
| 46 | Characters from *David Copperfield* | 111 |
| 47 | Dickens House Museum, Broadstairs | 114 |
| 48 | Office of *Household Words* | 116 |
| 49 | Fort House, Broadstairs | 118 |
| 50 | Tavistock House, London | 121 |
| 51 | Photograph of Charles Dickens, 1852 | 124 |
| 52 | *Bleak House* | 126 |
| 53 | Rockingham Castle | 128 |
| 54 | Birmingham Town Hall | 130 |
| 55 | Proofs of *Hard Times* with Dickens' Annotations | 132 |
| 56 | Letter Regarding Performance of *A Christmas Carol* from Dickens to his Wife | 134 |
| 57 | Le Meurice Hotel, Paris | 136 |
| 58 | No. 3 Albion Villas, Folkestone | 138 |
| 59 | Original Parts of *Little Dorrit* | 141 |
| 60 | Associated Locations in *Little Dorrit* | 144 |
| 61 | Gad's Hill Place, Higham, Kent | 147 |
| 62 | Thomas Carlyle's Statue | 150 |
| 63 | Illustration Depicting Dickens' Performance in *The Frozen Deep* | 153 |
| 64 | Admission Ticket | 155 |
| 65 | Dickens' Speech on Behalf of the Hospital for Sick Children | 157 |
| 66 | Publicity Photographs of Charles Dickens | 159 |
| 67 | The Garrick Club, London | 162 |
| 68 | Catherine Dickens | 164 |

| | | |
|---|---|---|
| 69 | Office of *All the Year Round* | 167 |
| 70 | *A Tale of Two Cities* | 169 |
| 71 | Dickens' Plaque, Campbell Square, Liverpool | 170 |
| 72 | Dickens' Writing Desk | 172 |
| 73 | Cooling Churchyard, Kent | 174 |
| 74 | Restoration House, Rochester | 176 |
| 75 | Rochester High Street | 179 |
| 76 | Music Hall, Newcastle | 181 |
| 77 | King's Arms Hotel, Berwick-upon-Tweed | 183 |
| 78 | Tombstone of Walter Landor Dickens, South Park Cemetery, Calcutta | 185 |
| 79 | *Our Mutual Friend* | 187 |
| 80 | Dickens' Swiss Chalet | 189 |
| 81 | Engraving Depicting the Staplehurst Railway Accident | 191 |
| 82 | St George's Hall, Liverpool | 193 |
| 83 | Door to Dickens' Room at the Parker House, Boston | 195 |
| 84 | Dickens' Mirror at the Parker House, Boston | 198 |
| 85 | Tremont Temple, Boston | 200 |
| 86 | Publicity Photographs of Dickens | 203 |
| 87 | The White House, Washington DC | 205 |
| 88 | Caricature of Dickens Astride the English Channel | 207 |
| 89 | Charles Dickens' Travelling Cutlery Kit | 209 |
| 90 | Dickens' Wooden Walking Stick | 211 |
| 91 | Programme of Dickens' Farewell Readings, St James's Hall | 213 |
| 92 | Dickens' Last Reading | 216 |
| 93 | *The Mystery of Edwin Drood* Locations | 219 |
| 94 | Queen Victoria Monument & Buckingham Palace | 222 |
| 95 | Charles Dickens' Court Suit | 225 |
| 96 | Dickens' Couch | 227 |
| 97 | Drawing Depicting Dickens in Death by Millais | 229 |
| 98 | Tablet indicating Dickens' wish to be buried in Rochester | 231 |
| 99 | Dickens' Grave | 234 |
| 100 | Statue of Charles Dickens, Portsmouth | 237 |

# Introduction

One hundred and fifty years after his death, Charles Dickens has left a substantial legacy of fifteen novels, various short stories and more than 1,500 interesting and diverse characters that were representative of Britain during the nineteenth century. Considered by some to be ranked second only to William Shakespeare, Dickens is regarded as one of Britain's greatest writers. He had the remarkable ability to write stories and create characters that would connect and resonate with his readers, which would touch their hearts. He had the ability to juxtapose tragedy with comedy that would arouse feelings of excitement and sorrow interspersed with joy and laughter. His books would promote kindness, decency and justice for everyone.

He was not only an author, but also a journalist and magazine editor who established the periodicals *Household Words* and *All the Year Round*. As a social reformer, Dickens used these magazines together with his novels as platforms to champion the causes that were close to his heart. Dickens was regarded as the 'Apostle of the Poor' and was able to depict their suffering and struggles in life with compassion. Living on the brink of poverty as a child, he was able to empathise with their plight. His detailed descriptions of squalid and impoverished existence of the less affluent in Victorian society acted as a prism to polarise their plight and raise awareness of the underprivileged in society among the ruling classes. Socially conscious of the injustices in King William IV's and Queen Victoria's Britain, the empathy that radiated throughout Dickens' novels would help bring about reforms and change. It was through his stories he was able to campaign against the Scrooges and the Dombeys who placed a boot on the necks of the poor. In a letter to the Reverend Thomas Robinson on 8 April 1841 Dickens wrote: 'I will pursue cruelty and oppression, the enemy of all God's creatures of all codes and creeds, so long as I have the energy of thought and the power of giving it utterance.'[1]

His understanding for the poor and the downtrodden alongside the inherent social problems in society was shown clearly throughout his novels, which echoed with his readers in those days. He used these novels to champion education for everyone, efficient hospitals, homes for all, the eradication of starvation, improvements in sanitary conditions and the reformation of the prison system.

---

1. Langton, Robert, *The Childhood & Youth of Charles Dickens* (Hutchinson & Co., London, 1891), p.166.

He was an advocate of gender equality and highlighted how women were not treated fairly in Victorian society. Paul Dombey neglecting his daughter Florence in favour of his son is one example where opportunities were granted to sons but not their daughters. Dickens highlighted the plight of the vulnerable in society, through characters entrapped in abusive relationships. Violent and mental abuse was seen in *Little Dorrit*, where Jeremiah Flintwinch abused his wife Affery. Daniel Quilp is another example of an odious man who mistreats his wife in *The Old Curiosity Shop*. Dickens also showed female domestic abuse against a male victim through the blacksmith Joe Gargery, the downtrodden husband threatened with violence by his wife in *Great Expectations*.

The sexual harassment and abuse by those in positions of responsibility and power over vulnerable individuals has been highlighted in recent years by the 'me too' campaign together with successful prosecutions and convictions of high-profile people. Dickens highlighted similar situations in his novels. The suggestive undertones made by Sir Mulberry Hawk to Kate Nickleby in the presence of her uncle, Ralph Nickleby, at the dinner table are reprehensible, and so is Ralph's inability to accept that his titled friend's behaviour is abhorrent. Dickens demonstrated that some men did not have respect for women and that some in powerful positions thought that they could behave as they desired without challenge. Dickens gives Sir Mulberry the surname Hawk, a bird of prey, which can be interpreted as a metaphor of a sexual predator.

The risk of investing capital money in bad investments is still as much a concern today as it was during Dickens' time and he highlighted the consequences of investing unwisely through the experiences of characters in his novels such as Nicholas Nickleby, Arthur Clennam and William Dorrit.

Dickens enjoyed managing and performing in his own amateur dramatic productions, which he would use to raise funds for philanthropic causes such as the preservation of the birthplace of William Shakespeare in Stratford-upon-Avon, preserving the legacy of the esteemed Bard. Dickens' early readings were primarily for charity before he undertook them professionally as a business, and among the benefactors was Great Ormond Street Children's Hospital. He supported this cause from its beginning and his involvement is among his lasting legacies.

It has been testament to his ability as a great writer and storyteller that Dickens' novels have continually been in print since his death 150 years ago and are still popular. They have relevance today because many of the problems that he highlighted, such as child poverty, hunger, homelessness, drug addiction, disease, greed and the balance of wealth, and the lack of opportunity still exist.

George Bernard Shaw wrote that 'there is no "greatest book" of Dickens: all his books form one great life-work: a Bible, in fact.'[2] This body of work has stood the test of time because the advent of television and cinema in the twentieth century created another medium in which to present the novels, and they have been successively interpreted for a modern audience.

---

2. Anonymous, *Charles Dickens, Extra Number of the Bookman*, 1914 (Hodder & Stoughton, London, 1914), p.104.

A hundred versions of Dickens' work were produced during the early years of film and further adaptations have followed. The detailed descriptions of characters, scenes and locations become a substantial primary source for any director embarking on producing an adaptation of Dickens' work. His own serialisations of his novels were the precursor for modern soap operas such as *EastEnders* and *Coronation Street*. People today watch serialisations on television in a similar way as readers were excited to read each monthly instalment of Dickens' stories.

It was evident that Dickens was an able comedy writer, as evidenced in his creation of humorous characters and comic situations, and he possessed the ability to interweave that humour within the drama. He was also a great comedy performer during his readings, with the ability to extract the eccentricities, mannerisms and accents from the character, combined with adopting their facial expressions, comic timing and delivery; Dickens possessed the gift to make people laugh during his reading tours, and would inspire modern-day writers of sitcoms. One example was the late John Sullivan, the creator of *Only Fools & Horses*, who cited Dickens as an influence upon him in how he created characters and placed them in comic situations. Sullivan went on to write the serialisation *Micawber*, based on Dickens' creation Wilkins Micawber.

Dickens helped to purport the cultural phenomenon that surrounds Christmas. His Yuletide stories became the forerunners of Christmas literature and introduced a template of how the season of goodwill has been celebrated in more than 175 years since *A Christmas Carol* was published. His popular depictions of the festive period in *A Christmas Carol* and his sequential Christmas stories promoted kindness and goodwill, which has been adopted by successive generations, not only in Britain but across the world.

The book follows the life and legacy of Dickens within mini-chapters, immersing the reader in a journey back to his time through locations, buildings associated with his life, surviving artefacts, his novels and the characters that he created. They represent the various events in his interesting and creative life, and together they provide an insight into his world.

*Paul Kendall*
*Folkestone, 2020*

# Acknowledgements

I would like to thank Susan Wilson, house historian at the Omni Parker House Hotel in Boston, Massachusetts, for kindly allowing me to use photos supplied from the hotel's archives relating to Dickens' stay at the hotel. I thank Martin Mace and John Grehan, for giving me the opportunity to write this book and their encouragement, and Robert Mitchell for his help with the many images that follow. Finally, I thank my partner Tricia Newsome for her continued support in all my projects.

# 1
# No. 1 Mile End Terrace, Portsmouth

### Birthplace of Charles Dickens

**On 7 February 1812, Dickens was born in this house at No. 1 Mile End Terrace, Landport, Portsea, which is now No. 393 Commercial Road. The house was built in 1808 and was the first marital home of Dickens' parents, John and Elizabeth, who moved there in 1809. Situated in the suburb of Portsmouth and overlooking fields, this plain red-brick building contained four rooms and two attics. It is now the Charles Dickens Birthplace Museum.**

John Dickens worked as a clerk for the Navy Pay Office in Portsmouth Royal Naval Dockyard from 1807 to 1814. It was while working there that he met his wife, Elizabeth, the daughter of his colleague, Charles Barrow, Chief Conductor of Moneys in Town, who introduced them. Barrow abused his position and soon after John married Elizabeth on 13 June 1809 at St Mary-in-the-Strand Church, close to Somerset House in London, he was accused of embezzling the Navy Pay Office of £5,000 during the period of several years. Barrow confessed and absconded from the country.

John and Elizabeth's first child, Fanny, was born at 1 Mile End Terrace in November 1810, followed by Charles in 1812, becoming the second of eight children. On the night before Charles was born, Elizabeth had accepted an invitation to a ball. She enjoyed the evening dancing and then returned to this house to give birth to her first son during the early hours of 7 February in the front bedroom on the first floor.

On 4 March 1812, Dickens was baptised in St Mary's Church in Fratton Road. Although the original church was rebuilt in 1848 and 1887, the font used to baptise Dickens was preserved in the rebuilt church. He was baptised Charles John Huffham Dickens. Charles was the name of his maternal grandfather, Charles Barrow. The second name, John, was after his father. His third name, Huffham, was misspelt and should have been Huffam, after his godfather, who was an affluent rigger from Limehouse who was employed by the Royal Navy and was a friend of John Dickens.

The Dickens family only stayed in this house a further four months after Charles' birth because John Dickens was living beyond his means and was unable to afford the annual rent, which was £35, amounting to a quarter of his £140 annual salary. In June 1812, the Dickens family relocated to cheaper accommodation at 16 Hawke Street, which was close to the

*Above*: Birthplace of Charles Dickens at 393 Commercial Road, Portsmouth. (Shutterstock)

*Left*: Portsmouth home of Charles Dickens in Hawke Street, second house on the left, now demolished. (Author's Collection)

Royal Naval Dockyard. A brother, Alfred, was born in the house at Hawke Street, but he died in infancy. Charles Dickens spent the first two years of his childhood at this address in Portsmouth.

Sarah Pearce, the owner of 393 Commercial Road and the last surviving daughter of John Dickens' landlord, died in 1903 and the property was purchased by Portsmouth Town Council to preserve as the birthplace museum dedicated to Dickens' memory.

# 2
# No. 22 Cleveland Street, London

### Dickens' first London home

**Charles Dickens lived at 22 Cleveland Street, formerly 10 Norfolk Street, in 1815–16 and 1828–31. Situated close to Tottenham Court Road, this Georgian-built townhouse has been acknowledged as his first London residence.**

The defeat of Napoleon at the Battle of Waterloo during 1815 brought an end to the war with France, which meant that there was no requirement to employ a large team of administrators at the Royal Naval Dockyard at Portsmouth. Consequently, John Dickens was transferred to work at the Royal Navy's Administrative Headquarters at Somerset House in London. Charles Dickens was aged three when the family relocated to London and they moved to 10 Norfolk Street in Fitzrovia, which is now 22 Cleveland Street. Letitia, a fourth sibling, was born in this house during 1816.

When the Dickens family returned to live here between 1828 and 1831, Dickens gave 10 Norfolk Street as the address for his reader's ticket at the reading room at British Museum in 1830. He must have been eager to obtain access to the museum's archives because he read in the reading room on 8 February, the day after his eighteenth birthday, the required age to be eligible to apply for a reader's ticket. He was a frequent

Charles Dickens lived here at 22 Cleveland Street, London, as an infant in 1815–16 and later as an adolescent in 1828–31. (Author's Collection)

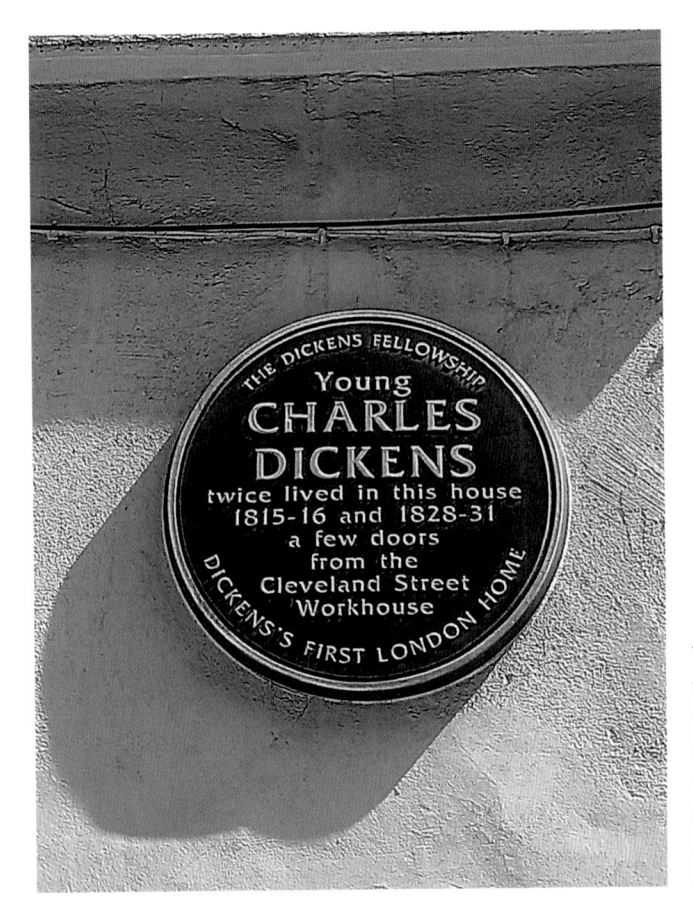

The Dickens Fellowship plaque that recognises 22 Cleveland Street as Dickens' first London home, which was unveiled on 8 June 2013 by his great-great-great-granddaughter Lucinda Dickens Hawksley. (Author's Collection)

visitor to the British Museum while he was living at this address and it is believed that he was studying to learn shorthand during this period.

Dickens would utilise Norfolk Street as the fictional Green Lanes, where the rioters in *Barnaby Rudge* sought refuge. The Strand Union Workhouse (referred to as the Cleveland Street Workhouse on the plaque) was at 44 Cleveland Street. It is conjectured that Dickens was aware of its existence and that he possibly used it as the workhouse in *Oliver Twist*, where Oliver asked the master of the workhouse for more gruel and where a notice offering to sell Oliver for £5 into an apprenticeship was displayed on its gates, although the location was set 70 miles from London in the story.

# 3
# Navy Pay Office, Chatham Royal Naval Dockyard

### John Dickens worked here as a pay clerk from 1817 until 1822

**This red-brick building served as an office for the pay clerks and other staff of the Clerk of the Cheque. John Dickens would frequently bring his infant son Charles to these premises, where he would play on the steps.**

Born the second son of William Dickens and Elizabeth Ball on 21 August 1785, John Dickens' parents worked as servants for John Crewe at Crewe Hall in Cheshire. Sponsored by Crewe, John received a good education and during 1805 he began a career with the Navy Pay Office at Somerset House. After working in Portsmouth, he returned to London, before being transferred to Chatham Royal Naval Dockyard during 1817. It was a nomadic existence, which meant that the Dickens family were unsettled and restless as they moved to different towns.

The Navy Pay Office at Chatham has not changed since John Dickens worked there on the ground floor. He received an increase in salary, rising to £200 per year and he was responsible for attending to the regular muster of labourers and craftsmen employed within the dockyard, as well as receiving arriving ships to pay the crews. William Thomas Wright was the head of the Navy Pay Office at Chatham Dockyard and remembered John Dickens to be 'a fellow of infinite humour, chatty, lively and agreeable; and believed him capable to have imparted to his son Charles materials for some of the characteristic local sketches of men and manners, so graphically hit off in the early chapters of Pickwick'.[3] It is believed that Dickens' father was the inspiration for the character of Wilkins Micawber in *David Copperfield*.

Charles Dickens used to frequent the Navy Pay Office as a boy between the ages of five and eleven. He was able to roam around and watch the rope-makers, anchor-smiths, sailmakers and shipwrights at work. In later life, he would write about Chatham Dockyard in an article entitled *One Man in A Dockyard*:

---

3. Langton, Robert, *The Childhood & Youth of Charles Dickens* (Hutchinson & Co., London, 1891), p.22.

The Cashier's Office at the Royal Naval Dockyard, Chatham, where Dickens accompanied his father as a boy. (Author's Collection)

*Inset*: The top plaque commemorates John Dickens working in this building during 1817–22. The bottom plaque was inaugurated in October 1963 during the time that Captain P.G.C. Dickens, Royal Navy, a great grandson of the author, was Captain of the Dockyard. (Author's Collection)

> It resounded with the noise of hammers beating upon iron, and the great sheds or slips under which the mighty men-of-war are built loomed business-like when contemplated from the opposite side of the river … Great chimneys smoking with a quiet – almost a lazy – air, like giants smoking tobacco; and the giant shears moored off it, looking meekly and inoffensively out of proportion, like the giraffe of the machinery creation.[4]

Dickens would also have seen the convicts labouring in Chatham Dockyard and led to boats that transported them to prison hulks anchored in the River Medway and Thames Estuary during the evenings. His father would allow him to accompany him on the Navy pay yacht on a short passage from the dockyard to Sheerness, where he observed those prison hulks and ships sailing in and out of the River Medway. He was able to see the prison hulks in the River Medway that would inspire him when writing about Abel Magwitch, the convict who escaped from a similar hulk in *Great Expectations*.

Dickens' son Sydney joined the Royal Navy when he was aged 13 and he would visit when the ship he served on was at Chatham Dockyard. Sydney was a lieutenant in the service when he died while travelling aboard HMS *Topaze*. He was buried at sea on 2 May 1872.

---

4. *Household Words*, 6 September 1851.

# 4
# No. 11 Ordnance Terrace, Chatham

## The Dickens family home between 1817 and 1821

**John Dickens was transferred to Chatham Royal Dockyard, which meant he had to relocate his family from London to Chatham and they lived in this house when Charles Dickens was aged between five and nine. He regarded this period of his childhood with happiness.**

The salary earned at the Navy Pay Office allowed John Dickens to afford two servants to live with the family in this house. Mary Weller was employed as a nursemaid, while the elder, Jane Bonner, was hired as a domestic servant. Mary later remembered the young Charles to be 'a lively boy of a good, genial, open disposition, and not quarrelsome as most children are at times'.[5]

Charles Dickens held fond memories of his childhood that he spent in Chatham. His mother, Elizabeth, taught him English and elementary Latin while living in this house, which was No. 2 at the time, and Dickens, together with his sister Fanny, attended a local preparatory day school in Rome Lane, which is now Railway Street, albeit this building no longer exists. While living at 11 Ordnance Terrace, Dickens developed a passion for reading books such as *Tom Jones*, *Don Quixote*, *Robinson Crusoe* and the *Arabian Nights*, and for playing the characters within them. Dickens' interest in drama was awakened while he lived in Chatham because it was here that he first experienced the theatre. Dr Matthew Lamert, a serving army surgeon who was courting his widowed Aunt Fanny, took Dickens to see pantomimes and dramas at the Theatre Royal in Rochester. In 1819 he saw Joseph Grimaldi, the clown, perform and years later as an adult he would edit his memoirs. Lamert's son, James, from a previous marriage, was involved in amateur dramatics and invited Dickens to watch rehearsals and their performances. After Matthew Lamert married his aunt and moved to Ireland, James Lamert lodged with the Dickens family at 11 Ordnance Terrace and he would take Charles to see Shakespeare productions such as *Macbeth* and *Richard III*. This experience would stand him in good stead for when he conducted his readings as an adult and produced his own theatre productions.

Dickens' exposure to theatre and books would inspire him to perform with his sister Fanny in their own plays and recitals for their father and for the benefit of family and friends who visited

---

5. Langton, p.26.

No. 11 Ordinance Terrace, Chatham. (Courtesy of Marathon; www.geograph.org.uk)

their Chatham abode. The seed was sown at an early age when as a boy he began to write when he was living at Ordnance Terrace. Dickens told John Forster that he wrote a tragedy entitled *Misnar, the Sultan of India*. The characters that Dickens created for *Sketches by Boz* were drawn from neighbours who lived in Ordnance Terrace. Mrs Newman who lived at the end of the terrace at No. 5 was the Old Lady and she treated the Dickens children with kindness.

Charles and Fanny Dickens would play with Lucy and George Stroughill, who lived next door to their home in Ordnance Terrace, and they enjoyed playing games in the fields next to Fort Pitt, which was close by. It was there that he set the scene for the duel between Dr Slammer and Winkle in *The Pickwick Papers*. Dickens would use his elder friend George Stroughill as the inspiration for James Steerforth in *David Copperfield*.

Elizabeth Dickens gave birth to two children at Ordnance Terrace; Harriet, who was christened on 3 September 1819 but died in infancy, and Frederick, who was christened on 4 August 1820. Despite receiving an increased salary at Chatham Royal Naval Dockyard, John Dickens was unable to live within his means and he was unable to afford the rent for 11 Ordnance Terrace. As a consequence, the family relocated to the Brook at 18 St Mary's Place, where they lived from 1821 to 1822. The move to cheaper accommodation was the start of John Dickens' downward spiral into debt and, before he was transferred to London, the family had to sell their furniture to pay off some of their debts.

# 5

# Window of the Little Attic from No. 16 Bayham Street, London

## Charles Dickens lived at this address in Camden Town, London

**John Dickens was transferred to Somerset House during 1823 and the family had to relocate to London. Dickens made the sombre journey that lasted five hours by stagecoach from Chatham to London when he was aged eleven.**

Dickens was not happy with the transition from Chatham to London. In later life he recalled his misery at the prospect of arriving in the capital when he wrote, 'there was no other inside passenger, and I consumed my sandwiches in solitude and dreariness, and it rained hard all the way, and I thought life sloppier than I expected to find it'.[6] He arrived at Cross Key, Wood Street, Cheapside, and would live with his family in a small tenement building at 16 Bayham Street. The house where Dickens lived was demolished in 1911, but there is a plaque on the wall of the current building (now No. 141 Bayham Street) that stands on the same site, which states that 'CHARLES DICKENS LIVED IN A HOUSE ON THIS SITE WHEN A BOY IN 1823'. However, it is difficult to see because it is now concealed by wire netting. Located in Camden Town, this was one of London's poorest area in the suburbs and it was here that Dickens would first encounter poverty and deprivation. The building at No. 16 Bayham Street was considered new, given that it was built in 1812, eleven years before Dickens' arrival during 1823.

The original house contained four rooms on two floors, together with a basement and a garret. It had to accommodate Dickens' parents, six children, a maid and their lodger, James Lamert, which was overcrowded. There was a small courtyard that acted as a garden and, with no one to play with, Dickens felt lonely and isolated, especially when his sister Fanny won a scholarship to attend the Royal Academy of Music. Dickens was saddened to leave Chatham, the River Medway, the open spaces and his school. Dickens later confided to his friend John Forster: 'As I thought in the little back-garret in Bayham Street, of all I had lost in losing

---

6. Dickens, Charles, *The Uncommercial Traveller* (Chapman & Hall, 1861), pp.170–1.

*Above*: The window of the little attic from 141 Bayham Street, London. (Author's Collection)

*Left*: No. 16 Bayham Street, Camden Town, London, photographed in 1905, six years before it was demolished in 1911. (Author's Collection)

Chatham, what would I have given, if I had had anything to give, to have been sent back to any other school, to have been taught something anywhere.'[7]

Dickens was so unhappy because his father's financial problems were not resolved and he still had to pay off debts incurred from when they lived in Chatham. It caused Dickens great distress to sell the books that he loved to read. John was unable to provide for his family. Elizabeth Dickens moved from Bayham Street to 4 Gower Street North when they were unable to evade creditors and John Dickens was imprisoned in the Marshalsea debtors' prison in Southwark during February 1824. Dickens would use Bayham Street as the setting for Mr Micawber's house in *David Copperfield* and the home of Tiny Tim and Bob Cratchit in *A Christmas Carol*.

Although the house that Dickens lived in at 16 Bayham Street no longer exists, the window of the little attic has survived and is exhibited in the Dickens' House Museum at Doughty Street.

---

7. Forster, Vol. 1, op. cit., p.30.

# 6

# Marshalsea Prison Wall, Southwark, London

## Dickens' father imprisoned for debt

Beyond this old wall was the site of the old Marshalsea Prison for debtors where John Dickens was imprisoned for fourteen weeks during 1824. This wall formed part of the southern boundary of the prison. The alleyway known as Angel Place to the north of the old wall was the narrow exercise yard, which separated the inmates' building from the wall. The wall stopped sunlight from entering the yard and made it a dismal place.

John Dickens' salary from the Navy Pay Office while working at Somerset House should have enabled him to pay for his family's living expenses, but for reasons undetermined he descended further into debt. Dickens Senior was originally arrested and imprisoned in a 'sponging house' where the opportunity was given to the family to attempt to obtain the value of the outstanding debts. However, they failed and on 20 February 1824 he was sent to the Marshalsea Prison, where he would be treated as a criminal until he could pay his debt. Society regarded anyone sent to the Marshalsea as being in disgrace. Charles recalled the heart-breaking first time that he visited his father there:

> My father was waiting for me in the lodge, and we went up to his room (on the top storey but one), and cried very much. And he told me, I remember, to take warning by the Marshalsea, and to observe that if a man had twenty pounds a year, and spent nineteen pounds nineteen shillings and sixpence. He would be happy; but that a shilling spent the other way would make him wretched.[8]

The Navy Pay Office was still paying John Dickens a salary for the first month of his imprisonment, but fearing that he could be dismissed as a consequence of his insolvency, he made an application for ill health retirement and pension. Dickens' mother tried to earn income through running a school for girls at the family lodgings at No. 4 Gower Street North, but that venture failed when no students arrived and she resorted to pawning domestic possessions to

---

8. Trumble, Alfred, *In Jail with Charles Dickens* (Suckling & Galloway 1896), p.115.

The surviving wall of the Marshalsea Prison, Borough, Southwark. (Shutterstock)

Courtyard of the Marshalsea Prison taken in 1897. (Public Domain)

One of six plaques that line Angel Place along the old Marshalsea Prison wall. (Courtesy of Stephen Craven; www.geograph.org.uk)

survive. Once she had exhausted all their possessions, Elizabeth Dickens was forced to leave Gower Street and join her husband John in the prison, taking the family with her. They were not allowed to leave the prison, although they needed to pay for rent, food and maintenance expenses while they were confined within its walls. The responsibility for supporting the family fell upon the shoulders of Charles Dickens.

This was a dark period in Dickens' life because he was working at Warren's Blacking Factory during the day and visiting his family at the Marshalsea Prison each evening until the bell was rung at ten o'clock to warn visitors that the prison gates would be closed. It was during those visits that Dickens would become familiar with the other prisoners and their stories.

John Dickens would have remained in prison for the remainder of his life, however, his mother died on 26 April 1824 and left him a sum of money, which combined with his ill health retirement pension due for his long service with the Navy Pay Office meant he was able to pay his debts and leave the prison on 28 May 1824.

The Marshalsea Prison was closed during November 1842, but it affected Dickens emotionally and he would tap into his experience as material for *Little Dorrit*, *David Copperfield* and *Pickwick Papers*. His father, John, would be the stimulus for the creation of Wilkins Micawber and William Dorrit. Dickens visited the site in 1857 because he wrote in the preface to *Little Dorrit*:

> But whosoever goes into Marshalsea Place, turning out of Angel Court, leading to Bermondsey, will find his feet on the very paving-stones of the extinct Marshalsea jail; will see its narrow yard to the right and to the left, very little altered if at all, except that the walls were lowered when the place got free; will look upon the rooms in which the debtors lived; and will stand amongst the crowding ghosts of many miserable years.[9]

Angel Court is now Angel Place and was inside the Marshalsea Prison. Although the cobblestones of the prison have gone, the southern wall still exists and on the pavement of Angel Place there are six plaques positioned on the ground with references to Dickens and *Little Dorrit*.

---

9. Dickens, Charles, *Little Dorrit* (Bradbury & Evans, London, 1857), p.vii.

# 7
# Warren's Blacking Factory Bottle

## Charles Dickens employed at Warren's Blacking Factory

**While John Dickens was struggling to manage his debts, Charles Dickens, being the eldest son, was expected to support the family. Employment was found for him at Warren's Blacking Factory in 1824, before John Dickens' incarceration in the Marshalsea Prison. This is one of the bottles from the factory and is similar to those that Dickens would paste labels and lids on.**

Warren's Blacking Factory was a boot polish factory situated at 30 Hungerford Stairs on the north side of the River Thames where Charing Cross Station now stands. James Lamert, former lodger with the Dickens family, was employed there as the chief manager. Lamert could see that the Dickens family were struggling with finances and offered Charles employment at the factory. He was initially paid six shillings a week, which was later increased to seven. Charles' education was temporarily halted as he began work when he was aged twelve. He later recalled this moment in his life to John Forster:

> The blacking warehouse was the last house on the left-hand side of the way, at old Hungerford Stairs. It was a crazy, tumble-down old house, abutting of course on the river, and literally overrun with rats. Its wainscoted rooms, and its rotten floors and staircase, and the old grey rats swarming down in the cellars, and the sound of their squeaking and scoffing coming up the stairs at all times, and the dirt and decay of the place, rise up visibly before me, as if I were there again. The counting house was on the first floor, looking over the coal barges and the river. There was a recess in it, in which I was to sit and work. My work was to cover the pots of paste-blacking; first with a piece of blue paper; to tie them round with a string; and then to clip the paper close and neat, all round, until it looked as smart as a pot of ointment from an apothecary's shop. When a certain number of grosses of pots had attained this pitch of perfection, I was to paste on each a printed label, and then go on again with more pots.[10]

---

10. Forster, Vol. 1, op. cit., p.51.

Dickens would use the experience at Warren's Blacking Factory in *David Copperfield*, where the protagonist was put to menial work at Murdstone and Grinby's Warehouse near Blackfriars in Chapter 11. One of the other boys, Bob Fagin, who also worked at the factory in a similar job, would provide Dickens' inspiration for the name of Fagin in *Oliver Twist*.

During the period that Dickens worked at Warren's, the business expanded and the premises moved from Hungerford Stairs to Chandos Place. This building was demolished during 1889, but a plaque marks the spot and states 'As a boy Charles Dickens worked here 1824–25'. He would be positioned by the window as passers-by in the street stared through the window to watch him work. Dickens felt so embarrassed by his experience at the blacking factory that in his adult life he would cross the street in The Strand to avoid walking directly past Robert Warren's office because the smell of cement that they put upon the blacking corks reminded him of the factory.

The public were unaware of this part of his life until two years after his death, when John Forster published his biography. Working at the blacking factory and his father's imprisonment in the Marshalsea Prison instilled a strong determination within Dickens to work hard to attain personal success and financial security. After Dickens left the factory, he returned to being a student as a pupil at the Wellington House Academy in Hampstead.

*Above*: A bottle from Warren's Blacking Factory. (Author's Collection)

*Right*: Illustration depicting Charles Dickens at the factory. (Author's Collection)

WARREN'S BLACKING FACTORY BOTTLE

# 8
# The Sign of the Dog's Head in the Pot

### Replica sign familiar to Dickens

As a boy, Dickens walked past an ironmonger's shop with the sign of a dog's head in a pot, which stood on the corner of Blackfriars Road and Union Street, when he walked from Warren's Blacking Factory to his lodgings in Lant Street, Borough, close to the Marshalsea Prison.

While Dickens continued to work at Warren's Blacking Factory, he initially resided at Little College Street, Camden Town. Feeling isolated from his parents and his siblings, he found lodgings at Lant Street, Borough, which was closer to Warren's Blacking Factory and was near to the Marshalsea Prison so that he could visit his family each night. Dickens later wrote of his journey home after work and referred to a shop at the junction of Blackfriars Road and Charlotte Street (Now Union Street) where there was a sign of a dog licking a pot. The shop no longer exists, but this is a replica of that sign on the site where the shop once stood and where Dickens walked. Dickens' words are inscribed on the pavement beneath it. 'My usual way home was over Blackfriars Bridge and down that turning in the Blackfriars Road, which has Rowland Hill's chapel on one side, and the likeness of a golden dog licking a golden pot over a shop door on the other.' The replica sign and the inscribed pavement were unveiled by Charles Dickens' great-great-grandson, Mark Dickens, in 2013.

Sign of the dog licking a golden pot on the junction of Blackfriars Road and Union Street where the ironmonger's shop was situated, which was familiar to Charles Dickens when he walked past it as a boy. (Author's Collection)

Charles Dickens' Dog and Pot Sculpture at Blackfriars Road. (Courtesy of Matt Brown)

Lant Street, Borough where Dickens lived while working in the blacking factory and during his father's incarceration in the Marshalsea Prison. (Author's Collection)

# 9

# Ellis & Blackmore Offices, No. 1 Raymond Buildings, Gray's Inn, London

**Dickens worked as a clerk at Ellis & Blackmore in 1827–28.**

After completing his studies at Wellington House Academy, Dickens' father secured him a position as a clerk for a solicitor named Edward Blakemore, who was a family friend and a partner at Ellis & Blackmore attorneys, based at No. 1, Raymond Buildings, Gray's Inn. Dickens' office was on the second floor and overlooked the road. He worked there from May 1827 until November 1828.

On his first day working for Ellis & Blackmore, Dickens arrived wearing a military-style cap and was sent on an errand. While he was crossing Chancery Lane from Lincoln's Inn Gateway, a man knocked his cap from his head. Dickens retaliated by striking him, but then the man hit him, which meant that he returned to the office with a black eye.

Dickens gave a negative impression of his workplace in *The Uncommercial Traveller*, because he wrote of 'a highly suicidal set of chambers in Gray's Inn' and 'the large square of Melancholy'.[11] It is clear that Dickens was not happy working as a clerk, the office junior, in a law firm. He continued his bleak impression of Gray's Inn in *The Uncommercial Traveller*:

> Indeed, I look upon Gray's Inn generally as one of the most depressing institutions in brick and mortar, known to the children of men. Can anything be more dreary than its arid Square, Sahara Desert of the law, with the ugly old tiled-topped tenements, the dirty windows, the bills To Let To Let, the door posts inscribed like gravestones, the crazy gateway giving upon the filthy Lane, the scowling iron-barred prison-liken passage into Verulam Buildings …[12]

---

11. Dickens, Charles, *The Uncommercial Traveller* (Chapman & Hall, London, 1861), p.200.

12. Ibid., p.203.

No. 1 Raymond Buildings, Gray's Inn. The building on the corner housed the offices of Ellis & Blackmore, where Dickens was employed as a legal clerk. (Author's Collection)

Part of Dickens' duties as a clerk was to maintain the accounts book that contained the office expenses. In one of these books dated between January to March 1828, in his handwriting the names listed in the book are Corney, Rudge, Bardell, Weller and Newman Knott. These were people who interacted with Ellis & Blackmore that Dickens would reincarnate as characters in his future novels. It is certain that during the eighteen months that he worked here that he met people in the legal community who would inspire creations of characters such as Tulkinghorn in *Bleak House*, Sampson Brass in *The Old Curiosity Shop* and Solomon Pell in *The Pickwick Papers*.

Although law did not excite Dickens, he was able to garner some experience and knowledge about the legal profession that he would incorporate within his work. He was able to analyse the characteristics and mannerisms of lawyers and clients. Dickens used that knowledge to write *Bleak House*, which revolved around the Jarndyce and Jarndyce case, a long, drawn-out case where lawyers profited and abused the Court of Chancery. Among his creations in the book is William

Entrance to Gray's Inn and the building where Dickens worked as a legal clerk at Raymond Buildings. (Courtesy of Mike Quinn; www.geograph.co.uk)

Guppy, who, like Dickens, worked as a legal clerk. According to George Lear, there was a woman who had been the victim of a protracted Chancery case who Dickens would immortalise in *Bleak House* as Miss Flite. In *Great Expectations* he created Mr Jaggers, the criminal lawyer who represented Abel Magwitch and informed Pip of his great expectations. Dickens associated the legal profession with darkness, as he placed Jaggers' office in 'a gloomy street',[13] situated in Little Britain, near Smithfield, and described his office as 'a dismal place'. Even Jaggers' 'high backed chair was of deadly black horse hair, with rows of brass nails round it, like a coffin'.[14]

He was not suited to a career in law, so he sought alternative career options. Since John Dickens had been pensioned off by the Admiralty he had learnt shorthand and was employed as a parliamentary reporter. Dickens decided to follow his father and he also learned shorthand. It was difficult for Dickens because during the day he was working for Ellis & Blackmore and persevered to learn shorthand in the reading room at the British Museum. During November 1828, Dickens left Ellis & Blackmore to work briefly at Lincoln's Inn Law firm Charles Molloy. He then became a shorthand writer at Doctors' Commons, which dealt with wills and probate and was situated between the River Thames and St Paul's Cathedral.

---

13. Dickens, Charles, *Great Expectations* (Collier, New York, 1890), p.168.

14. Ibid., p.169.

# 10

# The House of Commons

**During 1832, Charles Dickens joined the parliamentary staff reporting for the periodical *The Mirror of Parliament*.**

**Dickens was a regular visitor to the Houses of Parliament between 1832 and 1836, but the Old Palace of Westminster had burnt down in 1834. The only surviving part of the palace that would have been familiar to Dickens is Westminster Hall. The current building, designed by Sir Charles Barry, was completed and opened in 1852.**

Once Dickens had completed his experience at Doctors' Commons, he found employment as a reporter for a London morning newspaper entitled the *True Sun* in 1832, which involved travelling around the country recording public speeches. It was during this period that he met John Forster in the office of the *True Sun*. He was a contributor to the newspaper and would become Dickens' lifelong friend. During that same year, Dickens joined the reporting staff of a newly established newspaper called the *Mirror of Parliament*, which was created by his uncle, John Henry Barrow, and where his father was employed. Dickens joined ninety other parliamentary reporters in the gallery of the House of Commons reporting on the daily machinations of the lower house, including the final debates of the Reform Bill. He established a good reputation as a reporter and was later employed in 1834 by the *Morning Chronicle*, which was a popular Liberal newspaper of the period that rivalled *The Times*. When Parliament was not sitting, Dickens was sent across the country to cover by-elections, public meetings and ceremonies. On his return journey to London, he would industriously write up the articles for the following day's edition of the newspaper. At the second annual dinner of the Newspaper Press Fund in 1865, he spoke of his career as a reporter:

> I went into the gallery of the House of Commons as a parliamentary reporter when I was a boy, and I left it – I can hardly believe the inexorable truth – nigh thirty years ago, and I have pursued the calling of a reporter under circumstances of which many of my brethren at home in England here ... can form no adequate conception. I have often transcribed for the printer, from my short-hand notes, important public speeches, in which the strictest accuracy was required, and a mistake in which would have been to a young man severely compromising, writing on the palm of my hand, by the light of

The Speaker presiding over debates in the House of Commons, as depicted in this print commemorating the destruction of the Commons Chamber by fire in 1834. Dickens would have been familiar with this view of the House of Commons as he sat in the upper gallery. (Author's Collection)

a dark-lantern, in a post-chaise and four, galloping through a wild country, all through the dead of the night, at the then surprising rate of fifteen miles an hour ... I have worn my knees by writing on them on the old back row of the old gallery of the House of Commons; and I have worn my feet by standing to write in a preposterous pen in the old House of Lords, where we used to be huddled together like so many sheep – kept in waiting, say, until the woolsack might want restuffing.[15]

While working as a reporter, his father, John, was once again experiencing difficulties in managing his finances and Dickens had to step forward to ensure that his family did not return to the Marshalsea Prison. Dickens ended his career as a parliamentary reporter during the close of session of 1836. He was twenty-four years old and the experiences of the blacking factory, the Marshalsea debtors' prison, Ellis & Blackmore law firm and as a parliamentary reporter would provide him with experiences that he would use when writing his novels. Living in London would also give him local knowledge of these places, and the various social levels, that he would use as settings for the various characters that he created.

---

15. *Londonderry Standard*, 27 May 1865.

# 11

## *Sketches by Boz*

### Dickens' first commercial work published.

**Literature during the early nineteenth century focused upon the dark Gothic horror and romance within the aristocracy in country estates. *Sketches by Boz* marked a radical change from these genres in which Dickens focused upon the everyday life and people.**

During the autumn of 1833 Dickens wrote the first of nine sketches. He posted one sketch entitled *A Dinner at Poplar Walk*, which was later retitled *Mr Minns and his Cousin*, at the office of the *Monthly Magazine* in Johnson Court, which was published in December 1833. Dickens recalled that:

> My first copy of the magazine in which my first effusion – a paper in the 'Sketches,' called 'Mr Minns and his Cousin' – dropped stealthily one evening at twilight, with fear and trembling, into a dark letter-box, in a dark office, up a dark court in Fleet Street – appeared in the glory of print; on which occasion I walked down to Westminster Hall, and turned into it for half an hour, because my eyes were so dimmed with joy and pride that they could not bear the street, and were not fit to be seen there.[16]

In August 1834, Dickens first assumed the pseudonym of Boz, which originated from the family nickname given to his younger brother, Augustus. Dickens wrote: 'Boz was a very familiar household word to me, long before I was an author, and so I came to adopt it.'[17]

On 31 January 1835, Dickens' piece on Hackney coach stands appeared in *The Evening Chronicle*. Dickens' sketches were later continued in *The Morning Chronicle* and *Bell's Life* during 1836. The sketches were a collection of short pieces containing scenes of daily life in London and its people during the reign of William IV. The sketches were categorised into sections entitled 'Our Parish', 'Scenes', 'Characters' and 'Tales', with the last section containing fictional stories. The sketches were the precursors to his novels. He wrote of the Beadle in 'Our Parish', for which he would later create Mr Bumble, the parish beadle in *Oliver Twist*. In the

---

16. *Tamworth Herald*, 18 June 1870.
17. Forster, Vol. 1, op. cit., p.104.

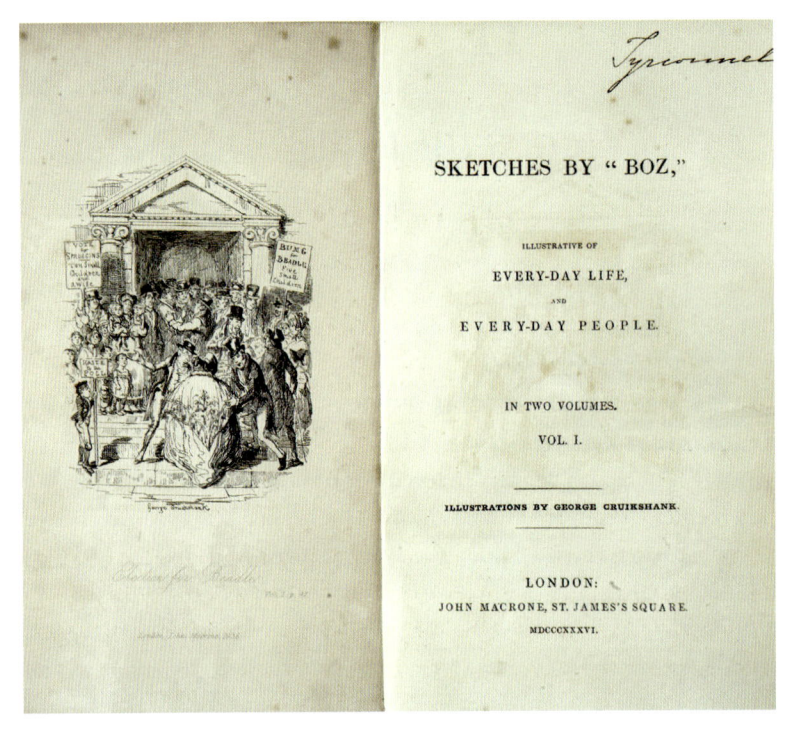

Frontispiece of *Sketches by Boz* by Charles Dickens. (Author's Collection)

'Scenes', Dickens focused upon the streets, shops, Scotland Yard, Seven Dials, Hackney Coach stands, the river, pawnbroker's shops and the criminal courts. Dickens would have written these early writings when he was living at Ordnance Terrace in Chatham and Bayham Street in London. It was from this material that Dickens would develop from writing short sketches to longer novels.

While employed as a legal clerk at Ellis & Blackmore, Dickens would act in minor amateur dramatic parts in the evenings with a fellow clerk named Mr Potter. When *Sketches by Boz* was published, Potter recognised that Dickens had featured him in the chapter entitled *Making a Night of It*, in which Potter is named, and *The Misplaced Attachment of Mr. John Dounce*, where Potter was the inspiration for the character named Jones, 'capital-company, full of anecdote'.[18] Jones would suggest excursions to the theatre to see a play or a farce, just as Potter did with Dickens. It is also thought that the character of Jones, aka Potter, was the prototype for Mr Alfred Jingle in *The Pickwick Papers*.

Dickens was introduced to publisher John Macrone by the novelist William Harrison Ainsworth. By 1836 Dickens had written fifty-six sketches and at Macrone's suggestion he collated the series into two volumes, which would be entitled *Sketches by Boz*. Macrone also brought Dickens together with the illustrator George Cruickshank. Dickens had retained the copyright of the sketches and sold this to Macrone for £150. *Sketches by Boz* was published during February 1836 and it was positively received, with a second edition released six months later.

---

18. Dickens, Charles, *Sketches by Boz* (Chapman & Hall, London, 1854), p.149.

# 12

# Dickens' Memorial and Plaque, Furnival's Inn, London

**Dickens started to write *The Pickwick Papers* at Furnival's Inn.**

**Holborn Bars (the former Prudential Assurance building) is situated at 138–142 Holborn and it is the site of the Furnival's Inn building of the Inns of Chancery, where Dickens lodged within its chambers between December 1834 and March 1837. The building was demolished in 1897 to make way for the Prudential Assurance Building, but inside the courtyard Dickens' connection with Furnival's Inn is commemorated with a plaque and a bust depicting him in his later years.**

After receiving a modest fee for *Sketches by Boz* and together with his income as a parliamentary reporter for the *Morning Chronicle*, Dickens, who was aged 24, was able to consider living independently. He was living with his father at Bentick Street and after briefly living at Buckingham Street he found suitable lodgings at Furnival's Inn. Dickens initially resided at No. 13 as a bachelor. The lease stipulated that he was not permitted to have children living with him in the chambers. During February 1836, he relocated from his bachelor chambers to No. 15 Furnival's Inn, where he lived in three rooms and wrote later instalments of *Sketches by Boz*.

The location is significant because it was at Furnival's Inn where William Hall, partner of the publishers Chapman & Hall, visited Dickens with a proposal to write a monthly piece revolving around images produced by the artist Robert Seymour. That project would evolve into *The Pickwick Papers* and Dickens wrote the first instalments at Furnival's Inn. The popularity of *The Pickwick Papers* signalled the beginning of his successful literary career during 1835. Dickens worked extremely hard maintaining his job as a parliamentary reporter and writing serials for magazines, resorting to working into the early hours of the morning.

Dickens featured Furnival's Inn in his novels as the lodgings for John Westlock in *Martin Chuzzlewit*, in which he commented that 'there are snug chambers in those Inns'.[19] He later wrote in the novel that 'there is little enough to see in Furnival's Inn. It is a shady, quiet place, echoing the footsteps of the stragglers who have business there; and rather monotonous and

---

19. Dickens, Charles, *Martin Chuzzlewit* (Chapman & Hall, 1859), p.516.

*Above left*: Dickens' bust and plaque commemorating his residence at Furnival's Inn, at Holborn Bars, and where he wrote *The Pickwick Papers*. (Author's Collection)

*Above right*: Plaque at Holborn Bars commemorating that Dickens lived on this site. (Author's Collection)

gloomy on summer evenings.'[20] However, Westcott's existence in the chambers were not happy ones and maybe reflected Dickens' own perception of life at Furnival's Inn: 'It was a wretched life, he said, a miserable life. He thought of getting rid of those chambers as soon as possible.'[21] Thirty-four years after staying there, Dickens used Furnival's Inn in *The Mystery of Edwin Drood* as the chambers where Rosa resided, in which he described her room as 'airy, clean, comfortable, almost gay'.[22]

The chambers rented by Dickens were ideal for a young single man, but in 1836 he married Catherine Hogarth and on 6 January 1837 their first child, Charles Dickens Junior, was born at Furnival's Inn, which was contrary to the conditions of the lease forbidding children living on the premises. His sister-in-law, Mary Hogarth, and his brother Fred would sometimes stay with them, which made the lodgings at Furnival's Inn too small for a family. The success of *The Pickwick Papers* gave Dickens the financial freedom to look for a house in which to accommodate his family and he moved to 48 Doughty Street.

---

20. Ibid., p.519.

21. Ibid., p.517.

22. Dickens, Charles, *The Mystery of Edwin Drood* (Chapman & Hall, London, 1870), p.160.

# 13

# Manuscript of *The Pickwick Papers* and Dickens' Quill

### Dickens' first novel was serialised between March 1836 and November 1837.

Entitled the *Posthumous Papers of the Pickwick Club*, Dickens' novel is informally known as *The Pickwick Papers*. It was a record of the travels, adventures, farcical situations and escapades of the Pickwick Club led by its founder Samuel Pickwick. The story is set in 1827 and it was Dickens' most jocular work that would propel him, aged 24, into one of the most popular authors of the day. Here is an example of Dickens' handwriting and one of his writing quills that he used to write the story.

Dickens preferred to write with a quill. His daughter, Mamie, later recalled that:

> My father always wrote with a quill pen and blue ink, and never, I think, used a lead pencil. His handwriting was considered extremely difficult to read by many people, but I never found it so. In his manuscripts there were so many erasures, and such frequent interlineations that a special staff of compositors was used for his work, but this was not on account of any illegibility in his handwriting.[23]

In 1836, newly established publishers Chapman & Hall were looking for an author to write comic commentary to accompany sporting images drawn by an artist named Robert Seymour. They approached Dickens with a proposal for him to write 12,000 words a month for a series of twenty monthly parts. Dickens agreed on the condition that Seymour's drawings must match the text, instead of the text being written around the drawings. Despite protestations from Seymour, Chapman & Hall concurred with Dickens' stipulation. He was now contracted to deliver 12,000 words each month, while continuing to work as a reporter.

The first shilling edition of *The Pickwick Papers*, with four illustrations from Robert Seymour, was first sold on 31 March 1836. There was a verbal agreement that Chapman & Hall would pay fifteen guineas for a sheet and a half for each numbered edition. Dickens received an

---

23. Dickens, Mamie, *My Father as I Recall Him* (The Roxburghe Press, London, 1896), p.63.

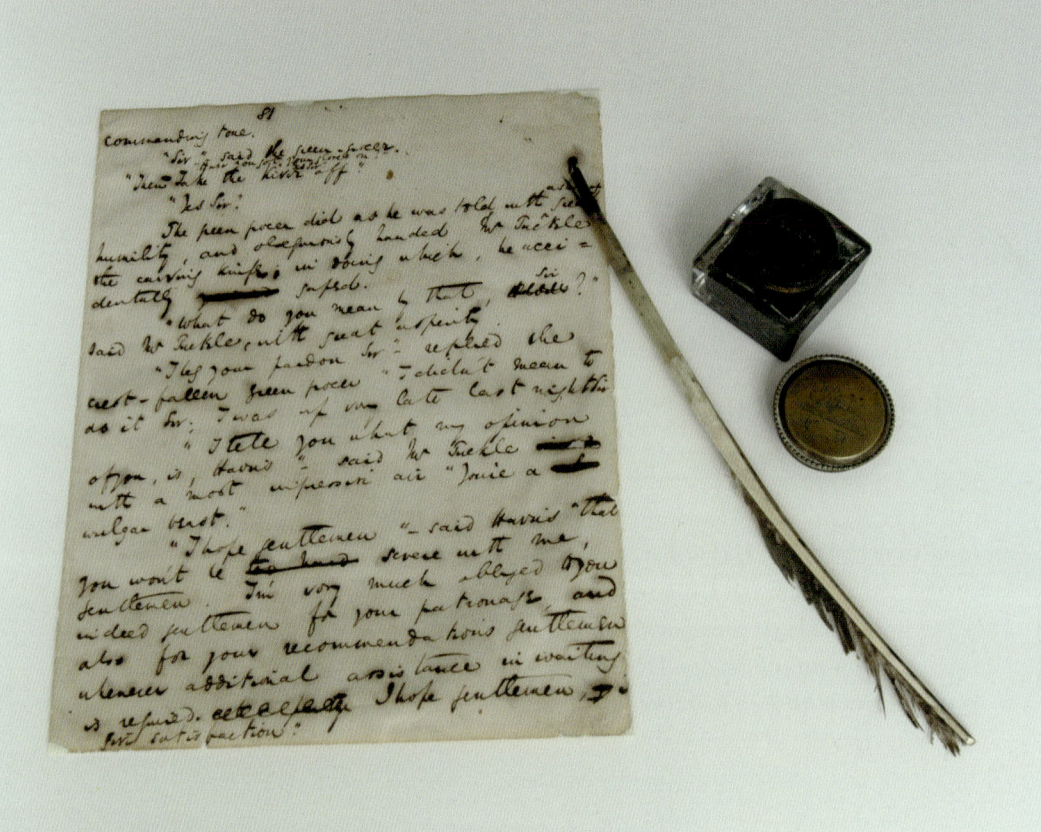

The manuscript of the Pickwick Papers and Dickens' Quill. (© Charles Dickens Museum, London/Bridgeman Images)

advance for the first two because he needed the money to marry Catherine Hogarth. They also agreed to pay more to the author if there was an increase in sales.

The number of pages written by Dickens increased to thirty per instalment after the second month. The success of *The Pickwick Papers* prompted Chapman & Hall to advise Dickens to take a share of the copyright.

Each monthly instalment, or as Dickens referred to them 'numbers', of each edition comprised either two or three chapters. *The Pickwick Papers* was a series of loosely connected stories that at the end of its run was published as a book. The first three numbers only sold 400 copies and there was a setback when the unsettled and dispirited Seymour committed suicide by shooting himself through the heart before the issue of the second instalment. Seymour had produced three illustrations for this issue, but a replacement illustrator had to be found. R.W. Buss was chosen and he produced two images for the No. 3 issue, but they were deemed inferior and he was dismissed from the project. Hablot Knight Browne, known as Phiz, was the chosen successor and he worked as Dickens' illustrator regularly from then on.

*The Pickwick Papers* followed the adventures of the Pickwick Club, which included Samuel Pickwick, Nathaniel Winkle, Augustus Snodgrass and Tracy Tupman, later joined by Sam Weller, who became Pickwick's valet. It was not until the first appearance of Sam Weller in the fourth instalment of *The Pickwick Papers* that sales increased from 400 to 20,000 copies. The popularity of *The Pickwick Papers* transcended across the social classes and generations within Britain, appealing to a wide variety of people from all ages and backgrounds. It created commercial opportunities where Pickwick hats, gaiters, waistcoats, Weller corduroys and china figures of the characters were among the Pickwickian merchandise sold. The appeal of Pickwick inspired people to name their pets after characters from the story, and Sam, Jingle and Mrs Bardell were common names for dogs and cats during the time.

Dickens wrote *The Pickwick Papers* under the name of Boz, but in September 1837 when Part XVII was issued, Chapman & Hall issued a notice that confirmed that they had agreed Mr Dickens would write a new work in the same vein as *The Pickwick Papers*. This new serialisation would be Dickens' third book, entitled *Nicholas Nickleby*. It was the first acknowledgement from the publisher that identified Dickens as author of the serialisation.

As the serialisation progressed, *The Pickwick Papers* sold 40,000 copies.[24] The popularity of *The Pickwick Papers* extended abroad to America, France and Russia. The astounding success of the serial meant that Dickens could resign from his position as a reporter for the *Morning Chronicle* to concentrate on writing fiction.

---

24. Forster, Vol. 2, p.64.

# 14

# Characters from *The Pickwick Papers*

**Samuel Pickwick** is the delightfully innocent and lovable elderly, affluent, portly protagonist, who is the founder and chairman of the Pickwick Club. Its members travel around the country and report on their adventures to the club. Pickwick initially appears as a bumbling fool, but as the story progresses, his humanity, generosity, kindness and his view of the world, seeing the good in people, gained the affection of his friends and Dickens' readers. His amiable personality made him well loved by those who read each instalment, but his naivety made him vulnerable to scoundrels. His pursuit of adventure and sense of decency sometimes results in a loss of dignity as he finds himself going from one disastrous comic situation to another. According to Samuel Petherington, Dickens visited the White Hart Inn in Bath during 1836 and the name of Pickwick was taken from a coach owned by his uncle, Moses Pickwick, the proprietor of the White Hart Inn and a coaching company.[25] The physique, clothes and demeanour of the character of Samuel Pickwick was taken from John Foster, not Dickens' friend John Forster, but a friend of Dickens' publisher, Edward Hall. Foster resided in Richmond, was of portly appearance and who would wear drab tights with black gaiters.

Samuel Pickwick. (All Author's Collection)

**Sam Weller** cleans boots and later serves as valet to Samuel Pickwick. His cockney charm and humour brought a new dynamic to *The Pickwick Papers* that endeared readers and attracted new ones. Pickwick first encounters Weller cleaning a pair of boots at the White Hart Inn in Borough High Street, Southwark, when he accompanies Mr Wardle, who is searching for his sister after she has eloped with Alfred Jingle. Weller characteristically pronounces his Ws as a V.

---

25. *Bath Chronicle & Weekly Gazette*, 31 October 1936.

His appearance increased sales and elevated Dickens as an author. A popular comedian named Samuel Vale was the original model for Sam Weller. He performed at the Drury Lane Theatre during 1822 and he amused audiences with his comic acting and catchphrases.[26] It is probable that Dickens saw him perform as a boy. Pickwick is so endeared by Weller's personality and appearance, he employs him as his servant for twelve pounds a year and two suits of clothes as he travels around the country with fellow members of the Pickwick Club. The streetwise, astute Weller acts as a counterbalance to the naivety of his employer, but he is devoted and loyal to Pickwick.

**Alfred Jingle** leads a nomadic existence as a jobbing actor with very little money, who wears second-hand clothes that do not fit him. When Jingle attaches himself to Pickwick's party at the Golden Cross Inn as they embark aboard the Commodore, the London to Rochester coach, Pickwick observes 'the green coat had been a smart dress garment, in the days of swallow-tails, but had evidently in those times adorned a much shorter man than the stranger, for the soiled and faded sleeves scarcely reached to his wrists'.[27] Jingle introduces himself to Pickwick as Jingle of 'No-hall, Nowhere'.[28] He speaks in a staccato rhythm, which sounds like an announcement instead of a conversation when communicating. Jingle is a swindler and a charlatan who eats at the expense of the Pickwick Club. Pickwick refers to Jingle as 'an unprincipled adventurer – a dishonourable character – a man who preys upon society, and makes easily deceived people his dupes'.[29] Later in the story, Pickwick encounters Jingle in the Fleet Prison, destitute and imprisoned for debt. The benevolent Pickwick pays his debt and gains Jingle's liberty.

Sam Weller.

Alfred Jingle.

---

26. *Lake's Falmouth Packet & Cornwall Advertiser*, 14 March 1885.
27. Dickens, Charles, *The Pickwick Papers* (T. Nelson & Sons, London, 1900), p.10.
28. Ibid., p.99.
29. Ibid., p.363.

# 15

# The Royal Victoria & Bull Hotel, Rochester

**The current building is 400 years old and was a coaching inn on the London to Dover Road.**

Dickens was a frequent visitor to the Royal Victoria & Bull Hotel in Rochester High Street, Kent, and featured it in *The Pickwick Papers* and *Great Expectations*. It was unusual for Dickens not to change the name for his novels and he referred to it as the Bull in *The Pickwick Papers*. It was later called the Royal Victoria, because Princess Victoria spent the night in the inn during a journey between Dover and London during November 1836, two years before her accession to the throne.

The Royal Victoria & Bull Hotel was where Messrs Pickwick, Tupman, Winkle, Snodgrass and Jingle alighted from their coach journey from London and stayed on the recommendation of Alfred Jingle. It was where Jingle and Tupman attended a ball at the hotel. Jingle did not have a change of clothing and at the insistence of Tupman, he borrowed the suit belonging to Winkle, who had overindulged in wine at the dinner and had fallen asleep. Jingle makes an impression upon a wealthy widow in the ballroom of the hotel, much to the annoyance of Dr Slammer, who had amorous intentions towards her. It was on the staircase in the hotel where the altercation took place between Alfred Jungle and Dr Slammer. Jingle was borrowing Winkle's coat without his knowledge, and Slammer challenged Winkle to a duel, mistaking him for Jingle. Mr Pickwick stayed in room 17, which was used by Dickens.

Dickens later utilised the Bull in *Great Expectations* as the Blue Boar inn where, after Miss Havisham provided Pip with twenty-five guineas to be bound apprenticed to Joe Gargery as a blacksmith, his sister was so overwhelmed that they celebrated with a dinner at the Blue Boar, which was attended by Uncle Pumblechook, Mr Wopsle and the Hubbles. Pip returned to the Blue Boar as an adult and it was here that the lawyer Mr Jaggers informed him that Miss Havisham was not his benefactor.

Dickens stayed at the Bull Hotel during February 1845 with Catherine, Georgina Hogarth, John Forster, Douglas Jerrold and Daniel Maclise. The party visited Cobham Park. On 7 February 1846, Dickens celebrated his 34th birthday at the Bull Hotel, using it as a base to visit his favourite places in and around Rochester.

*Above*: The Royal Victoria & Bull Hotel, Rochester. (Author's Collection)

*Right*: Plaque denoting Dickens' connection on the façade of the Royal Victoria & Bull Hotel. (Author's collection)

While living at Gad's Hill Place, Dickens would mischievously walk with friends into Rochester High Street, where he would enter auction rooms and bid for various random items, then withdraw from the bidding at the right time to avoid making a purchase. On one occasion he was too late and bought a cane chair. He did not require the chair so he paid a boy to take it to the Bull Inn, requesting that it should be put in Mr Dickens' bedroom.[30]

---

30. Ward Catherine & H. Snowdon, *The Real Dickens Land* (Chapman & Hall Limited, London, 1904). p.78.

# 16

# Charles Dickens' Honeymoon Cottage, Chalk

## Cottage where Charles and Catherine Dickens spent their honeymoon for one week in Chalk, Kent.

**Dickens fell in love with the flirtatious Maria Beadnell during 1830. He courted Maria for three years, but she was the daughter of an affluent banker who did not approve of the relationship and considered that Dickens lacked prospects. Although he was smitten, Maria treated Dickens atrociously and the relationship broke down in 1833. Dickens would meet Catherine Hogarth in 1835.**

Dickens met his future wife through George Hogarth, who was Dickens' colleague at the *Morning Chronicle* and introduced her to his daughter, Catherine. He invited Catherine to his 23rd birthday celebrations at Furnival's Inn during February 1835 and later that year their friendship developed into a romance, resulting in their engagement. Dickens married Catherine at St Luke's Church, the parish church of the Hogarth family in Chelsea, on 2 April 1836, two days after the publication of the first edition of *The Pickwick Papers*. The wedding ceremony was a low-key, quiet affair. Thomas Beard, a reporter and colleague from the *Morning Herald*, performed the role of Dickens' best man. Henry Burnett, husband of Fanny Dickens and Dickens' brother-in-law, recalled the wedding:

> As for the wedding … the breakfast was the quietest possible. The Dickens family, the Hogarth family, and Mr Beard … comprised the whole of the company. A few common, pleasant things were said, healths drunk, with a few words said by either party – yet all things passed off pleasantly, and all seemed happy, not the least so Dickens and his young girlish wife. She was a bright and pleasant bride, dressed in the simplest and neatest manner, and looked better perhaps than if she had been enabled to aim at something more.[31]

---

31. Kitton, Frederick G., *Charles Dickens: His Life, Writings and Personality* (T.C. & E.C. Black, London, 1902), p.36.

House on the Dover Road at Chalk where Dickens spent his honeymoon and later holidays. This is not the house where there is currently a plaque. (Author's Collection)

Dickens was so busy with work commitments, being a reporter and committed to writing monthly instalments of *The Pickwick Papers*, that he could only spare one week for their honeymoon. Dickens decided to spend it in the place where he had fond childhood memories: in a cottage in Chalk, near Gravesend. The cottage was situated at the junction of the lower Higham Road and Chalk Road.

Although there is a bronze plaque on a house in Chalk stating Dickens' connection, it is believed that the actual cottage was a few doors down the same street but has been demolished. The plaque, dedicated by Dickens' friend Percy Fitzgerald, is accompanied by a marble plate above the door with the inscription: 'Charles Dickens. Born 1812. Died 1870. Spent his honeymoon in this house (1836). Here also were written some early chapters of Pickwick.'

On 4 February 1837, Dickens returned to Chalk when he brought his family for a brief stay in this cottage where he previously spent his honeymoon, before moving from Furnival's Inn to 48 Doughty Street. The experiences of Dickens would be shared by Tommy Traddles in *David Copperfield* and Walter Gay in *Dombey & Son*, who both spend their honeymoons in Kent.

# 17

# No. 48 Doughty Street, London

**Dickens' London home from March 1837 until November 1839.**

The move to Doughty Street reflected the next phase of Dickens' success for he had leased a three-storey house containing twelve rooms with a small garden at the rear. Built towards the end of the eighteenth century, the house was in an exclusive street, with gates at both ends and with a lodge that was manned by a porter. It is now the Charles Dickens Museum.

During the two and a half years that he lived at Doughty Street; Dickens completed the last five monthly numbers of *The Pickwick Papers* between April and November 1837. He worked on *Oliver Twist* from the fifth number in April 1837 until the last number published during April 1839 for *Bentley's Miscellany*. He wrote *Sketches of Young Gentlemen* and edited the *Memoirs of Grimaldi* in 1838. He also wrote twenty monthly numbers of *Nicholas Nickleby* from April 1838 to October 1839. Dickens also wrote a farce entitled *The Lamplighter*, written specifically for his actor friend Macready, but this was never published nor performed during Dickens' lifetime. A small portion of *Barnaby Rudge* was also written in this house, but because he could not reach a satisfactory agreement with Richard Bentley, Dickens did not resume work on this book until 1841, two years after he had left Doughty Street. The building is significantly important because he established his reputation as an author in Britain and attained international acclaim for the novels that he wrote during the time that he lived here. Many of his peers from the literary world, including George Henry Lewes, Leigh Hunt and John Forster, visited him and dined with him in this house.

Dickens was continually thinking about his work, even in the presence of visitors. Dickens' brother-in-law, Henry Burnett, visited Doughty Street when he was writing *Oliver Twist*, recalled observing 'the mind and the muscles working (or, if you please, playing) in company, as new thoughts were being dropped upon the paper – and to note the working brow, the set of mouth, with the tongue tightly pressed against the closed lips, as was his habit.'[32]

Dickens' residence in this house was overshadowed by tragedy. His sister-in-law Mary Hogarth also lived with the family and within weeks of moving into their new home she died there. Mary was suddenly taken ill after spending the evening of 6 May 1837 at

---

32. Kitton, *Life*, p.54.

No. 48 Doughty Street was Dickens' London home between March 1837 and November 1839. It is now the Charles Dickens Museum. (Author's Collection)

Plaque on the wall at 48 Doughty Street. (Author's Collection)

St James's Theatre with Charles and Catherine, where they had watched an operetta *The Village Coquettes*, for which Dickens had written the libretto, while John Pyke Hullah had written the music. Mary died from a heart seizure in Dickens' arms during the following afternoon. Dickens was grief-stricken. He paid for the funeral expenses and wrote the epitaph on her gravestone in Kensal Green Cemetery, which read: 'Young, beautiful, and good, God numbered her among his angels at the early age of seventeen.' Her death had an immense impact upon Dickens because he was so distraught he was unable to write, which meant that the publication of instalments of *The Pickwick Papers* and *Oliver Twist* was interrupted for two months. In a letter to William Harrison Ainsworth, he wrote: 'I have been so much unnerved and hurt by the loss of the dear girl whom I loved after my wife, more deeply and fervently than anyone on earth, that I have been compelled for once to give up all idea of my monthly work, and to try a fortnights rest and quiet.'[33]

The intensity of the bereavement suffered from the loss of Mary would resonate throughout his life. Dickens' true feelings for his deceased sister-in-law have been the subject of speculation, for he would wear her ring for the remainder of his life. When George Hogarth, her brother, died in 1841, Dickens wrote to his mother-in-law that he wanted to be buried next to Mary, but gave that space to George.

There were moments of joy at Doughty Street because Dickens' two daughters were born in the house. Mary was born on 6 March 1838 and was named after her deceased aunt. Dickens would call her Mamie. On 29 October 1839, Catherine Elizabeth Macready Dickens was born. Dickens referred to her as Kate or Katey and her middle name Macready, was named after his friend and theatre manager, William Macready. After the birth of Kate, it was necessary to move to a larger house and during November 1839, the family moved from Doughty Street to No. 1 Devonshire Terrace, Marylebone.

The house at Doughty Street was threatened with demolition in 1922 and it was the Dickens Fellowship that raised sufficient funds to purchase No. 46 and the adjacent house to preserve it as a museum dedicated to Dickens. In 1925 the museum was opened and became a shrine in London to commemorate Dickens' life and work.

---

33. Kitton, *Life*, p.43.

# 18

# Frontispiece of *Oliver Twist*

## Publication of *Oliver Twist*.

**On 22 August 1836 Dickens signed an agreement with Richard Bentley to edit a new monthly magazine entitled *Bentley's Miscellany* and to write a story to be serialised within that publication from January 1837. That story was *Oliver Twist* and it was written from 1837 to 1839. Dickens had increased his workload because when the first number of *Oliver Twist* was issued, he was still writing installments of *The Pickwick Papers*.**

*The Pickwick Papers* was a collection of loosely connected stories, but *Oliver Twist* was Dickens' first full-scale novel. Dickens wanted the piece to be published monthly in *Bentley's Miscellany* because many literate working classes were living on low incomes and the magazine was more affordable to the less affluent in society.

The first instalment of *Oliver Twist* was published during February 1837 with the subtitle *The Parish Boy's Progress*. The story chronicled the childhood of Oliver Twist from being orphaned at birth in a workhouse, through the injustices and abuses he suffered within the workhouse to running away 70 miles to London, where he falls into the clutches of Fagin and his gang of thieves.

In London, Oliver meets the Artful Dodger, who introduces him to Fagin. He offers Oliver food and warmth, something that neither the workhouse nor the undertaker Mr Sowerberry could offer. However, these gestures of kindness have sinister undertones, for those who accept Fagin's generosity are expected to go into the London streets and pick pockets for his benefit. It is here that the story focused upon vulnerable children living on the streets and how children were recruited into the criminal world. The nation was enthralled by the story of *Oliver Twist* as they read each instalment and it was positively received by literary critics, such as George Henry Lewes, who recognised Dickens' talent in his review of *Oliver Twist*:

> Boz should be compared to no-one as no-one has ever written like him – no-one has ever combined the nicety of observation, the fineness of tact, the exquisite humour, the wit, heartiness, sympathy with all things good and beautiful in human nature, the perception of character, the pathos, and accuracy of description, with the same force that he has done.[34]

---

34. *National Magazine and Monthly Critic 1837*, pp.445–9.

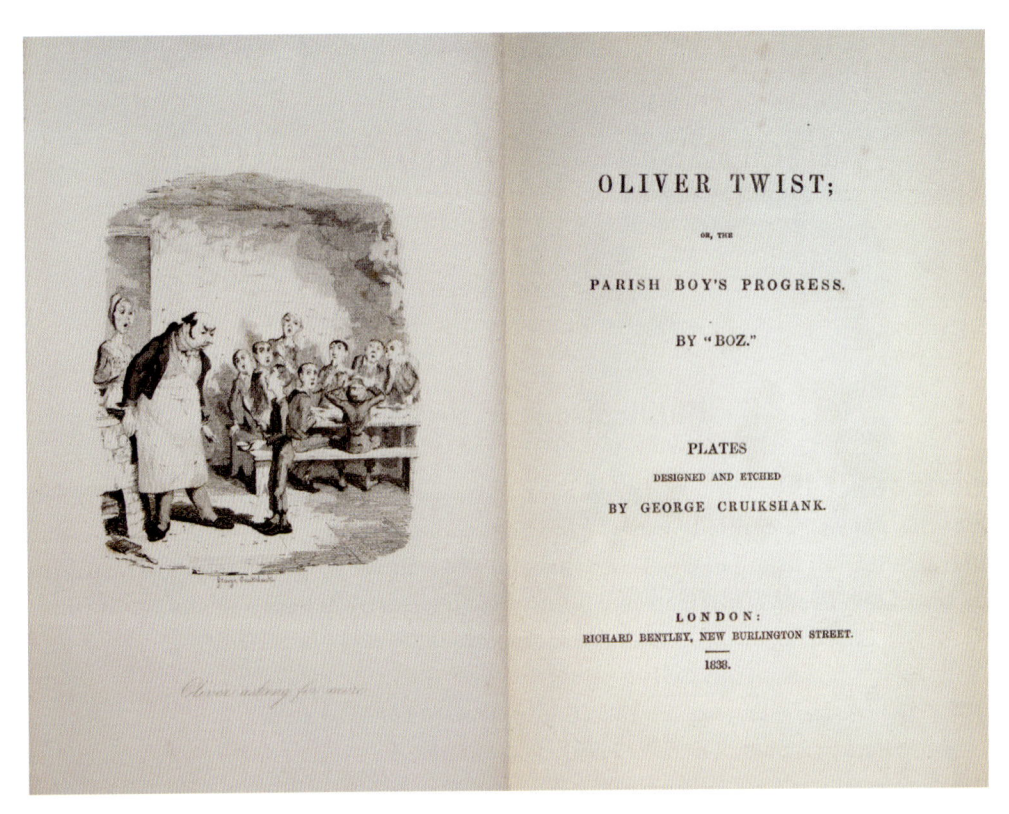

Frontispiece from the first edition of *Oliver Twist*, 1838. (Author's Collection)

Dickens had produced a story that was written in a way that was groundbreaking in English literature. Another reviewer commented that: 'This admirable story by "Boz," which will take its stand among the highest prose fictions of the language, and which has become so universally popular … We have never read anything so real.'[35]

Later in 1838 the novel was published in one volume and this is the frontispiece, which showed that it was written under Dickens' pseudonym, Boz, and illustrated by George Cruickshank. The frontispiece also included Cruickshank's illustration of the famished Oliver Twist asking for more gruel from the less than empathetic workhouse master. Dickens experienced a turbulent relationship with Bentley and was unhappy with how he was treated by this publisher. As the serialisation of *Oliver Twist* came to a conclusion, he resigned as editor of *Bentley's Miscellany* and with the help of Chapman & Hall, his successive publisher, Dickens was able to purchase the rights of *Oliver Twist*.

---

35. *Leeds Intelligencer*, 28 October 1837.

# 19

# Characters from *Oliver Twist*

## Dickens established some of his iconic, well-known characters within this novel

**O**liver Twist is the protagonist of Dickens' second novel. Born in a workhouse in a town outside London, Oliver is orphaned when his mother, Agnes Fleming, dies shortly after childbirth and is robbed by Old Sally, a nurse at the workhouse, on her death bed. As an infant he is 'farmed' out to be cared for at a baby farm run by Mrs Mann with twenty other infants until aged nine, when he is taken by Mr Bumble to the workhouse to learn a trade. However, Oliver is forced to pick oakum to seal warships instead.

Oliver asking for more food was used by Dickens as a mechanism to highlight that people, especially children in workhouses, were suffering malnutrition and to criticise the meagre diet provided. The master of the workhouse's response is brutal as he strikes Oliver with a blow across the head for having the audacity to request more food. The board of the workhouse offers £5 to anyone willing to apprentice Oliver, which leads to him being apprenticed to Mr Sowerberry, the undertaker. Although Sowerberry treats Oliver kindly and appoints him as a mourner at children's funerals, he is mistreated by his wife, who underfeeds him, and he is bullied by fellow apprentice Noah Claypole.

After running away to London, a chance encounter with the Artful Dodger leads him into a world of vice and criminality in which he is taken in by Fagin, the receiver of goods stolen by a number of children who he employs as thieves. Oliver is present when the Artful Dodger robs Mr Brownlow and is arrested. At his trial Brownlow confirms that Oliver was not the culprit and takes him under his wing. Fagin's gang finds Oliver and drags him back into the streets. A chain of events leads Oliver to finding his aunt and details of his parentage, as well as being rescued by Brownlow.

Oliver Twist. (All Author's Collection)

**Mr Bumble** is the Parish Beadle who brings Oliver Twist to the workhouse from where he was farmed. Dickens derived his name from the word bumptious, which is an ambiguous word for conceited, arrogant, pompous and consumed within one's own self-importance, clearly unsavoury qualities that were associated with Mr Bumble. He is a man who preaches Christian virtues but lacks compassion or empathy for the orphans under his guardianship. After accessing the valuables of Mrs Corney, the matron of the workhouse, he succeeds in wooing and marrying her, only to discover that she is an acid-tongued tyrannical woman who makes his life uncomfortable. Bumble ascends to the position of master of the workhouse, albeit he becomes a suppressed husband and is humiliated by his wife in front of the paupers. When Bumble learns from Mr Brownlow that the husband is lawfully responsible for the actions of his wife, Bumble retorts that 'if the law supposes that … the law is an ass – a idiot. If that's the eye of the law, the law's a bachelor, and the worse I may wish the law is, that his eye may be opened by experience – by experience.'[36]

Mr Bumble.

Bumble's wife Mrs Corney is present when workhouse inmate Old Sally confesses to stealing items belonging to Agnes Fleming when she died after giving birth to Oliver. The Bumbles sell these items to Oliver's half-brother Edward Monks, who throws them in the River Thames to ensure that Oliver's true identity remains concealed. When their complicity with Monks' plot is discovered, the Bumbles lose their positions at the workhouse and they find themselves reduced to poverty and living in a workhouse.

**Jack Dawkins (alias the Artful Dodger)** is a young pickpocket who works for Fagin. He is the leader of the gang of thieves and Dickens portrayed him as a child who behaved like a streetwise adult, living off his wits:

> He was a snub-nosed, flat-bowed, common-faced boy enough; and as dirty a juvenile as one would wish to see; but he had about him all the airs and manners of a man. He was short of his age: with rather bow-legs, and little, sharp, ugly eyes. His hat was stuck on the top of his head so lightly, that it threatened to fall off every moment – and would have done so, very often, if the wearer had not had a knack of every now and then giving his head a sudden twitch, which brought it back to its old place again.[37]

---

36. Dickens, Charles, *Oliver Twist* (Harper & Brothers publishers, New York, 1872), p.164.

37. Ibid., p.29.

Jack Dawkins, the Artful Dodger.   Fagin.   Bill Sikes.

He befriends Oliver and tries to teach him the skill of pilfering, to no avail. The luck of the Artful Dodger runs out when he is caught stealing and is sentenced to transportation for life.

**Fagin** is a villainous fence who trains vulnerable children to steal and receives the results of their pilfering. Despite appearing jovial and friendly, he is capable of violence, which he demonstrates in the beating of the Artful Dodger when Oliver is first rescued by Brownlow. He fails in his attempt to lead Oliver Twist into a life of crime and after a life lived in crime, he is condemned to death by hanging for complicity to murder.

**Bill Sikes** is a former pupil of Fagin who has evolved into a violent burglar. Accompanied by his bull terrier named Bulls-eye, Sikes is devoid of any redeeming features. He is violent towards Nancy, his lover, and the relationship concludes with him brutally beating her to death. When the police search for a man with a dog resembling his description, he attempts to drown his faithful animal.

# 20

# Cleveland Street Workhouse, London

## Inspiration for the workhouse in *Oliver Twist*.

**Despite Oliver Twist being born in a workhouse 70 miles from London, it is believed that Dickens was aware of this workhouse at No. 44 Cleveland Street because he lived at No. 22 when it was called Norfolk Street on two occasions during his youth.**

Dickens also used the story of *Oliver Twist* as a vehicle to highlight the unfairness of the Poor Law introduced by Parliament in 1834. The aim of the law was to provide support to the vulnerable, destitute and underprivileged in society. The workhouse, such as the one at Cleveland Street, was meant to have been the institution that would facilitate that assistance to those who were unable to support themselves. However, the workhouse system was deliberately created to make them unpleasant, and administered with a harsh regime used as a deterrent to encourage the disadvantaged to support themselves.

Dickens exposed the deficiencies of the workhouse system and showed how they broke up and segregated families, with husbands separated from their wives, children from their parents and infants sent to be cared for in baby farms. The workhouse was an oppressive environment, while the wealthy administrators who preached religion and applauded their own perverted perception of philanthropy while being well fed, were unsympathetic, uncaring and behaved negligently to those children under their care and guardianship, who were poorly fed and worked to exhaustion. These institutions were meant to provide assistance to those in need; instead it broke their spirits and resolve. Dickens attacked these civil institutions that kept children malnourished and laws that allowed these children to be sold like slaves and exploited for child labour through the story of Oliver Twist.

It was ironic that Lord Melbourne, who was Home Secretary when the Poor Law was passed through Parliament, read the beginning of *Oliver Twist* when he was serving as Prime Minister and discarded it, commenting that 'it is all among workhouses and pickpockets and coffin makers. I do not like those things: I wish to avoid them. I do not like them in reality and therefore do not like to see them represented.'[38]

---

38. Cecil, David, *The Young Melbourne* (The Bobbs-Merrill Company, 1939), p.263.

Although Lord Melbourne was reluctant to read *Oliver Twist*, Dickens' influence as a writer touched all echelons of society. Queen Victoria mentioned in her journal on several occasions that she read *Oliver Twist*.

*Right*: Cleveland Street Workhouse, which cared for the sick and poor of the local parish. (Author's Collection)

*Below*: Cleveland Street Workhouse. (Courtesy of Matt Brown)

# 21

# Jacob's Island

**Scene of Bill Sikes' demise in *Oliver Twist*.**

**Sikes received a violent end when he was pursued by the police to his refuge at Jacob's Island. As he tried to evade them by using a rope to climb down from the roof of a warehouse, he was hanged by that rope and died.**

Jacob's Island was a notorious slum in Bermondsey, just south-east from Tower Bridge. The area, located east of St Saviour's Dock, was a dangerous place to be and Dickens had to be escorted to Jacob's Island by the officers of the River Police when he visited the place for research.

Dickens wrote in *Oliver Twist*:

In the borough of Southwark, stands Jacob's Island, surrounded by a muddy ditch, six or eight feet deep and fifteen or twenty feet wide when the tide is in, once called Mill Pond, but known in the days of this story as Folly Ditch … Crazy wooden galleries common to the backs of half a dozen houses, with holes from which to look upon the slime beneath; windows, broken and

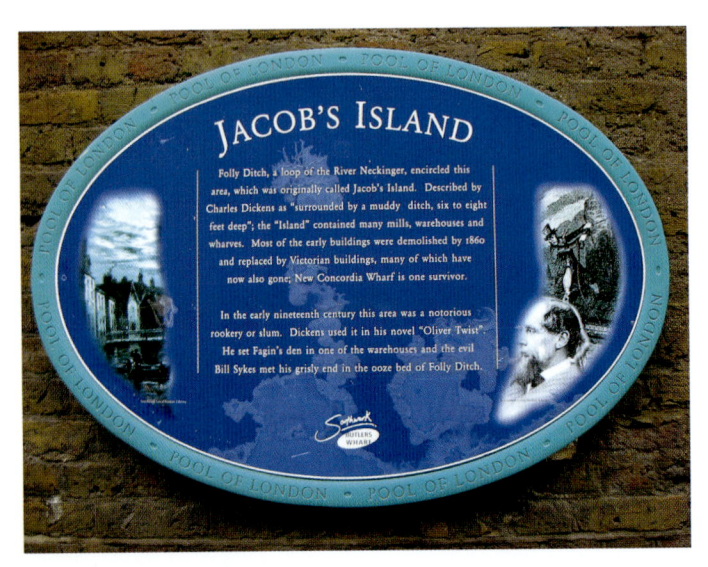

The plaque denoting the site of Jacob's Island, Bermondsey. (Courtesy of T.P. Holland)

St Saviour's Dock and site of Jacob's Island. (Courtesy of John Sutton; www.geograph.org)

patched, with poles thrust out, on which to dry the linen that is never there; rooms so small, so filthy, so confined, that the air would seem to be too tainted even for the dirt and squalor which they shelter; wooden chambers thrusting themselves out above the mud and threatening to fall into it – as some have done; dirt-besmeared walls and decaying foundations, every repulsive lineament of poverty, every loathsome indication of filth, rot, and garbage: all these ornament the banks of Folly Ditch. In Jacob's Island the warehouses are roofless and empty; the walls are crumbling down; the windows are windows no more; the doors are falling into the streets; the chimneys are blackened, but they yield no smoke … now it is a desolate island indeed. The houses have no owners; they are broken open and entered upon by those who have the courage; and there they live and die. They must have powerful motives for a secret residence, or be reduced to a destitute condition indeed, who seek a refuge in Jacob's Island.[39]

A plaque commemorates Dickens' association with this site. However, the statement that Fagin's den was at Jacob's Island is incorrect. Dickens set Fagin's den in Field Lane, Saffron Hill, where the Holborn Viaduct now stands. Jacob's Island was, however, where Fagin's thieves took refuge when he was arrested. Today Jacob's Island has been replaced by modern apartments and to the west is Butler's Wharf, where Dickens set the location for Quilp's yard in *The Old Curiosity Shop*.

---

39. Dickens, *Twist*, op. cit., p.157.

# 22

# No. 14 Market Place, Barnard Castle

### Place where Dickens conducted research for *Nicholas Nickleby*.

The blue plaque by the door states that Dickens stayed at this Grade II listed building, then the King's Head, in 1838 while collecting material for *Nicholas Nickleby*.

Dickens was commissioned to write *The Life and Adventures of Nicholas Nickleby* on 19 November 1837. It was agreed that the first number was to be delivered to Chapman & Hall on 15 March 1838 and on the 15th of each successive nineteen months. Dickens received £150 per issue.[40] The first instalment of *Nicholas Nickleby* was published in April 1838 and ended in October 1839. This placed enormous pressure upon Dickens as a writer. He had begun writing the first instalments of *Nicholas Nickleby* while he was continuing to write numbers of *Oliver Twist*.

Before writing *Nicholas Nickleby*, Dickens, accompanied by his illustrator, H.K. Browne, known as 'Phiz', visited boarding schools in North Yorkshire where poor children unwanted by their parents were housed in oppressive conditions. They would provide the inspiration for Dickens to create Dotheboys Hall in the novel.

During the visit, Dickens stayed at the King's Head at Barnard Castle for two nights on 1 and 2 February 1838 while he was exploring the area, which was covered with snow. Dickens was writing from personal experience when he referred to it in *Nicholas Nickleby* when Newman Noggs concluded a letter: 'If you should go near Barnard Castle, there is good ale at the King's Head.'[41] The public house no longer exists but the building has remained as it was during Dickens' visit and a plaque commemorates his stay.

*Nicholas Nickleby* repeated the success of his previous work and sold 50,000 copies of the serial.[42] The book was dedicated to his friend, the actor William Macready, who was also

---

40. Forster, Vol. 1, op. cit., p.146.

41. Dickens, Charles, *Nicholas Nickleby* (Chapman & Hall, 1839), p.64.

42. Forster, Vol. 2, op. cit., p.64.

*Above*: No. 14 Market Place, Barnard Castle, was formerly the King's Head where Dickens stayed during February 1838. The building is now a Grade II listed property. (Courtesy of Eiran Evans; www.geograph.org.uk)

*Right*: The blue plaque by the door of 14 Market Place states that Dickens stayed at this establishment in 1838 while collecting material for *Nicholas Nickleby*. (Courtesy of Bob Harvey; www.geograph.org.uk)

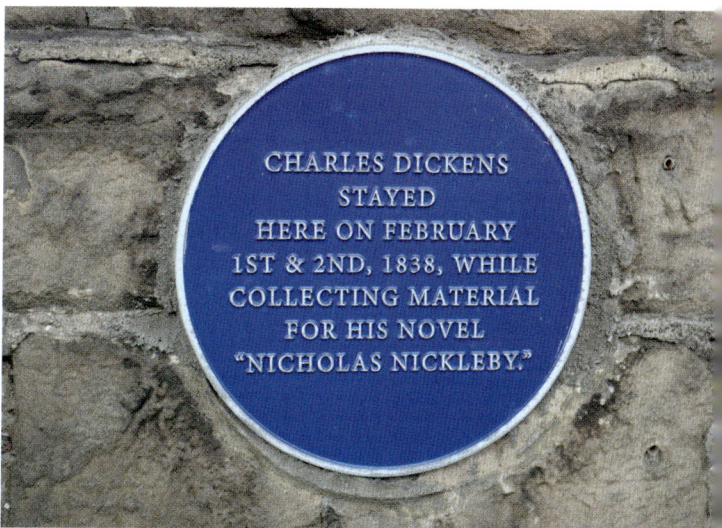

godfather to Kate. It was also the only book that Dickens wrote that features the town of his birth, when Nicholas and Smike walk 75 miles from London to Portsmouth. The success of *Nicholas Nickleby* surpassed the sales of *The Pickwick Papers* and *Oliver Twist*, so Chapman & Hall paid Dickens an additional £1,500.[43]

---

43. Forster, Vol. 1, op. cit., p.197.

NO. 14 MARKET PLACE, BARNARD CASTLE | 59

# 23

# Bowes Academy, Yorkshire

**The original school known as Bowes Academy or Shaw's Academy was immortalised by Dickens as Dotheboys Hall in *Nicholas Nickleby*.**

Bowes Academy was established in 1817 at Great Bridge, Yorkshire. An advert in *The Times* stated that it did not allow vacations, which meant that parents could leave their unwanted children at the school. It was a hellish place and its headmaster, William Shaw, was prosecuted in 1823 for negligence after two students went blind as a result of poor hygiene and treatment. Dickens visited Bowes Academy to carry out research for *Nicholas Nickleby* and he would use the novel to expose the unsatisfactory conditions and the agonies, neglect, cruelty and disease suffered by the students at these boarding schools, to condemn them and campaign for their closure.

In *Nicholas Nickleby*, Dickens describes Dotheboys Hall as 'a long cold-looking house, one storey high, with a few straggling out-buildings behind, and a barn and stable adjoining'.[44] It is a cheap boarding school where unwanted children are left by their uncaring parents and guardians. The children are oppressed with violence and malnourished. On 2 February 1838, Dickens visited Bowes Academy and saw the one-eyed headmaster, William Shaw. Dickens based the character of Wackford Squeers, the sadistic headmaster of Dotheboys Hall, on Shaw, for both men shared the same initials and both had one eye. Dickens wrote, 'Shaw, the headmaster we saw today, is the man in whose school several boys went blind some time since from gross neglect. The case was tried, and the verdict went against him. It must have been between 1823 and 1826.'[45]

William Jones was an eleven-year-old pupil at Shaw's Academy and testified against Shaw at one of those trials. He recalled:

On one occasion in October I felt a weakness in my eyes and could not write my copy. Mr Shaw said he would beat me. On the next day I could not see at all and I told

---

44. Dickens, *Nickleby*, op. cit., p.59.

45. *Penrith Observer*, 21 September 1954.

Bowes Academy was the inspiration for Dickens' Dotheboys Hall in *Nicholas Nickleby*. (Author's Collection)

Mr Shaw who sent me and three others to the wash house. I stayed in the wash house about a month. The number of boys when I left it was 18. I was then put into a room. There were nine boys totally blind.[46]

The jury went in favour of William Jones against Shaw and Jones was awarded £300 damages. Despite losing various legal cases brought against him, Shaw's Academy continued to operate when Dickens visited in 1838. Dickens was quite precise in his research of Bowes Academy and the shenanigans of Mr Shaw. In a letter written on 29 December 1838 he wrote:

Depend upon it that the rascalities of these Yorkshire schoolmasters cannot easily be exaggerated, and that I have kept down the strong truth and thrown as much comicality over it as I could, rather than disgust and weary the reader with its fouler aspects. The identical scoundrel you speak of, I saw curiously enough – His name is Shaw: the action was tried (I believe) eight or ten years since, and if I am not much mistaken, another action was brought against him by the parents of a miserable child, a cancer in whose head he opened with an inky penknife, and so caused his death. The country for miles around was covered, when I was there, with deep snow.[47]

In the churchyard close to the school Dickens found the grave of George Ashton Taylor, who was a pupil and died while under the guardianship of William Shaw. It is speculated that Taylor was the inspiration for the story of Smike. Dickens wrote, 'I suppose the boy's heart broke – the camel follows down suddenly when they heap the last load upon his back – died at that wretched place. I think his ghost put Smike into my head, upon the spot.'[48]

Dickens' exposure of these abhorrent schools did encourage the closure of some of them, for in the preface of a later edition of the book he wrote that 'though it has not yet disappeared, it is dwindling daily'.

---

46. Ibid., 28 September 1954.
47. Ibid., 7 September 1915.
48. *Daily Herald*, 11 April 1933.

# 24

## Characters from *Nicholas Nickleby*

*Nicholas Nickleby* was published in instalments from April 1838 to October 1839. Dickens' third novel was about the protagonist coming of age, at the moment when he and his family fall into poverty.

**Nicholas Nickleby and Smike.** The young Nicholas Nickleby and his sister Kate are reduced to penury after his father's death and a legacy of bad investments. Their mother appeals for assistance from their uncle, Ralph Nickleby, who receives them coldly and, despite being affluent, refuses to support them. Ralph takes an instant dislike to Nicholas, but secures a position for him as an assistant teacher at Dotheboys Hall, administered by headmaster Wackford Squeers. It was here that Nicholas witnesses his brutality and ill treatment of the boys under his care. Smike is one of Squeers' victims, who is disabled and in modern terms would require special educational needs. Smike is brought to Dotheboys Hall, but after the first year no one comes to claim him or pay his fees, so Squeers uses him as a skivvy, and physically abuses and starves him. The treatment leaves Smike traumatised by the beatings, malnourished, half-witted with his spirit broken. Nicholas takes pity and treats him with kindness and gentleness. Unable to live under the oppressive regime of the Squeers, Smike runs away but is caught by Mrs Squeers and returned to Dotheboys Hall, where he is tied and beaten by her husband. Nicholas Nickleby intervenes and beats Squeers with the cane, with the same violence that he would have inflicted upon Smike, before Nickleby and Smike both depart from Dotheboys Hall. They join Mr Crummles' theatrical company and then venture to London, where Nicholas protects the honour of his sister Kate from the lecherous Sir Mulberry Hawk. Nicholas secures employment with the Cheeryble brothers, so he is able to support Kate and his mother. Smike is welcomed into Nicholas' family, which brings him comfort and allows him to heal from his troubled childhood. Squeers captures Smike in London, but he is rescued by Nicholas. Despite feeling accepted by Nicholas and his family, Smike never recovers from his traumatic childhood and dies before it is revealed that he is the discarded son of Ralph Nickleby and a cousin to Nicholas. The relationship between Nicholas and Smike is at the heart of the novel. Nicholas' compassion, friendship and loyalty to Smike is endearing and Smike's response touches the heart. Dickens showed that everyone deserves love, respect and friendship.

*Nicholas astonishes Mr. Squeers and family.*

This illustration by Hablot Knight Browne depicts Nicholas Nickleby saving Smike from Wackford Squeer's violent abuse. (British Library)

# 25

# Royal Albion Hotel, Broadstairs

## Dickens frequently stayed at this hotel.

**The plaque on the wall of the Royal Albion Hotel confirms that Dickens stayed at the hotel during 1839, 1840, 1845, 1849 and 1859, and that he wrote part of *Nicholas Nickleby* here.**

Dickens made his first visit to Broadstairs with his family during the summer 1837 and was lodging at 12 Albion Street, where he worked on some of the instalments of *The Pickwick Papers*. He wrote: 'I have walked upon the sands at low-water from this place to Ramsgate, and sat upon the same at high-ditto till I have been flayed with the cold.'[49] He also socialised at the Albion Hotel during this visit, when he was joined by John Forster, because Dickens wrote a letter to him in 1839, remembering his first visit to Broadstairs in which he referred to the 'Albion Hotel where we had a merry night two years ago'.[50]

In 1839, Dickens stayed at No. 40, also in Albion Street, which was two doors from the Albion Hotel where this plaque is located. During that visit Dickens completed the final instalments of *Nicholas Nickleby*. Broadstairs was a quiet seaside town where Dickens could write, walk, swim and enjoy the sea air. On 1 September 1843, Dickens described Broadstairs in a letter to Professor Felton:

> This is a little fishing village; intensely quiet; built on a cliff, where on – in the centre of a tiny semi-circular bay – our house stands; the sea rolling and dashing under the windows. Seven miles out are the Goodwin Sands … whence floating lights perpetually wink after dark, as if they were carrying on intrigues with the servants. Also, there is a big lighthouse called the North Foreland on a hill behind the village, a severe parsonic light, which reproves the young and giddy floaters, and stares grimly out upon the sea. Under the cliff are rare good sands, where all the children assemble every morning and throw up impossible fortifications, which the sea throws down again at high water.[51]

---

49. Forster, Vol. 1, op. cit., p.137.
50. Dexter, Walter, *The Kent of Dickens* (Cecil Palmer, London, 1924), p.181.
51. Dickens, Charles, *The Letters of Charles Dickens, Volume 1* (Chapman & Hall Limited, London 1882), p.105.

While staying at the Albion Hotel in 1849, he wrote *David Copperfield* and it was from his hotel room window that he could see Mary Pearson Strong objecting to donkeys passing in front of her home, which was across the road from the hotel and gave Dickens the inspiration for the character of Betsey Trotwood in the book.

In September 1859, Dickens was suffering from a cold and stayed at the Albion Hotel to recover. By that time, the house at No. 40 Albion Street had been bought by the landlord named Ballard and was incorporated as part of the expanding hotel.

*Above*: The white building in the centre of the photograph is the western side of the Albion Hotel in Broadstairs. Dickens stayed here on several occasions throughout his life. In 1839, Dickens lodged in a house two doors from the Albion Hotel. The eastern side of the hotel overlooks the sea. (Author's collection)

*Right*: A plaque on the wall of the Albion Hotel. (Author's Collection)

# 26

# Sculptured Panel Commemorating Dickens, Marylebone, London

**The site of Dickens residence at No. 1 Devonshire Terrace.**

**This memorial, situated at 15 Fergusson House, Marylebone Road, London, marks the site of the home that Charles Dickens leased from 1839 until 1851. It was demolished during 1958 and replaced with the current office block named Fergusson House.**

The plaque states that: 'While living on a house on this site Charles Dickens wrote six of his principal works, characters from which appear in this sculptured panel.' The characters that are featured on this mural are, left to right along the top: Scrooge with the head alongside the door knocker representing Marley's ghost from *A Christmas Carol*, Barnaby Rudge and Grip, his raven from *Barnaby Rudge*, Little Nell and her grandfather from *The Old Curiosity Shop*. On the middle row: Paul Dombey and his son, Little Paul, from *Dombey & Son*, Mrs Gamp from *Martin Chuzzlewit* and on the bottom, there is Mr Micawber and David Copperfield from *David Copperfield*.

The sculptured panel depicting Dickens and some of his characters at 15 Fergusson House, Marylebone Road, London, is today on the site of what was No. 1 Devonshire Terrace. (Author's Collection)

66 CHARLES DICKENS – PLACES AND OBJECTS OF INTEREST

Dickens' home at No. 1 Devonshire Terrace, Marylebone, London, from 1839 to 1851 – as it appeared then. St Marylebone Parish Church was adjacent to this building and it was there that he set the scene for the burial of Paul Dombey and his mother. It was also the setting for Mr Dombey's second wedding. (Author's Collection)

Dickens moved to No. 1 Devonshire Terrace during November 1839 and described it as 'a house of great promise (and great premium), undeniable situation, and excessive splendour'.[52] John Forster said that 'he cared most for Devonshire Terrace'.[53] His two daughters, Mamie and Katie, occupied the garret at the top of the building and Dickens' study had close access to the garden. Mamie described Dickens' writing environment in this house: 'The first study

---

52. Kitton, *Country*, op. cit., p.58.
53. Forster, Vol. 2, op. cit., p.457.

SCULPTURED PANEL COMMEMORATING DICKENS, MARYLEBONE, LONDON

that I remember is the one in our Devonshire Terrace home, a pretty room, with steps leading directly into the garden from it, and with an extra baize door to keep out all sounds and noise.'[54]

The garden was a prime attraction for Dickens because he was able to play shuttlecock and bowls with his family and friends. Lady Sawle provided details of a visit to Dickens at this house during the spring 1840 in her diary:

> We dined with Mr and Mrs. Charles Dickens in Devonshire Terrace, and there met Dr Quin, Walter Savage Landor, Mr John Forster, Mr Kenyon, the poet and Daniel Maclise, the artist. The house had a small enclosure at the back, with a grass plot, and a tree in the centre. It was very hot that day, and we found Dickens lying on his back, on the turf under the tree, deep in composition of *The Old Curiosity Shop*. He told me he had received scores of letters imploring him not to kill Little Nell. In the evening we had charades en action. Charles Dickens was a born actor. With a turn down of his cuffs, or a turn up of his collar, or coat thrown back from his shoulder, he so metamorphosized himself that he could personate at will any character … Charles Dickens was a very showy dresser, and wore his hair long.[55]

The year 1849 was a pinnacle moment for Dickens with the publication of *David Copperfield* and prominent members of the aristocracy and eminent writers, actors and scientists would be honoured to receive an invitation to dine with him at No. 1 Devonshire Terrace, including Thomas Carlyle, William Thackeray, Charles Babbage, Isambard Kingdom Brunel, Charles Kemble, Edward Bulwer-Lytton and Elizabeth Gaskell. Dickens relished entertaining his guests at his home. Mamie wrote that 'he was delightful as a host, caring individually for each guest, and bringing the special qualities of each into full notice and prominence, putting the very shyest at his or her ease, making the best of the most humdrum, and never thrusting himself forward'.[56]

On 21 September 1845, Dickens and his friends performed a private amateur dramatics production of Ben Jonson's play *Everyman in his Humour* at Devonshire Terrace. It was very successful and there was demand for it to be performed in a larger theatre where the public was admitted.

The Dickens family continued to expand while at Devonshire Terrace, with the birth of four sons named, Walter Landor, Francis Jeffrey, Alfred Tennyson, Henry Fielding and a daughter, Dora Annie, who died prematurely shortly after her birth. By 1851, Dickens and Catherine were the parents to six sons and two daughters. They decided that Devonshire Terrace could no longer accommodate the family and did not renew the lease.

---

54. Dickens, Mamie, op. cit., p.49.

55. Sawle, Rose Paynter Graves, *Sketches from the Diaries of Rose Lady Graves Sawle* (W.H. Smith, London 1908), p.53.

56. Dickens, Mamie, op. cit., p.16.

# 27

# The Old Curiosity Shop, London

*The Old Curiosity Shop* **first appeared in** *Master Humphrey's Clock* **during 1840.**

The shop was not the inspiration for the shop in the novel. However, Dickens was aware of this corner shop because he would regularly visit his friend John Forster, who lived nearby in Lincoln's Inn Fields.

*Master Humphrey's Clock* was a weekly periodical written and edited by Dickens, financed by Chapman & Hall. The premise for the project was a collection of short stories where Master Humphrey wrote about his friends, including Mr Pickwick. On 4 April 1840, the first edition was published, but the sales for the initial three numbers were poor. Dickens was writing occasional articles and his readers expected more content from him, which reduced sales. He was compelled to give his readers what they wanted and to salvage the project by including a new serialised story of similar length and depth as his previous work. He would begin to include the story of Little Nell and her grandfather in the weekly serialisation that would become *The Old Curiosity Shop*. As the story of the adventures of Nell and her grandfather progressed, the sales of *Master Humphrey's Clock* increased weekly. Before the serialisation ended, a version of the story was being prepared to be performed on stage at the Theatre Royal, Sadler's Wells, London.

The shop in Portsmouth Street, London, attracts tourists from around the world, but despite its audacious signing on its wall 'immortalised by Charles Dickens', it was not the inspiration for the novel. A newspaper article in the *Sheffield Weekly Telegraph* in 1884 mentioned an interview with Georgina Hogarth regarding the issue:

> The controversy rages meanwhile with unabated vigour. But when all is said we fear the Old Curiosity Shop at No. 14 Portsmouth Street, is a sham. We have ventured to ask Miss Hogarth for any information respecting the house, but the locality was unfortunately never pointed out to her, and she is unable to speak authoritatively. 'My impression is,' she writes, 'that the identifying of this particular house is a mistake, but I always imagined the place to be more remote. I do not suppose that anyone lives now

The Old Curiosity Shop in Portsmouth Street, London. (Alexandre Rotenberg/Shutterstock)

who could throw any light on the matter. Mr Forster might have known, and George Cattermole and Hablot Brown, certainly.[57]

Charles Tessyman was a bookbinder who owned the shop in Portsmouth Street between 1868 and 1877 and knew Thackeray and Dickens. The statement was painted upon the façade of the shop around 1870 by Tessyman for commercial purposes and it worked because many American tourists who read the book came to visit the building that they had been led to believe was the Old Curiosity Shop.

---

57. *Sheffield Weekly Telegraph*, 5 January 1884.

# 28

# Characters from *The Old Curiosity Shop*

### Published between April 1840 and November 1841 in eighty-eight weekly parts.

**Nell Trent (Little Nell)** is the focal character in the story. In the preface Dickens explained:

> I had it always in my fancy to surround the lonely figure of the child with grotesque and wild, but not impossible, companions, and to gather about her innocent face and pure intentions, associates as strange and uncongenial as the grim objects that are about her bed when her history is first foreshadowed.[58]

Little Nell is an orphan looked after by her elderly grandfather, who is the proprietor of the old curiosity shop and whose name is never revealed in the book. In his pursuit of ensuring his granddaughter's future and happiness, he turns to gambling, but persistently loses each time at the gaming table. He resorts to borrowing money from Daniel Quilp and sends Little Nell to collect money from him. She feels uncomfortable in his presence as she is only a child, being fourteen years old, but is in danger of being sexually and violently abused by Quilp, who lusts after her and suggests that she could become the second Mrs Quilp after he has disposed of his first wife. Also, her brother Freddie introduces Dick Swiveller in the hope that he will marry Little Nell and they both share the inheritance that they mistakenly believe she would inherit from her grandfather. It is uncomfortable to read that Quilp and Swiveller are adults who are in fact contemplating marriage with a child. There were no social services to protect a child in this dubious situation in the nineteenth century and Dickens was highlighting that children were at risk of being abused. With the grandfather unable to pay off the debts, Quilp takes possession of everything, including the old curiosity shop, and the grandfather and Little Nell are reduced to destitution and forced to escape from his clutches. Dickens explored the dynamic between generations, with her grandfather belonging to the older generation, while Little Nell represented youth. There is a role reversal where Little Nell, who is a child, acts like an adult in looking after her grandfather, the person who is meant to be her guardian and look after her well-being. Little

---

58. Dickens, Charles, *The Old Curiosity Shop* (Chapman & Hall Limited, London), p.vi.

*Above left*: Detail of Little Nell and her grandfather that can be seen on the sculptured panel depicting Dickens and his characters at 15 Fergusson House. (All author's Collection)

*Above right*: Little Nell.

*Left*: Sampson Brass.

Nell is a kind-hearted, fearless child who acts as the guardian angel to her wandering, reckless, irresponsible grandfather. She leads him from London and towards the Midlands. During that journey her grandfather gambles away their last possessions and she is forced to beg on the streets.

**Sampson Brass** is a low-rate, corrupt lawyer who practises with his sister and partner, **Sally Brass**, from an office in Bevis Mark in London. He serves Quilp as his legal advisor, preparing the legalities to enable the unscrupulous moneylender to take possession of the old curiosity shop as payment for outstanding debts owed

Sally Brass.

Dick Swiveller.

The Marchioness.

by Little Nell's grandfather. On behalf of Quilp he helps to falsely incriminate Christopher Nubbles, known as Kit, for which he is arrested and thrown into prison for larceny.

**Dick Swiveller** is a friend of Fred Trent, Little Nell's brother. Fred brings Swiveller to the old curiosity shop intent on him meeting Little Nell. When Little Nell and her grandfather disappear, Swiveller becomes friends with Quilp, who secures him a position as a clerk for Sampson Brass. This is where he met the Marchioness. After Kit Nubbles is arrested as a consequence of Sampson Brass's false testimony, the Marchioness informs Swiveller of Kit's innocence and Swiveller helps to procure the young boy's release. Swiveller receives an annual annuity and marries the Marchioness when she eventually reaches nineteen years of age.

**The Marchioness** is a malnourished maid who works in service of Sampson and Sally Brass. Dick Swiveller observes her looking through the key hole in the Brass office, and he calls her the Marchioness. It is through what she views through the keyhole that Kit is exonerated from the crime for which Sampson Brass has set him up.

CHARACTERS FROM *THE OLD CURIOSITY SHOP*

# 29

# Butler's Wharf

**The site of Quilp's Wharf in *The Old Curiosity Shop*.**

**Daniel Quilp was the fiendish, malformed dwarf who menacingly pervaded the story.**

Butler's Wharf is just west of Jacob's Island where Bill Sikes dies in *Oliver Twist* and Dickens returned to this stretch of the Thames to create the home for the antagonist in *The Old Curiosity Shop*. It was at Butler's Wharf that he located Quilp's Wharf, the business address of Daniel Quilp, where he is officially listed as a ship breaker, but there is no evidence that he is active in this occupation. He does not have a trade but earns his income from various enterprises. He collects rents from the dwellings along the riverside and is a money lender. Dickens described Quilp's business premises as 'a rat-infested dreary yard called "Quilp's Wharf," in which there were a little wooden counting-house burrowing all awry in the dust as if it had fallen from the clouds and ploughed into the ground; a few fragments of rusty anchors; several large iron rings; some piles of rotten wood; and two or three heaps of old sheet copper, crumpled, cracked and battered.'[59]

---

59. Dickens, *Curiosity*, op. cit., p.23.

Butler's Wharf, site of Quilp's Wharf in *The Old Curiosity Shop*. It shows the River Thames looking east. The site of Butler's Wharf is near Tower Bridge, though the latter did not exist during Dickens' lifetime. (Author's Collection)

Residents who lived in the vicinity of Butler's Wharf could remember an individual who resembled Dickens' villain, but Lady Sawle provided an insight into where Dickens obtained his inspiration for the creation of Quilp outside of London:

> Dickens loved to wander about the back streets of Bath, picking up the queer names which appear so often in his books. We introduced him to the original of Quilp, a frightful little dwarf named Prior, who let donkeys on hire, and whose temper was as ugly as his person. He always carried with him a thick stick, with which he belaboured his donkeys and his wife.[60]

Quilp was one of Dickens' most unsavoury characters. He described him:

> As an elderly man of remarkably hard features and forbidding aspect, and so low in stature as to be quite a dwarf, though his head and face were large enough for the body of a giant. His black eyes were restless, sly and cunning; his mouth and chin, bristly with the stubble of a coarse hard beard; and his complexion was one of that kind which never looks clean or wholesome. But what added to the grotesque expression of his face, was a ghastly smile, which, appearing to be the mere result of habit and to have no connection with any mirthful or complacent feeling, constantly revealed the few discoloured fangs that were yet scattered in his mouth, and gave him the aspect of a panting dog.[61]

Daniel Quilp. (Author's Collection)

Quilp was the most repulsive of Dickens' creations for he was the incarnation of devilish malignity, distorted spite and foul mischievous delight. He was a narcissist who revelled in the misfortunes of others. Quilp lived in Tower Hill opposite the entrance into the Tower of London. He is a domineering, violent, cruel husband to Betsey, his wife. Suggestive comments to Little Nell, who is a girl, not a woman, reveal Quilp to be a sexual predator, regardless of age and without a care if he feels his comments will make a person feel uncomfortable. He relentlessly pursues Little Nell and her grandfather for his money, but fails to find them. Quilp drowns in the Thames at Quilp's Wharf as he attempts to evade policemen who are about to arrest him for various crimes. His wife inherits his property and she goes on to marry a man who will love and treat her with the respect that she deserves.

---

60. Sawle, Rose Paynter Graves, *Sketches from the Diaries of Rose Lady Graves Sawle* (W.H. Smith, London 1908), p.55.
61. Dickens, *Curiosity*, op. cit., pp.17–18.

BUTLER'S WHARF

# 30

# Statue of Dickens and Little Nell

**The death of Little Nell was felt across the world and this statue of Dickens with his heroine was erected in Philadelphia, USA.**

**Dickens had not considered killing the character of Little Nell until John Forster suggested a tragic conclusion to the novel when he was halfway through writing the story. He was reluctant to kill her character but eventually accepted Forster's suggestion.**

As the health of the fragile Little Nell deteriorated towards the end of the serialisation, there was concern amongst readers that she would meet an unfortunate end and Dickens received many letters appealing to him not to kill her character in the story. Writing the death of Little Nell affected Dickens emotionally, because it reminded him of the personal bereavement he felt for the loss of Mary Hogarth, and according to John Forster he took some time to commit her demise to the page. Dickens wrote that:

> I am the wretchedest of the wretched. It casts the most horrible shadow upon me, and it is as much as I can do to keep moving at all. I tremble to approach the place … I sha'nt recover it for a long time. Nobody will miss her like I shall. It is such a very painful thing to me, that I really cannot express my sorrow. Old wounds bleed afresh when I only think of the way of doing it: what the actual doing it will be, God knows … Dear Mary died yesterday when I think of this sad story.[62]

Dickens eventually completed writing the last moments of Little Nell in *The Old Curiosity Shop*. He wanted to write her death in a sensitive manner, where those readers who were suffering from a similar bereavement would identify with that feeling and find some solace and comfort that everyone at some point in their lives feels this sense of loss for a loved one. The death of Little Nell affected Dickens deeply and although she was a fictional character, he mourned her as if she was his child. Dickens confirmed to John Forster on 17 January 1841:

---

62. Forster, Vol. 1, op. cit., p.210.

I resolved to try and do something which might be read by people about whom Death had been, with a softened feeling, and with consolation ... After you left last night, I took my desk upstairs, and, writing until four o'clock this morning, finished the old story. It makes me very melancholy to think that all these people are lost to me forever, and I feel as if I never could become attached to any new set of characters.[63]

*Master Humphrey's Clock* was deemed as Dickens' first failure, but sales increased when he featured *The Old Curiosity Shop* within this publication. He learned from the episode and began to know his audience and what they wanted from him. The story affected the nation and the demise of Little Nell caused many readers to shed a tear.

The appeal of the story of Little Nell became global as soon as editions became available. It reverberated across the Atlantic Ocean, where avid readers of the story waited on the piers of New York Harbour and hollered to English sailors on arriving ships if Little Nell was dead as if she was a real person. Dickens achieved international success and through *The Old Curiosity Shop* he enshrined the memory of his deceased sister-in-law, Mary Hogarth, through the character of Little Nell.

The American sculptor Francis Edwin Elwell sculptured this bronze statue of Dickens with Little Nell in 1891. Dickens is seated gracefully, combing his beard as he is absorbed in contemplative thought as Little Nell gazes up to her creator. It was first exhibited in Philadelphia, where it was awarded a gold medal. Elwell then brought the statue to England. Former British Prime Minister William Gladstone admired the work and Dickens' family were impressed. There was interest in raising funds to purchase the sculpture to display in England, but it could not be carried out because it would violate Dickens' wish that there would be no monuments erected in his honour after his death. Elwell received offers from affluent families in England offering to purchase the statue for private display, but he was reluctant to sell it for this purpose. The statue featuring Dickens and Little Nell was unveiled twenty-one years after his death in 1891 in Philadelphia.

The Dickens and Little Nell Memorial in Philadelphia. (Courtesy of Bruce Anderson)

---

63. Ibid., p.211.

# 31
# Lawn House, Broadstairs

***The Old Curiosity Shop* and *Barnaby Rudge* were written in this house.**

Dickens returned to Broadstairs on two occasions during June and September 1840 and stayed at a villa called Lawn House, which is now known as Archway House. The alley that skirts along the garden wall of Fort House passes through the archway.

Dickens lived at Lawn House (now known as Archway House) during 1840–41. This alleyway runs along the southern wall of Fort House, where Dickens also lived. (Author's Collection)

Dickens would rearrange the furniture at every home in which he lived, even if it was for a few days, to ensure that he created a suitable environment in which to write. On 2 June 1840 Dickens wrote after the day he arrived at Lawn House: 'I set out my writing table with extreme taste and neatness, and improved the disposition of the furniture generally.'[64] He wrote much of *The Old Curiosity Shop* while residing in Broadstairs during the summer of 1840.

Dickens returned to Lawn House in 1841 when he was writing *Barnaby Rudge*. A plaque on the wall of the villa commemorates this visit. On 2 August 1841 he wrote to John Forster from Broadstairs, 'it is the brightest day you ever saw. The sun is sparkling on the water so that I can hardly bear to look at it. The tide is in, and the fishing boats are dancing like mad.'[65]

While at Broadstairs he would walk along the beach, beneath the chalk cliffs at low tide to Ramsgate.

In a letter to his wife dated 3 September 1850 he mentioned 'Lawn House Archway', when he opened the gate to the garden of Fort House and Sydney bolted through it, along the alley to the archway.[66]

*Above*: Lawn House photographed in 1905. (Author's Collection)

Plaque on the wall of Lawn House, Broadstairs. (Author's Collection)

---

64. Ibid., p.215.

65. Ibid., p.281.

66. Dickens, *Letters*, Vol. 1, op. cit., p.239.

LAWN HOUSE, BROADSTAIRS

# 32

# Barnaby Rudge

## *Barnaby Rudge* was Dickens' first historical novel.

Dickens had committed to writing *Barnaby Rudge* for Richard Bentley several years before working on it. The novel was set during the Gordon Riots, which took place in London on 7 June 1780 as a response to anti-Catholic sentiment. During that night a mob set ablaze Newgate Prison and set free the prisoners. Dickens used the novel to discuss the morality of capital punishment.

During 1836, Dickens considered writing *Barnaby Rudge*, which he originally entitled *Gabriel Varden*, for *Bentley's Miscellaneous*, but he struggled to progress with this project. He was working full capacity while he was focused on *The Pickwick Papers*, *Oliver Twist* and *Nicholas Nickleby* and kept Richard Bentley waiting for a draft. After writing the initial chapters, Dickens was annoyed that Bentley had advertised this new serial, because he was not ready to advance the story because of his other commitments. As a consequence, Dickens agreed that Chapman & Hall should publish the work. *Barnaby Rudge* first appeared in *Master Humphrey's Clock* in weekly instalments between February and November 1841.

Lithograph depicting Barnaby Rudge seated at a table, holding a basket with one arm and feeding his pet raven, Grip, with the other. Grip is perched on Barnaby's head. (Courtesy Library of Congress)

**Barnaby Rudge** is a demented, reckless youth who becomes embroiled in the Gordon Riots when he joins the mob and its destruction during the riots in London. He shows determination as he continues fighting until he was overpowered and arrested. Rudge is condemned to death for his involvement in the riots but receives a pardon.

**Simon Tappertit**, known as Sim, is an apprentice to the locksmith Gabriel Varden. The ambitions Sim has aspirations of greater things and resents his employer. He is also in love with Varden's daughter, Dolly. Sim has a rival for her affections in Joe Willet. Tappertit is the captain of the group known as the "Prentice Knights', later called the 'United Bull-Dogs' who seek vengeance against their employers and aim to fight for the restoration of ancient rights and holidays. Sim is one of the leading agitators who takes part in the Gordon Riots, where he is shot and his legs are crushed. His legs are amputated and he is rejected by Dolly Varden. After a period of convalescence in hospital, Sim is sent to prison. He escapes the hangman for his involvement in the riots and at his trial he is discharged. He acquires two wooden legs and is helped by Gabriel Varden to establish a business as a bootblack, which becomes successful. Sim marries the widow of a rag and bone man at the end of the novel.

This playing card features the character Sim Tappertit from *Barnaby Rudge*. The popularity of Dickens' novels meant that there were opportunities to capitalise upon that public esteem in using characters from the novels for commercial purposes. This card originates from a pack of cards that contained the characters and scenes from Dickens' novels set in a neo-rococo framework, produced around 1855. (Smithsonian Design Museum)

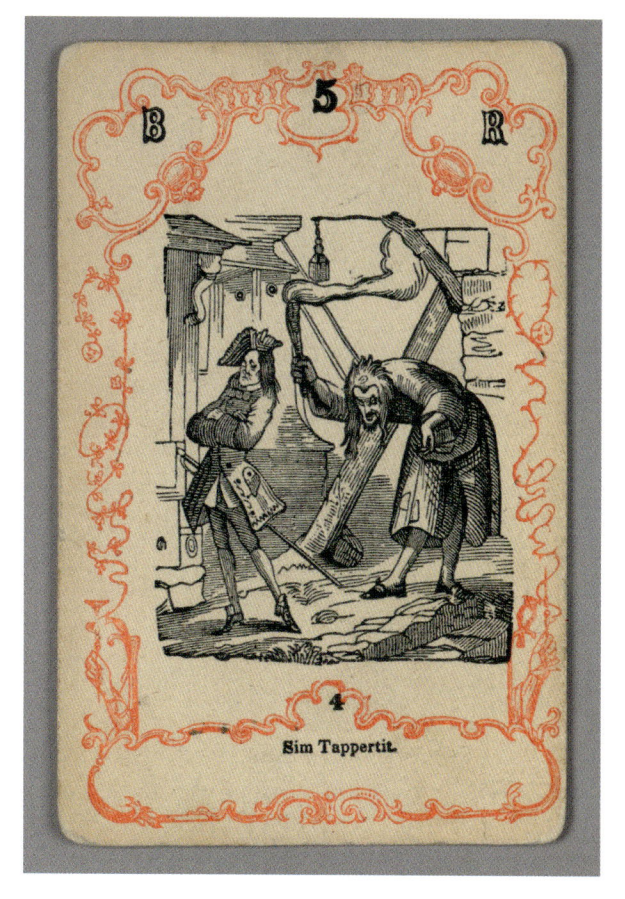

# 33

# Dickens' Pet Raven named Grip

### The taxidermized raven that inspired Dickens to feature in *Barnaby Rudge*.

**Grip was Dickens' beloved pet and when the raven died, he had him professionally taxidermized and mounted. Dickens immortalised Grip as the companion of Barnaby Rudge in the novel.**

Dickens adored animals and among the pets he kept at No. 1 Devonshire Terrace was an eagle and a raven. The eagle was kept in a grotto made especially for him in the garden, to which he was chained. Grip, the raven, was kept in a stable in the garden. When the American poet Henry Longfellow stayed at Devonshire Terrace as Dickens' guest he wrote in a letter: 'I write this from Dickens' study, the focus from which so many luminous things have radiated. The raven croaks in the garden, and the ceaseless roar of London fills my ears.'[67]

The raven was able to speak with an extensive vocabulary. He was very mischievous, chasing the children and biting their ankles. He became a source of amusement for the Dickens family. When the eagle was being fed, the raven would swoop down upon the food and place it out of reach. The raven tormented the eagle, mounting guard over the food, dancing around it and chuckling, before slowly devouring it in front of the eagle and then hopping away. During the summer 1840, the bird became ill when it swallowed some white paint, but recovered. The bird's comical ways made such a strong impression that Dickens featured the bird as a prominent character in *Barnaby Rudge*. As Dickens was writing the novel, the bird became ill once again and died.

Topping the coachman had brought a doctor to attend to the pet, but it was too late and it was the doctor who had to inform Dickens of the raven's death. The bird had deposited various bits of food and coins around the garden of No. 1 Devonshire Terrace, and his mischief was revealed when it was uncovered by a new raven that was given to Dickens by friends in Yorkshire. In a letter to Angela Burdett-Coutts, Dickens wrote:

> The raven's body was removed with every regard for my feelings, in a covered basket. It was taken off to be stuffed, but it has not come home yet. He has left a considerable property

---

67. Kitton, *Country*, op. cit., p.60.

Dickens' pet raven Grip. (Author's Collection)

(chiefly in cheese and half pence) buried in different parts of the garden, for I have a successor – administer to the effects. He had buried in one place a brush, a very large hammer, and several raw potatoes, which were discovered yesterday. He was very uneasy just before death, and wandering in his mind talked amazing nonsense. My servant thinks the hammer troubled him. It is supposed to have been stolen from a carpenter of vindictive disposition – he was heard to threaten – and I am not without suspicions of poison.[68]

After the taxidermist had preserved the remains of Grip, Dickens placed him in his study. The American writer and poet Edgar Poe Allen reviewed *Barnaby Rudge* and his only complaint was that he wanted to see Grip featured more in the novel. Poe became Dickens' friend and he too would be inspired by Grip when he wrote the poem entitled *The Raven*.

The raven remained with Dickens throughout his life and it was sold for £110 at the auction of his possessions after his death by Christie & Manson's auction room during July 1870. One journalist who viewed those items being sold commented, 'some disappointment will be felt by the admirers of "Grip" in "Barnaby Rudge," the favourite raven of Mr. Dickens. It is not much bigger than an ordinary crow, and badly stuffed, still, it is Charles Dickens' raven and the original of "Grip."'[69] The raven is displayed in the rare books Department of the Philadelphia Free Library.

---

68. Osbourne, Charles C., *Letters of Charles Dickens to the Baroness Burdett-Coutts* (John Murray, London, 1931), pp.33–4.

69. *Pall Mall Gazette*, 6 July 1870 and *Glasgow Evening Citizen*, 7 July 1870.

# 34

# Bust of Charles Dickens

## Dickens' first visit to the United States of America.

**Dickens was aged thirty and the success of** *The Pickwick Papers, Oliver Twist, Nicholas Nickleby* **and** *The Old Curiosity Shop* **was meteoric for they were not only successful in Britain, but they were also being sold around the world including the United States of America. In 1842 he took the opportunity to visit America to gauge that success in person. Henry Dexter sculptured this bust of Charles Dickens when he arrived in Boston.**

On 3 January 1842, Dickens and Catherine began a passage aboard the Cunard steamship *Britannia* across the Atlantic Ocean from Liverpool to Boston. The passage took eighteen days and the *Britannia* encountered a bad storm that swept away the paddle-boxes. Dickens and Catherine were ill for six days during the journey. The steamship ran aground near Halifax, Nova Scotia, and they had to wait until it was refloated by the rising tide. Dickens arrived in Boston on 22 January to a rapturous welcome. The extensive tour took Dickens from Boston along the eastern coastline through New York, Philadelphia, Washington and Richmond. He ventured west as far as St Louis before heading north towards Niagara Falls, Toronto, Montreal and Quebec in Canada.

While in Boston, Dickens permitted Henry Dexter to sculptor his image in the form of a bust. He granted this privilege to two artists during this tour. G.B. Putnum,

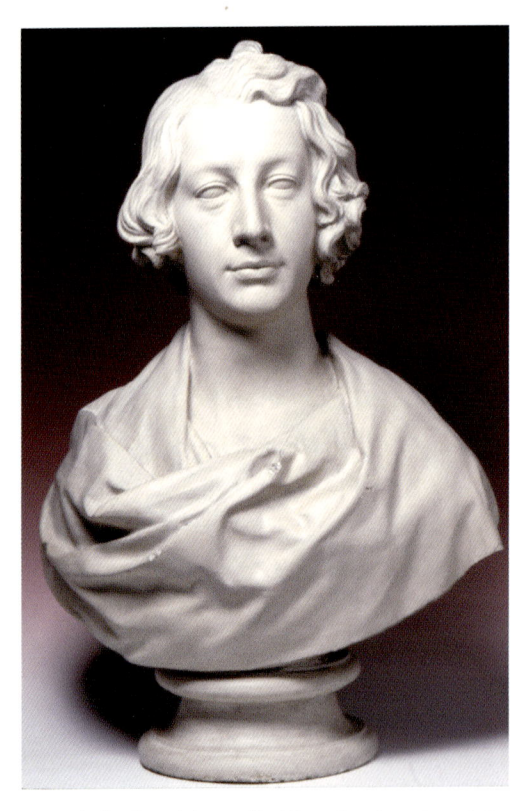

Bust of Charles Dickens. (Smithsonian American Art Museum and its Renwick Gallery)

Dickens' private secretary, was present in the author's Boston hotel room when Dexter created the bust, and wrote an article in the *Atlantic Monthly* in 1870:

> On Friday morning I was there at nine o'clock, the time appointed. Mr. and Mrs. Dickens had their meals in their own rooms, and the table was spread for breakfast. Soon they came in, and, after a cheerful greeting, I took my place at a side-table, and wrote as he ate his breakfast, and meanwhile conversed with Mrs. Dickens, opened his letters and dictated his answers to me.
>
> In one corner of the room, Dexter, was earnestly at work modelling a bust of Mr. Dickens. Several others of the most eminent artists of our country had urgently requested Mr. Dickens to sit for them for his picture and bust, but having consented to do so to Alexander and Dexter, he was obliged to refuse all others for want of time.
>
> While Mr. Dickens ate his breakfast, read his letters, dictated the answers, Dexter was watching him with the utmost earnest the play of every feature, and comparing his model with the original. Often during the meal, he would come to Dickens with a solemn, business-like air, stoop down, and look at him sideways, pass round and take a look at the other side of his face, and then go back to his model and work away for a few minutes; then come again and take another look, and go back to his model; then come again with the callipers and try the width of the temples, or the distance from the nose to the chin, and back again to his work, eagerly shaping and correcting his model. The whole soul of the artist was engaged in his task, and the result was a splendid bust of the great author. Mr. Dickens was highly pleased with it, and repeatedly alluded to it during his stay as a very successful work of art.[70]

Catherine Dickens praised Dexter's work in a letter: 'I was delighted with your bust of my husband, which I think is a beautiful likeness.'[71]

---

70. Albee, John, *Henry Dexter, Sculptor, A Memorial* (Privately Published, 1898), p.65.

71. Ibid., p.66.

# 35

# *American Notes*

## Dickens' travelogue, published 19 October 1842.

**On his return to England, Dickens set about writing his first travelogue detailing his experiences and perceptions of his first American tour.**

Dickens' visit to United States of America attracted much attention from the Americans. His presence attracted large crowds on a par with modern-day music or movie stars and he realised very quickly how popular he had become together with the consequences of being a celebrity. He wrote:

> I can give you no conception of my welcome here. There never was a king or emperor upon earth so cheered and followed by crowds, and entertained in public at splendid balls and dinners, and waited on by public bodies and deputations of all kinds. I have had one from the Far West – a journey of two thousand miles! If I go out in a carriage, the crowd surround it and escort me home; if I go to the theatre, the whole house (crowded to the roof) rises as one man, and the timbers ring again. You cannot imagine what it is. I have five great public dinners on hand at this moment, and invitations from every town and village and city in the States.[72]

The popularity Dickens attracted was at first a novelty, but it soon overwhelmed him. In each town he visited, he was invited to attend a reception that attracted many people with the expectation of shaking his hand. These functions would last two hours each day and it was too arduous for the exhausted Dickens as he had to engage with his enthusiastic admirers, who had so many questions for him. He was reluctant to be on view. He confided in Angela Burdett-Coutts, 'that they never leave me alone, that I shake hands every day when I am not travelling, with five or six hundred people. That Mrs Dickens and I hold a formal levee in every town we come to, and usually faint away (from fatigue) every day while dressing for dinner.'[73]

Dickens wanted to see if American democracy was a better model than the restrictive, oppressive, prejudiced class system in Britain. He did not appreciate the American custom of

---

72. Dickens, *Letters*, Vol. 1, op. cit., p.62.

73. Osbourne, op. cit., p.38.

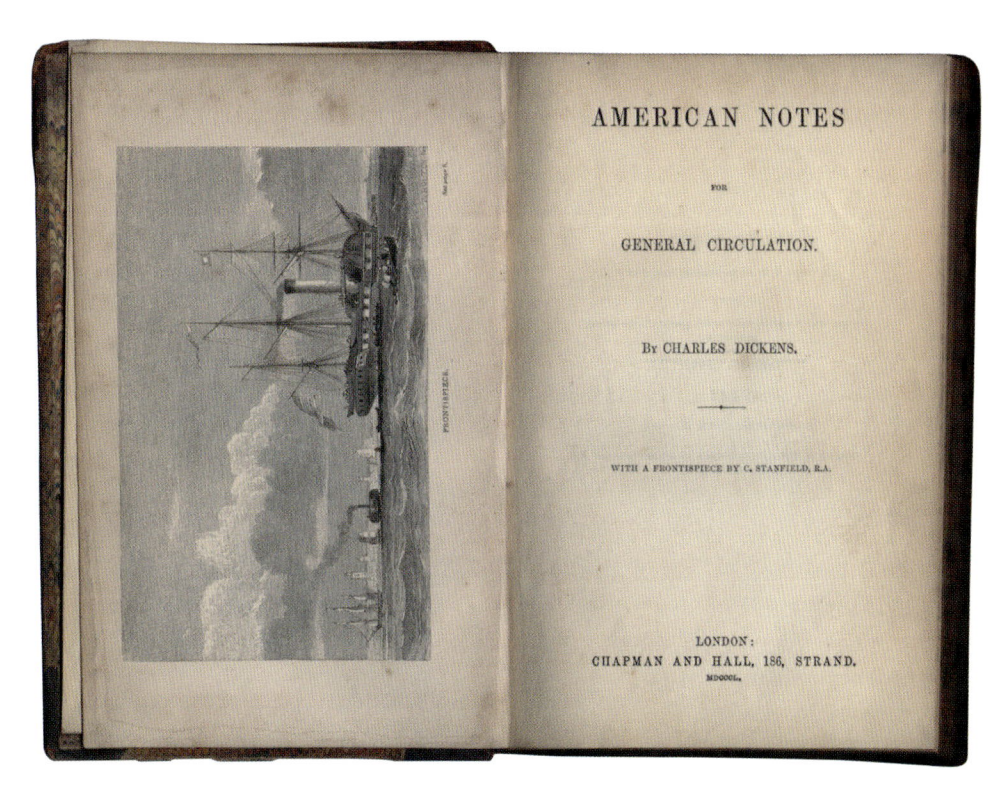

Copy of Dickens' *American Notes*. (Author's collection)

chewing tobacco and spitting. As a supporter of the Anti-Slavery League, Dickens was able to witness the slave trade and the traumatic effects it had upon those enslaved. It cemented his abhorrence of the unsavoury practice. He wrote of his first encounter with slaves:

> We stopped to dine in Baltimore, and now being in Maryland, were waited on, for the first time by slaves. The sensation of exacting any service from human creatures who are bought and sold, and being, for the time, a party as it were to their condition, is not an enviable one. The institution exists, perhaps, in its least repulsive and most mitigated form in such a town like this; but it is slavery; and though I was with respect to it, an innocent man, its presence filled me with a sense of shame and reproach.[74]

Dickens' tour of America ended on 7 June 1842 when he sailed from New York, returning on the *Britannia* and experiencing another rough transatlantic crossing before arriving in Liverpool. On his return to Britain, Dickens used the experience of travelling across America to write his first travelogue entitled *American Notes*, which was published on 19 October 1842. His British readers were not enamoured by the work, nor did it impress the Americans.

---

74. Dickens, Charles, *American Notes* (Chapman & Hall. London, 1850), p.607.

# 36

# *Martin Chuzzlewit*

**Dickens began writing *Martin Chuzzlewit* towards the end of 1842 after his first visit to the United States.**

*Martin Chuzzlewit* appeared as a serial between January 1843 and June 1844 and was dedicated to his friend and fellow philanthropist Angela Burdett-Coutts. In the preface of the novel, Dickens sets out his aim 'to exhibit in a variety of aspects the commonest of all the vices; to show how selfishness propagates itself, and to what a grim giant it may grow from small beginnings.'[75]

Selfishness is a regular theme that is displayed in various forms throughout the novel. Avarice is the common motivator for the egotistic actions of many of the characters within the story. Martin Chuzzlewit Senior is an affluent, eccentric gentleman, who has to deal with sycophantic relatives who are positioning themselves to inherit his legacy and he has to seek ways of identifying who would be worthy and genuine beneficiaries of that legacy.

Jonas Chuzzlewit attempts to murder his father, Anthony, using poison, in order to inherit his property and assets. He believes that he has succeeded, but he has died from other reasons because the elderly clerk, Mr Chuffey, has removed the poison. Montague Tigg, the unscrupulous director of a life insurance company, knows of Jonas's attempt to murder Anthony and uses that information to blackmail him to ensure that the secret does not become public knowledge. To maintain his liberty and retain his father's wealth, Jonas eventually murders Tigg. Jonas is also brutally cruel towards Pecksniff's daughters, Charity, called Cherry, and Mercy, named Merry, when he seduces Cherry while arguing with Merry, but then announces to Seth Pecksniff that he wants to marry Merry and asks that the £4,000 dowry that Pecksniff has pledged to Jonas to marry Cherry is increased by £1,000 for him to marry Merry. Merry accepts Jonas' proposal for egotistical reasons, to spite her sister and because of Jonas' affluence. However, Merry's acceptance of the marriage proposal is ill-judged because he treats her harshly and she becomes trapped in an abusive marriage.

---

75. Pierce, Gilbert A., *The Dickens Dictionary* (Chapman & Hall, London, 1891), p.226.

Sales of *Martin Chuzzlewit* declined when the fifth number had been published in which Martin and Mark go to America, which lost a lot of his readers. Dickens caused offence to the people of Cairo in Illinois, on which he based the fictional town of Eden, and he received further letters of complaints from disgruntled Americans disappointed with his perception of their country both in *American Notes* and *Martin Chuzzlewit*. Sales of *Martin Chuzzlewit* never exceeded 23,000 copies per month and did not match the popularity of his previous novels. Dickens was disappointed that sales fell below that of *Nicholas Nickleby*, however, there was some interest as the story concluded. The novel was adapted for the stage and Dickens took part in the supervision of rehearsals, but embarked on his tour of Italy before the production opened during the autumn 1844 at the Lyceum Theatre in London.

**Seth Pecksniff** is an architect and land surveyor who has never designed or constructed anything, and who lives in Salisbury. He is the cousin of Martin Chuzzlewit Senior. Dickens introduced Pecksniff as a man of moral fibre, but as the story progresses he is revealed to be selfish, egotistical, sycophantic and without a moral compass. Pecksniff's name became a synonym for hypocrisy. Martin Chuzzlewit Senior tests Pecksniff's morality when he intimates that he would benefit financially if he turns out his grandson Martin, who is being trained by Pecksniff as an engineer. Pecksniff, thinking of himself, banishes the young Martin Chuzzlewit immediately.

**Sairey Gamp** is the exuberant cockney nurse in *Martin Chuzzlewit* who is a partly trained midwife who comforts the lying in of pregnant women before childbirth, but also relishes the laying out of the deceased. Her competency as a nurse is questionable and she is portrayed

Seth Pecksniff. (Author's Collection)

Sairey Gamp is depicted on the Dickens memorial tableau at 15 Fergusson House, the site of Dickens' home at 1 Devonshire Terrace, where he wrote *Martin Chuzzlewit*. (Author's Collection)

as a snuff-taking alcoholic who often refers to an imaginary friend named Mrs Harris. Dickens was inspired by a nurse who was employed by his friend, Angela Burdett-Coutts, to tend upon her ill friend, Hannah Brown. It was through Sairey Gamp that Dickens highlighted the problems with health care during the time and the need for reform. The character was created a decade before the reforms implemented by Florence Nightingale, which improved the standards and care provided by nurses. Gamp carried an unwieldly large umbrella and after the publication of *Martin Chuzzlewit*, umbrellas would be known as gamps.

# 37

# *A Christmas Carol*

**Dickens' first Christmas story was published by Bradbury & Evans during December 1843.**

**The celebration of Christmas at the beginning of the nineteenth century was in decline, but books such as *A Christmas Carol* would bring a revival. Therefore, Dickens played an integral role in influencing the way that people celebrated Christmas and that would become one of his most significant legacies.**

Poor sales of *Martin Chuzzlewit* impacted significantly upon Dickens' mental state, confidence and his finances. He wanted to write a book that would match the commercial success of his earlier novels. During 1843 Dickens read a parliamentary report that highlighted the poor treatment of child labour in Britain's factories and coal mines. Incensed by the abuses of employers, Dickens decided to write a morality story entitled *A Christmas Carol* that would address this injustice and speak on their behalf. He wanted to tackle the issue of financial greed and show the impact of affluent men's power over the poor in society. Dickens also wanted to show that having money does not bring happiness. The story focused upon the spirit of Christmas and Dickens showed the importance of compassion, kindness and benevolence. He described it as 'a whimsical kind of masque, which the good humour of the season justified, to awaken some loving and forbearing thoughts, never out of season in a Christmas Land'.[76]

The season of Christmas meant so much to Dickens. On Christmas Eve he would take his children to a toy shop in Holborn, where he allowed them to choose presents for themselves and their friends. Sometimes they would spend an hour in the shop but Dickens was not impatient. His daughter Mamie testified:

> Christmas was always a time which in our home was looked forward to with eagerness and delight, and to my father it was a time dearer than any other part of the year. He loved Christmas for its deep significance as well as for its joys, and this he demonstrates in every allusion in his writings to the great festival, a day which he

---

76. Pierce, op. cit., p.220.

Ebenezer Scrooge being visited by Marley's ghost, illustrated by John Leech. Scrooge and Marley's ghost are also depicted on the Dickens memorial tableau at 15 Fergusson House, Marylebone Road, London which commemorates the site of Dickens home at 1 Devonshire Terrace, where he wrote *A Christmas Carol*. The old knocker that changed into the face of Marley's ghost was on a door in Craven Street, Strand. (British Library)

considered should be fragrant with the love that we should bear one to another, and with the love and reverence of his Saviour and Master.[77]

Dickens wrote *A Christmas Carol* within six weeks, completing it during November 1843. The low revenues received for *Martin Chuzzlewit* meant that his publishers retained a lot of the profit, which aggrieved Dickens. It resulted in disagreement with Chapman & Hall and a temporary cessation of business relations. *A Christmas Carol* was published by Bradbury & Evans on 19 December 1843 and proved to be more popular than *Martin Chuzzlewit*. It was commercially successful, selling 6,000 copies at five shillings on the first day of publication and selling 15,000 copies overall by Christmas Eve. However, it did not resolve Dickens' financial problems because he was expecting to receive £1,000, but was disappointed to receive only £726.[78]

**Ebenezer Scrooge** is a money lender and the surviving partner of the firm Scrooge and Marley. He is a reclusive, uncaring miser, and his unfriendly demeanour makes him unapproachable. At the beginning of the story, he is visited by two gentlemen seeking charitable donations and he dismisses them with the words 'Bah! Humbug!'. His nephew, Fred, then visits him to wish him a Merry Christmas. Scrooge responds: 'If I could work my will … every idiot who goes about with "Merry Christmas" on his lips should be boiled with his own pudding and buried with a stake of holly through his heart!'[79] Dickens also questioned whether money made a person happy. Scrooge asks Fred why should he be merry when he is impoverished, and Fred cannot understand why his uncle should be so morose when he is financially comfortable. Scrooge then declines an invitation to Christmas dinner with his nephew and wife. He is unfair to his employee, Bob Cratchit. During the cold winter Scrooge has a large fire in his office with a large coal box, while Cratchit is allowed just a small fire with one piece of coal, which he could not replenish. He is also reluctant to give him one day's holiday for Christmas. Scrooge is unaware that Cratchit has a family to support including a disabled child named Tiny Tim. There are two possibilities as to how Dickens created the name Scrooge. The word screw sounds similar, but it was a term associated with a miser during that period. There is also the word scourge, which means to punish or oppress.

The story has a supernatural feel to it as the ghost of Scrooge's deceased business partner, Jacob Marley, visits him on Christmas Eve, followed by three ghosts representing Christmas Past, Christmas Present and Christmas Future. They show him the meaning of Christmas through showing him how in the past he used to celebrate Christmas, how in the present his uncaring nature has an impact upon the people around him and the consequences in the Christmas Future. This persuades Scrooge to be kinder and he wakes up on Christmas Day a transformed man, who becomes kind-spirited and shows generosity to the Cratchit family, thereby redeeming himself.

---

77. Dickens, Mamie, op. cit., p.25.

78. Ward, op. cit., p.162.

79. Dickens, Charles, *A Christmas Carol* (William Heinemann, London 1915), p.8.

# 38

# Palazzo Peschiere, Genoa

### Dickens' home during his tour of Italy in 1844.

**Depressed by his financial problems, Dickens embarked upon a tour of Italy for twelve months from July 1844.**

Dickens and his family travelled by coach across France to Marseille, where they boarded a ship to Genoa. They arrived at Albaro near Genoa on 16 July 1844. Dickens wrote his second travelogue entitled *Pictures from Italy*, which recorded their journey to Genoa. Dickens chose to stay at Albaro because it was where Lord Byron, the poet that he admired, once lived; and his friend, Angus Fletcher, the Scottish sculptor, resided. Dickens actually wanted to lease Byron's house but it had not been maintained and was not suitable, so they resided at the Villa Bagnarello. The visit to Italy was private and Dickens could wander around without interference. He had learnt to speak Italian and could communicate with the locals. While in Genoa, he met the Marquis di Negri, who was a friend of Byron. After being entertained by the Marquis, he had to run home in order to leave the gates of Genoa before they were closed for the night. In his first sketch of Genoa, which was published in newspapers across Britain, Dickens wrote:

> I may part Genoa with anything but a glad heart. It is a place that 'grows upon you' every day. There seems to be always something to find in it. There are the most extraordinary alleys and by ways to walk about in. You can lose your way ... twenty times a day, if you like; and turn up again, under the most unexpected and surprising difficulties. It abounds in the strangest contrasts; things that are picturesque, ugly, mean, magnificent, delightful, and offensive, break upon the view at every turn.[80]

Dickens was disappointed with the Villa Bagnarello and on 1 October 1844, once the three-month lease had expired, they moved to a floor in the villa named Palazzo Peschiere on the suburbs of Genoa. It was the largest palace in Genoa, with the walls and ceilings decorated

---

80. *Northern Whig*, 19 February 1846.

Palazzo Peschiere. (Courtesy of Carlo Dell'Orto)

with frescos by Michelangelo. Dickens tried to encourage Douglas Jerrold to visit him and described the Palazzo Peschiere:

> I am lodged in quite a wonderful place, and would put you in a painted room, as big as a church and much more comfortable. There are pens and ink upon the premises; orange trees gardens, battledores and shuttlecocks, rousing woodfires for evenings and a welcome worth having.[81]

In a letter to Angela Burdett-Coutts he wrote of Genoa and his new abode. 'The city of Genoa is very picturesque and beautiful, the house we live in, is really like a Palace in a fairy Tale.'[82] Dickens could overlook Genoa Harbour, the Mediterranean Sea and the Alps from the garden of the Palazzo Peschiere, but it did not inspire him to write. Dickens yearned for London, for he wrote, 'I seem as if I had plucked myself out of my proper soil when I left Devonshire Terrace; and could take root no more until I return to it.'[83]

---

81. Dickens, *Letters*, Vol. 1, op. cit., p.120.

82. Osbourne, op. cit., p.63.

83. Anonymous, Bookman, op. cit., p.90.

# 39

# John Forster's Home – 58 Lincoln's Inn Fields, London

**Dickens gave his first reading in this house.**

Dickens often visited his friend John Forster, who lived at this address from 1834 until 1856. Forster was a close confidant and he exerted considerable influence upon Dickens' life and business decisions. Forster was a former barrister, slightly younger than Dickens, who changed his career to journalism, working as a theatre critic for *The Examiner*, and became an author. He would go on to write Dickens' biography after his death and he bequeathed his collection of Dickens' original manuscripts to the South Kensington Museum, which would evolve into the Victoria & Albert Museum.

During November 1844, Dickens briefly interrupted his tour of Italy to return home to London and read his new book *The Chimes* from the newly written manuscript to a select group of friends before its publication. On 2 December Dickens gave his first reading at John Forster's home at 58 Lincoln's Inn Fields. Among those who were present were historian Thomas Carlyle, Douglas Jerrold, Laman Blanchard, Dickens' brother Frederick, Unitarian minister, journalist and MP, W.J. Fox, artists Daniel Maclise and Stanfield; and Shakespearean scholars William Harness and Alexander Dyce. Maclise drew a sketch of Dickens reading to the group and wrote 'there was not a dry eye in the house, shrieks of laughter … and floods of tears as a relief to them – I do not think that there was ever such a triumphant hour for Charles.'[84]

Dickens also wrote of the effect that his performance had upon his audience during that first reading: 'If you had seen Maclise last night – undisguisedly sobbing, and crying on the sofa, as I read, you would have felt (as I did) what a thing it is to have Power.'[85]

The evening was a resounding success and this power not only awakened Dickens' previous passion for acting and performing, he realised the effect upon his audience, so when he was asked to give a second reading during that week, he was happy to oblige. Ingoldsby Barham

---

84. Tillotson, Kathleen, *Pilgrim Edition, Letters of Charles Dickens, 1844–6, Volume IV* (Oxford, 1977), p.234.

85. Ibid., p.235.

*Above*: Nos 57–58 Lincoln's Inn Fields, the home of John Forster and where Dickens gave his first reading. (Roy Harris/Shutterstock)

*Right*: A contemporary view of Nos 57–58 Lincoln's Inn Fields. (Author's Collection)

Dickens reading *The Chimes* on 2 December 1844. Daniel Maclise produced this sketch, including a halo over Dickens' head. (Author's Collection)

was present and recorded in his diary. 'December 5, 1844 – Dined with Charles Dickens, Stanfield, Maclise and Albany Fonblanque at Forster's. Dickens read with remarkable effect his Christmas story, *The Chimes* from the proofs.'[86]

The reading gave Dickens the opportunity to act the parts of the characters that he had created. He was a frustrated actor and he excelled at the experience of performing. He enjoyed the instant response from his audience. Dickens was pleased with the readings and said to Forster: 'I swear I wouldn't have missed that week, that first night of our meeting, that one evening of the reading at your rooms, aye and the second reading too, for any easily stated or conceived consideration.'[87]

This private experience would motivate Dickens to initially give readings for charity. When he realised their popularity, he eventually decided to undertake readings of excerpts from his novels in public tours around Britain and America for profit. Dickens spent a week in London and left on 9 December 1844 before returning to Italy to resume the tour. While Dickens was in Italy, *The Chimes* sold 20,000 copies and was a success.

Forster's residence would become the home and office of Mr Tulkinghorn in *Bleak House*. Tulkinghorn was a solicitor of the Court of Chancery who represented Sir Leicester Dedlock as a legal advisor and it was within this house that Dickens set the scene for his murder. Dickens wrote: 'Here, in a large house, formerly a house of state, lives Mr Tulkinghorn. It is let off in sets of chambers now; and in those shrunken fragments of its greatness, lawyers lie like maggots in nuts.'[88] Dickens also used Lincoln's Inn Field as the place where the rioters gathered in *Barnaby Rudge*.

---

86. Shore, W. Teignmouth, *Charles Dickens and his Friends* (Cassell & Company Ltd, London, 1909), p.130.

87. Ibid., p.130.

88. Dickens, Charles, *Bleak House* (Macmillan & Co., London, 1895). p.122.

# 40

# Rosemont Villa, Lausanne, Switzerland

## Dickens stayed here from June until November 1846, while he worked on *Dombey & Son*.

**Arriving at Lausanne on 11 June 1846, Dickens spent six months at Rosemont Villa, where he and his family enjoyed picturesque views of Lake Geneva and the Alps.**

Dickens described Rosemont Villa to Angela Burdett-Coutts in a letter on 25 June 1846:

> This is an odd little house, which I think might be easily put into the great hall of our old Genoese Palazzo – bodily. It stands in the midst of beautiful grounds, on the slope of the hill going down to the lake – and the blue waters thereof, and the whole range of mountains, lie in the front windows. I have a study, something larger than a plate warmer, opening onto a balcony and commanding a lovely view.[89]

While at Rosemont Villa, Dickens had various writing projects to complete including a piece on ragged schools for Lord John Russell, the Prime Minister, work for Angela Burdett-Coutts in relation to her philanthropy and a children's New Testament, as well as beginning another serialisation and Christmas book. Dickens was only able to write the first number of the serialisation entitled *Dombey & Son*. There was a small enclave of British citizens living in Lausanne and Dickens established good relations with some of them, including Mr and Mrs de Cerjat and the Honourable Richard and Mrs Lavinia Watson, who resided at Rockingham Castle in Northamptonshire. They would become lifelong friends and Dickens would dedicate *David Copperfield* to them. The Watsons would frequently call upon Dickens and they would have dinner parties, play card games, visit the local theatre and go on evening walks, which impeded upon his time to write *Dombey & Son*. Dickens gave a private reading of the instalment that he had written of *Dombey & Son* to his new-found friends in Lausanne. This also meant that he was unable to write two books simultaneously, which meant that he had to suspend work on *Dombey & Son* so that he could concentrate working on the next Christmas book,

---

89. Osbourne, op. cit., p.88.

Rosemont Villa, Lausanne, where Dickens lived for six months during 1846. The two middle windows open on the balcony were in Dickens' study. (Author's Collection)

which was entitled *The Battle of Life*, because such titles were more commercially successful and increased his income significantly.

During his stay at Lausanne, Dickens went on excursions to Chamounix and one to Great St Bernard, which he incorporated in *Little Dorrit*. He spent six months in Lausanne and the environment did not inspire him to continue writing *Dombey & Son* when he resumed that project, so he decided to relocate his family to Paris. A plaque was attached to Rosemont Villa in 1909 to commemorate Dickens' stay at Lausanne but the building no longer exists because it was demolished in 1938.

# 41

# No. 48 Rue de Courcelles, Paris

**Dickens lived in this building from November 1846 until March 1847.**

Paris was the ideal location to inspire Dickens to continue writing *Dombey & Son* in comparison to the quiet, subdued Lausanne. Dickens stayed at 48 Rue de Courcelles, which formed a junction with the Rue Rembrandt in the Faubourg Saint-Honoré district of Paris. The building was purchased by Ching Tsai Loo, an art dealer specialising in Chinese and Asian arts and antiquities, in 1925 and he transformed the building into the Pagoda that exists today.

It was a unique structure before its present incarnation as Dickens described the house to John Forster as the 'most ridiculous, extraordinary, unparalleled, and preposterous in the whole world, being something between a baby house, a shades, a haunted castle and a mad kind of clock, and not to be imagined by the mind of a man'.[90]

Dickens provided a further description of this unusual house in Paris in a letter written to the Honourable Richard Watson on 27 November 1846:

> I am proud to express my belief that we are lodged at last in the most preposterous house in the world. The like of it cannot, and so far as my knowledge goes does not, exist in any other part of the globe. The bedrooms are like opera-boxes. The dining-rooms, staircases, and passages, quite inexplicable. The dining-room is a sort of cavern, painted (ceiling and all) to represent a grove, with unaccountable bits of looking-glass sticking in among the branches of the trees. There is a gleam of reason in the drawing-room. But it is approached through a series of small chambers, like the joints in a telescope, which are hung with inscrutable drapery. The maddest man in bedlam, having the materials given him, would be likely to devise such a suite, supposing his case to be hopeless and quite incurable.[91]

Paris was enduring a hard winter with snow falling, for Dickens complained that he could not totally shut the windows of the house at 48 Rue de Courcelles.

---

90. Forster, Vol. 3, op. cit., p.318.
91. Dickens, *Letters*, Vol. 2, op. cit., p.169.

A postcard of Dickens' residence at 48 Rue de Courcelles, Faubourg Saint-Honoré, Paris (the house on the left).

Dickens was able to converse in French and was capable of delivering a speech praising the nation and the French in their language while in Paris. He would wander around the Parisian streets and immerse himself within the city and its people. This experience would enable him to write *A Tale of Two Cities*. Dickens wrote of his activities in Paris, 'I have been seeing Paris – wandering into hospitals, prisons, dead-houses, operas, theatres, concert-rooms, burial-grounds, palaces, and wine-shops. In my unoccupied fortnight of each month, every description of gaudy and ghastly sight has been passing before me in a rapid panorama.'[92]

John Forster joined Dickens for a fortnight in Paris. They went to the theatre and dined with French authors including Alexandre Dumas, and visited Victor Hugo at his home in Place Royale (now known as Place des Voges). Dickens wrote of his meeting with Hugo to the Countess of Blessington on 24 January 1847: 'We were at Victor Hugo's house last Sunday week, a most extraordinary place, looking like an old curiosity shop, or the property-room of some gloomy, vast, old theatre. I was much struck by Hugo himself, who looks like a genius as he is, every inch of him, and is very interesting and satisfactory from head to foot.'[93]

Dickens became fond of Paris and the French people, and in a letter to Emile de la Rue in March 1847 he wrote: 'Well! About Paris! I am charmed with the place and have a much greater respect for the French people than I had before.'[94]

Dickens' stay in Paris was curtailed when he had to return home because his eldest son was taken ill while studying at King's College School after succumbing to scarlet fever. Dickens returned to Paris at various times during his life. In 1863 he gave a reading of *David Copperfield* at the English Embassy for charity.

---

92. Ibid., p.174.

93. Ibid., p.169.

94. Fielding, K.J., & Storey Graham, *The Letters of Charles Dickens, Volume 5* (Oxford, Clarendon Press, 1981), p.42.

# 42

# Characters from *Dombey & Son*

**Bradbury & Evans published the first number of *Dombey & Son* on 1 October 1846.**

The story encompassed themes relating to child cruelty, female inequality, arranged marriages and relations between the different social classes in Victorian society. The twenty instalments of *Dombey & Son* sold well, 20,000 copies a month. The death of Paul Dombey repeated the emotional reaction among his readers felt at the death of Little Nell. Dickens rated *Dombey & Son* highly and believed that if any of his works 'are read years hence, "Dombey" will be remembered as among the best of them.'[95]

**Dombey & Son** Paul Dombey is an affluent London merchant who is stubborn, pompous, cold and devoid of emotion. He is socially inept as Dickens wrote that 'in all his life, he had never made a friend. His cold and distant nature had neither sought one, nor found one.'[96] Dombey is aloof and prejudiced against those not belonging to his social circle; he believes that 'the inferior classes should continue to be taught to know their position, and to conduct themselves properly'.[97] He is a successful businessman and longs for a son and heir. He is disappointed that his first child is his daughter Florence and, despite her being affectionate, she becomes a figure of indifference to Paul Dombey. His wife eventually gives birth to the son he has yearned for, but she dies after the boy is born. The boy is named after his father and is known as little Paul Dombey. He is frequently ill and an unhealthy child. Dickens' nephew Harry Burnett, inspired him to create little Paul Dombey. Harry was disabled and died when aged ten. Little Paul is loved by his sister Florence, but Dombey Senior keeps her away from him; Dombey's only concern is for his heir. Dickens' main theme within the story is to show the inequality between male and female children in Victorian society. Dombey Senior ignores

---

95. Kitton, *Life*, op. cit., p.163.

96. Dickens, Charles, *Dombey & Son* (Bradbury & Evans, London, 1848), p.35.

97. Ibid., p.44.

*Above left*: Dombey and his son are depicted on the Dickens memorial tableau at 15 Fergusson House, the site of Dickens' home at 1 Devonshire Terrace where he wrote *Dombey & Son*. St Marylebone Parish Church was situated close to 1 Devonshire Terrace. Dickens used this church for the wedding of Paul Dombey to Edith Granger, and for his son Paul Dombey's christening and burial. (Author's Collection)

*Above right*: Captain Edward Cuttle. (Author's Collection)

his daughter in favour of his son. Dombey hires Polly Toddle as a nanny to look after the infant Paul Dombey on the condition that she changes her surname from Toddle to Richards and that she sees as little of her family as possible.

**Captain Edward Cuttle** is a retired sea captain with a hooked hand. He is a friend and business partner of Solomon Gills. He loyally looks after Sol's nautical instrument shop, named the Wooden Midshipman, while Sol travels overseas to find his nephew, Walter Gay, whom is believed lost at sea. During that time, he offers Florence Dombey refuge when she flees her father's home.

# 43

# Children's New Testament

**Dickens completed *The Life of Our Lord* during 1849.**

**Dickens' New Testament was an abridged version of the Four Gospels specifically written for his children and not intended for publication.**

Religion played an important part in Dickens' life. His tour manager, George Dolby, wrote of Dickens' regard for the Bible, that 'no one had a greater reverence than himself, it being the book of all others he read the most, and "the one unfailing guide in life."'[98] Dickens favoured the New Testament and lived by Jesus Christ's ideals and values of compassion and justice. Writing *The Life of Our Lord* was a departure from writing novels and he wanted to instil in his children the importance of Jesus's existence. He began writing while living in Lausanne during 1846, completing the work in 1849. On the first page of the book, he stated his motivation for writing the book:

> My dear children, I am very anxious that you should know something about the History of Jesus Christ. For everyone ought to know about Him. No one ever lived, who was so good, so kind, so gentle, and so sorry for all people who did wrong, or were in anyway ill or miserable, as he was. And as he is now in Heaven, where we hope to go, and all to meet each other after we are dead, and here be happy always together, you never can think what a good place Heaven is, without knowing who he was and what he did.[99]

Dickens shared the values of Christ in that he wrote about those who were underprivileged, disadvantaged and in need, shining a spotlight upon their plight. His books were a way of encouraging those in a position of wealth, privilege and power to treat people with kindness and benevolence. In writing the *Life of Our Lord* he was leaving his children with a permanent record of his religious views and a point of reference on how they should live their own lives.

---

98. Dolby, George, *Charles Dickens as I Knew Him: The Story of the Reading Tours in Great Britain and America, 1866* (T. Fisher Unwin, London 1887), p.299.

99. Dickens, Charles, *The Life of Our Lord* (Associated Newspapers, London 1934), p.11.

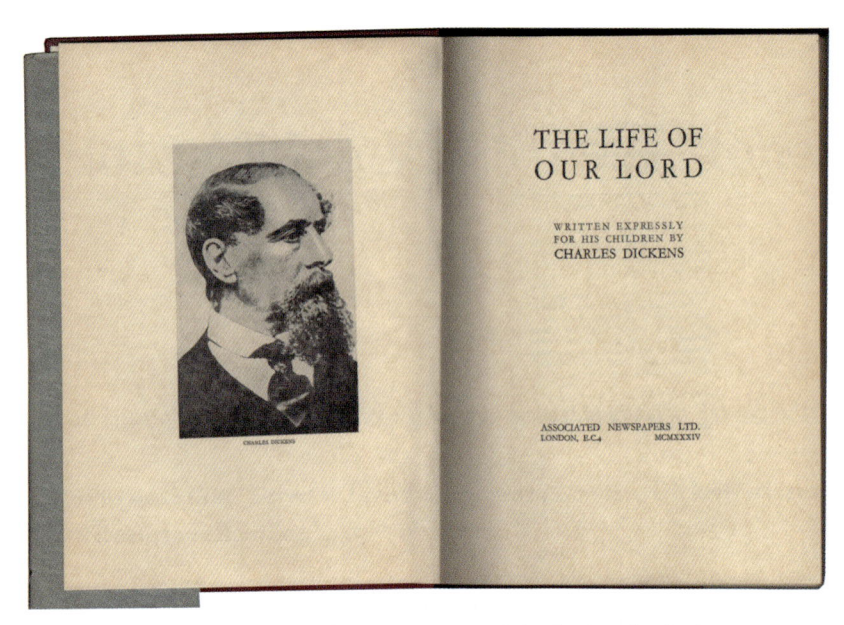

A first edition of Dickens' book, *The Life of Our Lord*. (Author's Collection)

On 15 October 1868, Dickens provided an insight into his faith and religion in a letter to his son, Henry, in which he referred to the work that he wrote for him and his siblings:

> I must strongly impress upon you the priceless value of the *New Testament*, and the study of that book as the one unfailing guide in life. Deeply respecting it, and bowing down before the character of our Saviour, as separated from the vain constructions and inventions of men, you cannot go very wrong, and will always preserve at heart a true spirit of veneration and humility. Similarly, I impress upon you the habit of saying a Christian prayer every night and morning. These things have stood by me all through my life, and remember that I tried to render the *New Testament* intelligible to you and lovable by you when you were a mere baby.[100]

Dickens wrote this letter nineteen years after writing *The Life of Our Lord* when he wanted to reinforce his religious beliefs upon his children. This book was never intended for public consumption. After his death, the manuscript remained in the possession of his sister-in-law, Georgina Hogarth, and when she passed away in 1917 it was bequeathed to Sir Henry Field Dickens. He was not enthusiastic about publishing the manuscript in his lifetime, but gave consent for this after his death. His will decreed that providing the majority of his family were in favour, it should be released for the public to read. He died on 21 December 1933 and *The Life of Our Lord* was published during March 1934, becoming the last published work written by Dickens.

---

100. Dickens, *Letters*, Vol. 2, op. cit., p.366.

# 44

# Theatre Royal Haymarket, London

**Dickens helped to preserve the legacy of the Bard.**

**In 1847 the birthplace of William Shakespeare in Stratford-upon-Avon was in danger of being sold to the American entertainer P.T. Barnum, who wanted to dismantle the building brick by brick and relocate it to his museum in New York. Dickens played a prominent part in saving the house for the nation by managing and performing two amateur dramatic productions to raise funds in a tour of England. Two of those performances took place at the Theatre Royal in Haymarket, London.**

Dickens was passionate about theatre since his childhood days in Chatham and was fond of acting. He performed in several amateur dramatic productions and during the spring 1848, he was the stage manager for amateur dramatic productions of Shakespeare's play *The Merry Wives of Windsor* and Ben Jonson's *Every Man in His Humour*. Dickens played Justice Shallow in *The Merry Wives of Windsor*, which toured for nine performances in Birmingham, Manchester, Liverpool, Glasgow, Edinburgh and London. Dickens' morale was high because he enjoyed the process of managing, acting, travelling and the camaraderie of a travelling acting company. It was a charity benefit tour to raise money for the 'Shakespeare House' fund, which was for the preservation of his birthplace in Stratford-upon-Avon, which was emphasised in the programme as being separate from the fund to purchase the actual house. Family and friends performed alongside Dickens, including Frederick Dickens as the host of the Garter Inn, Augustus Dickens as Nym, Mark Lemon as Sir John Falstaff, John Forster as Mr Ford and George Cruickshank as Pistol.

Two nights were performed at the Theatre Royal in London and according to John Forster, Queen Victoria and Prince Albert attended one of the performances on 15 May 1848. Mrs Cowden Clarke recalled Dickens' performance:

> The 'make up' of Dickens as Justice Shallow was so complete, that his own identity was almost unrecognisable, when he came onto the stage, as the curtain rose, in company with Sir Hugh and Master Slender; but after a moment's breathless pause, the whole house burst into a roar of applausive reception, which testified to the boundless delight of the assembled audience on beholding the literary idol of the day, actually before them.

The Theatre Royal Haymarket in London, where Dickens performed in *The Merry Wives of Windsor* and *The Frozen Deep*. (Author's Collection)

> His impersonation was perfect: the old stiff limbs, the senile stoop of the shoulders, the head bent with age, the feeble step, with a certain attempted smartness of carriage characteristic of the conceited Justice of the Peace – were all assumed and maintained with wonderful accuracy.[101]

It was at the Theatre Royal Haymarket, in 1857 that Dickens first noticed Ellen Ternan and on the recommendation of an actor friend he cast her, her mother and sister for two performances of *The Frozen Deep* in Manchester during August 1857. Dickens was aged forty-five, his twenty-two-year marriage to Catherine was falling apart and he was falling in love with Ellen, who was aged eighteen.

---

101. Ibid., p.166.

# 45

# Gates of Winterbourne, Bonchurch, Isle of Wight

## Dickens rented Winterbourne for six months.

**During the summer 1849, Dickens took his family to Bonchurch, near Ventnor on the Isle of Wight, where he rented the villa Winterbourne, the home of the Reverend James White, who was a friend and fellow author.**

The picturesque views on the Isle of Wight reminded Dickens of Italy and the Mediterranean coastline. In a letter to his wife, Catherine, dated 16 June 1849 from Shanklin, Dickens wrote: 'I have taken a most delightful and beautiful house, belonging to White, at Bonchurch; cool, airy, private bathing, everything delicious. I think it is the prettiest place I ever saw in my life, at home or abroad … A waterfall on the grounds, which I have arranged with a carpenter to convert into a perpetual shower.'[102]

It was within Winterbourne villa that Dickens began writing the early part of *David Copperfield*. He would establish a routine where he worked during the morning until 2 pm, when Dickens took advantage of walking the scenic terrain that the Isle of Wight offered and enjoyed picnics at Shanklin. He welcomed his friends William Makepeace Thackeray and Alfred Tennyson to Winterbourne villa.

There were eminent scientists staying at Sandown in 1849 who formed a select social group called the Red Lions. Dickens and the close circle of friends who visited him, including Mark Lemon and William Macready, created their own rival group from Bonchurch, which they named the Sea Serpents, and social gatherings were co-ordinated with each group, normally picnics that were held at Cook's Castle. Phoebe Lankester, the wife of Dr Edwin Lankester, member of the Red Lions, recalled one of those picnics:

> Well do I recollect the jolly procession from Sandown as it moved across the downs, young and old carrying aloft a banner bearing the device of a noble red lion painted in vermilion on a white ground. Winding up the hill from the Bonchurch side might be seen the 'Sea Serpents,' with their ensign floating in the wind – a waving, curling serpent, cut out of yards

---

102. Dickens, *Letters*, Vol. 1, op. cit., p.217.

The entrance gates to the Winterbourne villa, which was located in Bonchurch on the Isle of Wight. The building was made famous as a result of the brief period when Charles Dickens rented the villa from his friend, the Rev. James White, for writing *David Copperfield*. (Katherine Da Silva/Shutterstock)

and yards of calico, and painted of a bronzy-green colour with fiery red eyes, its tail being supported by a second banner-holder. Carts brought up the provisions on either side, and at the top the factions met to prepare and consume the banquet on the short, sweet grass under shadow of a rock or a tree. Charles Dickens delighted in the fun. He usually boiled the potatoes when the fire had been lighted by the youngsters, and handed them round in a saucepan, and John Leech used to make sketches of us ... I was very young then, and did not fully realise what it was to eat potatoes boiled by Charles Dickens.[103]

These social gatherings would usually end with both parties from the Red Lions and the Sea Serpents being welcomed to Winterbourne villa by Dickens to continue with tea and music.

Despite enjoying the beautiful surroundings that the Isle of Wight offered, the climate did not agree with Dickens and caused him insomnia and depression. He commented that: 'it's a mortal mistake – that's the plain fact. Of all the places I have ever been in, I have never been in one so difficult to exist pleasantly. Naples is hot and dirty, New York feverish, Washington bilious, Genoa exciting, Paris rainy, but Bonchurch – smashing. I am quite convinced that I should die here in a year.'[104]

Unable to bear the climate at Bonchurch, Dickens managed to complete the fifth number of *David Copperfield* before leaving in early October for Broadstairs.

---

103. Kitton, *Country*, op. cit., p.100.

104. Ibid., p.110.

# 46

# Characters from *David Copperfield*

**The first number of *David Copperfield* appeared during May 1849 and was serialised until November 1850.**

Sales of *David Copperfield* surpassed all other Dickens' previous books except for *The Pickwick Papers*, selling 25,000 copies per number. The book is semi-autobiographical and much of the experiences of Copperfield mirrored events and experiences that occurred during Dickens' life.

The leading protagonist shared the author's initials but in reverse, he worked in a blacking factory and his love for Dora reflected Dickens' love for Maria Beadnell. Unlike his previous books, it was written in the first person. *David Copperfield* was Dickens' personal favourite book. He wrote in the preface: 'Of all my books, I like this one the best. It will easily be believed that I am a fond parent to every child of my fancy, and that no one can ever love that family as dearly as I loved them. But, like many fond

David Copperfield and Wilkins Micawber are also depicted on the Dickens memorial tableau at 15 Fergusson House, this being where, when it was Devonshire Terrace, he wrote *David Copperfield*. (All Author's Collection)

David Copperfield.

parents, I have in my heart of hearts a favourite child. And his name is DAVID COPPERFIELD.'[105]

**David Copperfield** is born six months after the death of his father and raised by his widowed mother Clara Copperfield, supported by her nurse and servant Clara Peggotty. The young, sensitive David enjoys a warm, affectionate, loving relationship with both until the arrival of Mr Murdstone, who treats him brutally once under his guardianship, which breaks his mother's heart. Murdstone sends him to school, where he is bullied and violently abused by the headmaster Mr Creakle, under his sanction. It is Creakle who informs David, without compassion or empathy, that his mother has died. After her death, Murdstone sends David to work in Murdstone and Grimby's warehouse, where he is employed washing out empty wine bottles and pasting labels on them once filled. David is unhappy at the warehouse and runs away in search of his aunt, Betsey Trotwood. Before leaving London, he is robbed of his possessions. With no money, he is compelled to walk the 72 miles from London to Dover to find Betsey. He receives a warm reception from Betsey, who sends him to school in Canterbury. After completing his education, sponsored by his aunt, he learns to be a proctor in the firm of Mr Spenlow in London. Here he becomes acquainted with his daughter, Dora Spenlow. David falls in love with Dora, but her father disapproves of the friendship because he deems that David has few prospects and would make an unsuitable husband. When Betsey loses a large proportion of her fortune, David has to find ways to generate an income. He learns the skill of shorthand and becomes a parliamentary reporter. Before the death of Mr Spenlow, David becomes Dora's accepted suitor. He becomes a successful author, writing for periodicals, which provides regular employment and enables him to marry Dora. However, the relationship is not what David expects, proving to be unstable. Dora becomes ill and dies, which causes David anguish. David goes abroad for three years and on his return reignites a relationship with his friend Agnes Wickfield, who has had concealed feelings of love for him for many years. The novel ends with David marrying Agnes.

**Mr Edward Murdstone** is the stepfather of David Copperfield, who holds a sombre, gloomy, domineering influence upon Clara Copperfield. She accepts the security he provides as a husband, but his domineering, dictatorial manner, together with his interfering sister, will crush her gentle nature. The control of Murdstone will overwhelm the way she lives in her own home and the raising of her son, which is with harsh cruelty. Murdstone resents the love

---

105. Dickens, Charles, *David Copperfield* (Chapman & Hall, London) pp.v–vi.

Mr Murdstone.           Wilkins Micawber.           Uriah Heep.

that Clara bears upon David and acts with vengeance when she dies and David is orphaned. Murdstone repeats his controlling, dominant ways with his second wife, reducing her to lunacy.

**Mr Wilkins Micawber** has a cheery, jovial demeanour with the optimistic expectation of 'something turning up' during challenging times. The whole theory of civilised existence is compressed into his 'Twenty pounds income' advice with happiness or misery hinging on the displacement of a six-pence either way. David Copperfield lodges with Micawber at his home in City Road, while he works at Murdstone and Grimby's warehouse. Copperfield notices that the only visitors to the house are creditors. Micawber is eventually arrested and imprisoned in the King's Bench Prison. He is released under the Insolvent Debtors' Act and takes his family to Plymouth, where he hopes to obtain employment in the Customs House. Things do not work out for him and he reappears in David Copperfield's life when he sells corn and then works as a clerk for Uriah Heep. Micawber's story ends when he immigrates to Australia.

**Uriah Heep** is employed in the legal office of Mr Wickfield and later becomes his partner in the business. Recognising that the widowed Wickfield has an alcohol problem, Heep manipulates the situation to encourage him to drink more in an effort to take total control of the business, at the same time pursuing Agnes Wickfield, who has romantic feelings for David Copperfield. Heep ensnares Agnes and her father within his power, fraudulently taking control of the business. He also uses the company to commit other acts of fraud and forgery, which are uncovered by Micawber. Wickfield recovers from alcoholism, repossesses his property and Uriah Heep is imprisoned.

# 47

# Dickens House Museum, Broadstairs

### The house that became the inspiration for Betsey Trotwood's Home.

Dickens would visit Mary Pearson Strong, who owned this house, while he stayed in Broadstairs and her persona formed the basis for his formidable character Betsey Trotwood in *David Copperfield*. The house at No. 2 Victoria Parade, Broadstairs is now the Dickens House Museum, but there is a tablet inscribed as follows: 'In this house lived the original of Betsey Trotwood in *David Copperfield* by Charles Dickens 1849.'

Betsey Trotwood is David Copperfield's great-aunt. She is a strong-willed, austere, eccentric woman, but she is kind hearted and caring. She was hurt in a previous relationship and is wary of men, for when David is born, she is disappointed that he is not a girl and disappears from his life. After the death of his mother, David looks for Betsey because she is his last living relative and when he finds her she takes responsibility for being his guardian. She also pays Micawber's minor debt when he is arrested just as he is about to embark aboard a ship that transports him and his family to a new life in Australia.

Although Betsey Trotwood lives in Dover in the novel, this is the house in Broadstairs that inspired Dickens for her home. Miss Mary Pearson Strong lived in this house that overlooked the seafront and she was known to Dickens. He and his son, Charley, frequently were entertained by the charming and amiable Mary with tea and cakes in her parlour. Mary believed that she had the authority to stop donkeys passing the meadow land along the clifftop in front of her home and frequently exerted that right, which Dickens often saw from his room at the Albion Hotel. Dickens was inspired by Mary and she would be immortalised as Betsey in *David Copperfield*, which included the donkey incident. There is a letter written by Charley Dickens explaining that the owner of this house was the inspiration for Betsey. Since Mary was well known in Broadstairs, Dickens placed Betsey's character as living in Dover to protect Mary from any embarrassment or unwarranted attention.

The house fits the description described by David Copperfield in the novel: 'We soon came to a very neat little cottage with cheerful-bow windows; in front of it, a small gravelled court or garden full of flowers, carefully tended and smelling deliciously.'[106]

---

106. Dickens, *Copperfield*, op. cit., pp.150–1.

*Right*: Dickens House Museum was the home of Betsey Trotwood in Broadstairs. Note the building in the right of the photograph is the Albion Hotel where Dickens' frequently stayed and was able to see Betsey shooing away donkeys from in front of her home. (Author's Collection)

*Below*: Plaque on the wall of the Dickens House Museum. (Author's Collection)

The museum contains possessions owned by Dickens, including a writing box that was given to him as a gift by John Forster and a mahogany sideboard he purchased in 1836 and sold to solicitor Thomas Green in 1855. The Tattum family bought the sideboard in 1919 and bequeathed it to the town together with the house in 1952.

# 48

# Office of *Household Words*

**The magazine *Household Words* edited by Dickens ran from 1850 to 1859**

This photograph shows the entrance to Dickens' *Household Words* office in Wellington Street, The Strand, which has since been demolished.

*Household Words* was published by Bradbury & Evans, who provided financial backing, enabling Dickens to possess greater control of the content of the magazine, and he would capitalise on his celebrity status to attract readers. The concept of the magazine was 'designed for the instruction and entertainment of all classes of readers'.[107]

The first number appeared on 30 March 1850. Dickens championed new authors and invited them to write for the periodical, but their pieces were published anonymously within *Household Words*. George Meredith, Wilkie Collins, Edmund Yates and Elizabeth Gaskell were regular contributors from the first edition. George Eliot declined Dickens' offer to contribute because she was apprehensive about the prospect of writing a weekly serialisation. The magazine was expensive to produce, but it sold to a large circulation, approximately 100,000 copies, which covered its overheads and yielded a satisfactory profit.

The aim of the magazine was to raise awareness of social issues of the day. Dickens described the spirit of the periodical in a letter to Gaskell: 'No writer's name will be used, neither my own nor any other; every paper will be published without any signature, and all will seem to express the general mind and purpose of the journal, which is raising up of those that are down, and general improvement of our social condition.'[108]

Gaskell contributed the following novels to *Household Words*; *Lizzie Leigh* (in three parts during 1850), *Cranford* (December 1851 to May 1853), *North and South* (September 1854 to January 1855) and *My Lady Ludlow* (June to September 1858). Gaskell resisted being constrained to twenty instalments for *North and South* and was challenged by writing to deadlines. Her working relationship with Dickens was strained, and he was disappointed with her work. Towards the end of 1853, interest in *Household Words* had declined and Dickens

---

107. *The Sun, London*, 10 April 1850.

108. Dickens, *Letters*, Vol. 1, op. cit., p.216.

The *Household Words* office. (Author's Collection)

decided to feature his own novel within its pages. In April 1854, the first number of *Hard Times* appeared and resulted in a doubling of its circulation. Wilkie Collins also contributed the novels *A Rogue's Life* (1856) and *The Dead Secret* (1857).

*Household Words* did highlight the government's incompetency during the Crimean War, and advocated improvements in health, better sanitation and clean water. It also campaigned for education for all members of society. By 1858 Dickens grew tired of *Household Words* and when in June Bradbury & Evans refused to publish Dickens' letter in their other periodical, *Punch*, refuting rumours of his infidelity and separation from his wife, he tried to buy their shares in the magazine. Bradbury & Evans maintained that they had control of the brand *Household Words*, but after a legal challenge through the Court of Chancery, Dickens won the case and wound up the magazine, transferring his efforts into a new periodical he entitled *All the Year Round*. Dickens' eldest son married Elizabeth Evans, the daughter of his former publisher Frederick Evans in 1861, but the author refused to attend the wedding due to the acrimonious end to their business relationship.

# 49

# Fort House, Broadstairs

**Built in 1801, it was Dickens' home during the summer months from 1850 until 1859.**

Dickens made regular visits to Broadstairs annually and eventually searched for a house that he could lease for the duration of the summer. The alleyway that led from Lawn House Archway, which he occupied during 1840, passed along the southern wall of the garden of Fort House, which he was keen to occupy. An opportunity arose during the summer 1850, when Dickens obtained the lease for Fort House.

Fort House is perched on the cliffs at Broadstairs, having panoramic views of Viking Bay, the English Channel and the Goodwin Sands. There was a cornfield between the house and the beach, which made the sea easily accessible. Dickens invited the Reverend James White to Fort House during 1850 in the following letter:

> I have taken a house at Broadstairs, from early in August until the end of October, as I don't want to come back to London until I shall have finished 'Copperfield,' I am rejoiced at the idea of going there. You will find it the healthiest and freshest of places; and there are Canterbury, and all varieties of what Leigh Hunt calls 'greenery,' within a few minutes railroad ride. It is not very picturesque ashore, but extremely so seaward; all manner of ships continually passing close inshore.[109]

Dickens and his family took possession of Fort House during August 1850. His wife, Catherine, remained in London until she gave birth to their third daughter during that month and joined them in Broadstairs in September. Mamie Dickens recalled: 'For many consecutive summers we used to be taken to Broadstairs. This little place became a favourite of my father. He was always very happy there and delighted in wandering about the garden of this house, generally accompanied by one or other of his children.'[110]

---

109. Dickens, *Letters*, Vol. 1, op. cit., p.221.

110. Dickens, Mamie, op. cit., p.12.

*Above*: Fort House in Broadstairs. Fort House has undergone several modifications since Dickens occupied the property, in particular through the addition of the west wing, which was built in 1901. During the 1850s, there was a meadow between the house and the beach from where Dickens swam. (Author's Collection)

*Right*: A bust of Dickens that can be seen at Fort House. (Author's Collection)

It was within the study on the first floor at Fort House that looked out to sea that Dickens continued to work on *David Copperfield* throughout that summer and completed the final instalment in October 1850. After the death of his father, John, on 31 March 1851, he wrote to Macready that he 'was pining for Broadstairs',[111] and he would spend May to November 1851 at Fort House to avoid London, which was deluged with crowds visiting the Great Exhibition. This was the longest period he stayed in Broadstairs.

---

111. Dickens, *Letters*, Vol. 1, op. cit., p.271.

Fort House, Broadstairs as Dickens would have known it during the 1850's, before the west wing was built. (Author's collection)

Dickens took advantage of the sandy beach that Fort House overlooked and when lacking motivation to write he would swim in the sea. On 1 June 1851 he wrote:

> For the last two or three days I have been rather slack in point of work, not being in the vein. Today I had not written twenty lines before I rushed out (the weather being gorgeous) to bathe. … It is more delightful here than I can express. Corn growing, larks singing, garden full of flowers, fresh air on the sea – O, it is wonderful![112]

Dickens gave an idyllic description of Broadstairs in an article entitled 'Our Watering Place', which featured in *Household Words* in 1851:

> Half awake and half asleep, this idle morning in our sunny window on the edge of a chalk cliff in the old-fashioned watering place to which we are a faithful resorter, we feel a lazy inclination to sketch its picture. The place seems to respond. Sky, sea, beach and village, lie as still before us as if they were sitting for the picture. It is dead low-water.[113]

The advent of railways had made Broadstairs accessible to holidaymakers, which transformed the tranquillity of the seaside town into a bustling, noisy place to Dickens prior to leasing Fort House. It certainly impacted upon his ability to write. In 1847, Dickens lamented, 'vagrant music is getting to that height here and is so impossible to be escaped from, that I fear Broadstairs and I must part company in time to come. Unless it pours with rain, I cannot write half an hour without the most excruciating organs, fiddles, bells, or glee-singers. There is a violin of most torturing kind under the window now (time, ten in the morning), and an Italian box of music on the steps, both in full blast.'[114]

Despite the noise, Dickens continued to visit Broadstairs. He returned to Fort House for his last visit in 1859, while he recuperated from illness for a week. The building was renamed by a successive owner as Bleak House in the early part of the twentieth century, however Fort House was not the home of Mr Jarndyce in the novel.

---

112. Kitton, *Life*, op. cit., p.186.

113. *Household Words*, 2 August 1851.

114. Kitton, *Country*, op. cit., p.196.

# 50

# Tavistock House, London

**A plaque commemorates Dickens' residence at Tavistock House from 1851 to 1860.**

Tavistock House once stood in the north-eastern corner of Tavistock Square in Bloomsbury, London. Dickens stayed in Broadstairs during the summer 1851 while renovations were carried out at the house. When he took possession of the premises in November 1851 the work had not been completed, to his dismay. Dickens began writing *Bleak House* shortly after he relocated there.

Hans Christian Andersen, the Danish author, visited Tavistock House in 1857 and provided a concise description of Dickens' abode, in which he wrote:

> In Tavistock Square stands Tavistock House. This and the strip of garden in front are shut out from the through fare (Gordon Place, on the east side) by an iron railing. A large garden, with a grass plot and high trees, stretches behind the house, and gives it a countrified look in the midst of this coal and gas-steaming London. In the passage from street to garden hung pictures and engravings. Here stood a marble bust of Dickens, so like him, so youthful and handsome; and over a bedroom door were inserted the bas-reliefs of Night and Day, after Thorwaldsen. On the first floor was a rich library, with a fireplace and a writing-table, looking out on the garden … The kitchen was underground, and at the top of the house were bedrooms. I had a snug room looking out on the garden, and over the tree tops I saw the London towers and spires appear and disappear as the weather cleared or thickened.[115]

Dickens penned *Bleak House, Hard Times, Little Dorrit, A Tale of Two Cities* and *Great Expectations* at Tavistock House. Mamie described the room where they were written: 'The study at Tavistock House was more elaborate; a fine large room, opening into the drawing-room by means of sliding doors. When the rooms were thrown together, they gave my father

---

115. Kitton, *Country*, op. cit., p.71.

The plaque attached to the offices of the British Medical Association at 20 Tavistock House, Bloomsbury, London, which indicates that Dickens lived at Tavistock House, a building that once stood close to this spot. (Author's Collection)

a promenade of considerable length for the constant indoor walking which formed a favourite recreation for him after a hard day's writing.'[116]

Dickens worked in solitude, however, while he was living at Tavistock House, his daughter, Mamie gives us a rare insight into how he worked at his desk:

During our life at Tavistock House, I had a long and serious illness, with an almost equally long convalescence. During the latter, my father suggested that I should be carried every day into his study to remain with him, and, although I was fearful of disturbing him, he assured me that he desired to have me with him. On one of these mornings, I was lying on the sofa endeavouring to keep perfectly quiet, while my father wrote busily and rapidly at his desk, when he suddenly jumped from his chair and rushed to a mirror which hung near, and in which I could see the reflection of some extraordinary facial contortions which he was making. He returned rapidly to his desk, wrote furiously for a few moments, and then went again to the mirror. The facial pantomime was resumed, and then turning toward, but evidently not seeing, me, he began talking rapidly in a low voice. Ceasing this soon, however, he returned once more to his desk, where he remained silently writing until luncheon time. It was a most curious experience for me, and one of which, I did not until later years, fully appreciate the purport. Then I knew that with his natural intensity he had thrown himself completely into the character that he was

---

116. Dickens, Mamie, op. cit., p.16.

A contemporary view of Tavistock House, Dickens' residence between 1851 and 1860. (Author's Collection)

creating, and for that time being he had not only lost sight of his surroundings, but had actually become in action, as in imagination, the creature of his pen.[117]

A large room on the ground floor at the rear of the house was used to perform amateur dramatics, where a stage was built. On 6 January 1852, Dickens performed in *Tom Thumb* by Henry Fielding, as the ghost of Gaffer Thumb, which amused William Makepeace Thackeray, who was in the audience. The date on Twelfth Night, also Dickens' eldest son's birthday, would regularly see Dickens perform in plays in Tavistock House in what he billed as 'The smallest theatre in the world'. Wilkie Collins wrote *The Lighthouse* and *The Frozen Deep*, which were performed here.

Catherine gave birth to their son, Edward Bulwer-Lytton Dickens, on 13 March 1852 at Tavistock House, but it was also there that the marriage with Dickens broke down and it split the family. He refused to sleep with Catherine and had the connecting door to his bedroom closed permanently. According to Dickens, it was he who cared for the children and he was left with his sister-in-law, Georgina Hogarth, to run the house. Catherine was living in the shadow of her husband's success as a celebrity author. The situation was so unbearable when the Hogarths visited Tavistock House, he walked 30 miles through the night to seek refuge at Gad's Hill Place. Georgina sided with Dickens and remained with him as his housekeeper. All his children remained at Tavistock House except for Charles Junior, who left the house with Catherine. Dickens vacated Tavistock House when he moved to Gad's Hill Place in 1860. Tavistock House was demolished in 1901 but there is a plaque that remembers Dickens' residence.

---

117. Ibid., p.49.

# 51

# Photograph of Charles Dickens, 1852

### This image of Dickens was taken by Antoine Claudet at his studios at 107 Regent Street, London.

Claudet's photograph captures a three-quarter-length pose of Dickens standing with his right hand in his pocket and his left hand, holding his gloves, resting on an urn. The majority of photographs show Dickens with a beard, but this image uniquely depicts the author clean-shaven.

The photograph was taken in 1852, the year that he began writing *Bleak House*, and Dickens looks gaunt, exhausted and anguished. During the previous year he had suffered various traumas that caused him nervous exhaustion. Catherine was ill and so was his baby daughter, Dora. The infant rallied but his wife remained ill. It was therefore decided in March 1851 that for health reasons she should stay in Malvern, Worcestershire, where the air and water might aid her recovery, and she was accompanied by her sister, Georgina. The children remained in their residence at Devonshire Terrace, which meant that Dickens was dashing between London and Malvern. The situation was complicated when his father, who was suffering from ill health, died on 31 March 1851, which caused him much distress. His father was aged 66 and was interred in Highgate Cemetery. Dickens returned to London on 14 April to attend the annual dinner of the General Theatrical Fund. Before attending the dinner, he spent some time with his children and played with his baby daughter at Devonshire Terrace, but soon after he left the house, Dora, who was aged eight months, died suddenly in the arms of her nurse. Thirty minutes prior to Dickens' speech, a servant brought the news to John Forster, who was also attending the dinner. Forster withheld the information until after Dickens delivered his speech. The distraught Dickens comforted his children, while he sent Forster to convey the heart-breaking news to his wife in Malvern and bring her home. Dora was also buried at Highgate Cemetery close to the grave of his father.

In 1852, the year that this photo was taken, Dickens celebrated the birth of his son, Edward, 'Plorn', and it was also the year that he met fellow author Wilkie Collins. During October 1852, Dickens invited the American author Sara Jane Lippincott (who wrote under the pseudonym Grace Greenwood) to his new London residence at Tavistock House for dinner with his family and she provided an insight into Dickens' domestic life during the year in which this photograph was taken. Greenwood wrote:

A portrait of Charles Dickens taken by Antoine Claudet in 1852. (Courtesy of Library Company of Philadelphia)

On Thursday evening last, I dined with Mr. and Mrs. Dickens, and a small but brilliant party, at the pleasant house of the novelist in Tavistock Square. Mr. Dickens is all I looked to see, in person, manner and conservation. He is rather slight, with a large symmetrical head, spiritedly borne, and eyes beaming alike with genius and humour. Yet for all the power and beauty of those eyes, their changes seemed to be from light to light. I saw in them no profound, pathetic depth, and there was round them no tragic shadowing. But I was foolish to look for these on such an occasion, when they were properly left in the author's study, with pens, ink, and blotting paper, and the last written pages of *Bleak House*. Mrs. Dickens is a very charming person – in character and manner truly a gentlewoman; and such of the children as I saw seemed worthy to hand down to coming years the beauty of the mother and the name of the father. Mr. Dickens looked in admirable health and spirits, has good for at least twenty more charming serials … I have no doubt from the confirming impression I have of the exhaustiveness of his genius … Mr. Dickens' style of living is elegant and tasteful, but in no respect ostentatious, or out of character with his profession or principles.[118]

---

118. *Kilkenny Moderator*, 23 October 1852.

# 52

## *Bleak House*

**The first instalment of *Bleak House* appeared in March 1852.**

**Dickens set *Bleak House* in the countryside outside St Albans in Hertfordshire, not his home at Fort House in Broadstairs. It is notably the only Dickens' novel to feature a female narrator through the heroine Esther Summerson.**

After working as a legal clerk as a young man, Dickens maintained an unfavourable attitude towards the legal profession throughout his life. In a letter in 1870 he wrote: 'I have that opinion of the law of England generally, which one is likely to derive from the impression that it puts all the honest men under the diabolical hoofs of all the scoundrels.'[119] *Bleak House* gave Dickens the opportunity to expose the unscrupulous activities of the legal profession during his day.

Cases existed that continued for years, such as constant delays during the contention of indeterminable complicated wills that would last for decades and would be contested across the generations of a family. These cases would result in expensive legal fees absorbing the costs of the estate in question and the abandonment of that case. Those who were the intended beneficiaries of inheritance were denied that legacy and the lawyers were the only people who prospered. While Dickens was writing *Bleak House* during August 1853, he referred to an ongoing case and although he does not identify it by name, it can be identified through Dickens' letters that he was alluding to the will of Charles Day, a boot blacking manufacturer, which was being contested after his death in 1836. During two decades, the case involved between thirty to forty counsels appearing at court, each representing a beneficiary who had a claim to the estate. This was a straightforward case, but the confusion and delays had incurred costs of £70,000 and it was not resolved until 1854. It was through the elongated proceedings of the case of Jarndyce and Jarndyce, which formed the central plot of *Bleak House*, that Dickens attacked the abuses of the Court of Chancery. The legal profession dismissed Dickens' criticism of the profession as an exaggeration. His friend, Lord Denman, who had previously been Chief Justice of the Queen's Bench, was not happy with Dickens' perception of the Court of Chancery.

---

119. Kitton, *Life*, op. cit., p.26.

Dickens highlighted the predicament of those waiting for a conclusion to cases brought before the Court of Chancery through the story of Richard Carstone and Ada Clare, who become wards of John Jarndyce while the case is being determined. They marry each other and Carstone enters the Chancery to see if he can push forward proceedings in the Jarndyce and Jarndyce case. When the case comes to a conclusion, the entire value of the estate is consumed by legal fees, leaving them with no legacy. Afterwards, Carstone dies.

*Bleak House* successfully started with sales of 10,000 for each number and as the series progressed, these increased to 40,000 copies per month. The serial outsold *David Copperfield*, which did not exceed 25,000 copies per issue.

**Jo** is an orphaned homeless boy who sweeps the streets around the Chancery Court. He is reliant upon measly acts of charity, a few coins from passers-by, in order to survive. He is unable to keep himself clean and is looked down upon because of his poverty and lack of hygiene, which is out of his control. Captain Hawdon, known as Nemo, takes pity on Jo and gives him some coins. When Hawdon dies, Jo is asked to give evidence at the inquest into his death, although he has no knowledge of his demise. Jo becomes embroiled in the story when Lady Dedlock becomes aware that Jo attended the inquest and asks Jo to show her Hawdon's grave. Dickens uses the death of Jo to highlight the squalor of child poverty that existed in city slums.

**Inspector Bucket** was one of the first detectives to feature in a work of English fiction. Originally commissioned by Tulkinghorn to search for Lady Dedlock's secret, he becomes embroiled in the investigation of the murder of Tulkinghorn. Dickens based the character upon Inspector Charles Field, who formed the Detective Branch at Scotland Yard. He also accompanied Field on a night patrol around the notorious Seven Dials district in London, and he subsequently featured in an article that Dickens wrote in *Household Words*.

Jo. (Author's Collection)

Inspector Bucket. (Author's Collection)

# 53

# Rockingham Castle

**The inspiration for Dickens' Chesney Wold in *Bleak House*.**

**Dickens was a frequent visitor to Rockingham Castle in Northamptonshire as a guest of its owners, the Honourable Richard and Mrs Watson, whom he had met in Lausanne in 1846. His first visit to the Watsons' took place in 1849 and Dickens would use Rockingham Castle as Chesney Wold, the home of the Dedlocks in *Bleak House*.**

Rockingham Castle was built under the instruction of William the Conqueror during the eleventh century. Henry VIII granted the castle to Edward Watson and it had remained under the ownership of the Watson family since the Tudor period. Dickens described Rockingham Castle as 'a large old castle approached by an ancient keep, portcullis, etc, filled with company waited on by six-and-twenty servants'.[120]

Dickens returned to Rockingham Castle with his amateur dramatic company during January 1851. The village carpenter constructed a small theatre in the Long Gallery within the castle under his supervision for the performances of the plays *Used Up* and *Animal Magnetism*, which Dickens stage managed and performed.

Rockingham Castle was believed to have been inspiration for the Chesney Wold, the home of Sir Leicester Dedlock and Lady Honoria Dedlock in *Bleak House*, in which Dickens described:

> Thus Chesney Wold. With so much of itself abandoned to darkness and vacancy; with so little change under the summer shining or the wintery lowering; so sombre and motionless always – no flag flying now by day, no rows of lights sparkling by night; with no family to come and go, no visitors to be the souls of pale cold shapes of rooms, no stir of life about it; passion and pride, even to the stranger's eye, have died away from the place in Lincolnshire, and yielded it to dull repose.[121]

Sir Leicester Dedlock is a representative of one of the affluent county families of England and loves his wife, who is much younger. Lady Dedlock is dignified but maintains a cold

---

120. *Northampton Mercury*, 27 March 1936.
121. Dickens, Charles, *Bleak House* (Macmillan & Co., London, 1895), p.811.

A view of Rockingham Castle. (Courtesy of Marion Haworth; www.geograph.org.uk)

composure. She is imprisoned within its walls in a life of boredom and dissatisfaction. Her husband is unaware of her past, that before their marriage, Lady Dedlock was in a previous relationship with Captain Hawdon, to whom she was engaged but did not marry, although she had conceived a child by him. The name of her child was Esther Summerson. To have a child without marriage was regarded as scandalous during the period, so on the evening prior to her secret being revealed, Lady Dedlock flees from Chesney Wold. Wracked with shame, she dies at the gates of the cemetery where her past love, Captain Hawdon, is buried in a pauper's grave.

Although Dickens portrayed Chesney Wold as a depressing and dismal place, he was fond of Rockingham Castle, for he wrote to Mrs Watson, 'somehow, I always think of Rockingham, after coming away, as if I belonged to it and had left a bit of my heart'.[122]

---

122. Dickens, *Letters*, Vol. 2, op. cit., p.159.

# 54

# Birmingham Town Hall

## Dickens performed the first of three charity readings for the Birmingham and Midland Institute.

A decade after giving his first reading to his friends at John Forster's home at Lincoln's Inn Fields, Dickens gave the first of three public readings at the Birmingham Town Hall on 27 December 1853.

Dickens followed advice from Forster in refraining from making any public appearance and not doing any further readings for fear of diminishing his work or his reputation as a writer, but in 1853 he returned to the spotlight to fulfil a long-standing promise to raise funds for the Birmingham and Midland Institute, which was a newly established literary and scientific institution. He read for three nights at the Birmingham Town Hall to 2,000 people on each night for three hours. Dickens read *A Christmas Carol* on the first and third nights' performances and the *Cricket on the Hearth* on the second night. Dickens stipulated that the audience of the third night should be composed of working people. Dickens was aware of the size of the venue and was able to project his voice to ensure that his voice was audible to every person sitting in the audience. According to the *Huddersfield Chronicle*, the audience responded warmly to Dickens, for it reported:

> On Friday evening, the *'Christmas Carol'* was repeated to a large assemblage of workpeople, for whom, at Mr. Dickens' special request, the major portion of the vast edifice was reserved. The story appeared, if possible, to be more keenly appreciated than by the audience on Tuesday – Loud applause followed, in the midst of which a working man rose and proposed three cheers, with three times three, for Mr Dickens.[123]

Dickens addressed the audience on the third night with the words, 'you have heard so much of my voice since we met tonight, that I will only say, in acknowledgement of this affecting

---

123. *Huddersfield Chronicle*, 7 January 1854.

Birmingham Town Hall, as seen in this view from Chamberlain Square, was opened in 1834. (Courtesy of Julian Osley; www.geograph.org.uk)

mark of your regard, that I am truly and sincerely interested in you; that any little service I have rendered to you I have freely rendered from my heart.'[124]

After the success of the Birmingham public readings, Dickens was inundated with requests to give similar readings for other charitable causes. He soon realised the lucrative potential of being paid for these events. He continued non-professional readings sporadically for charitable causes until 29 April 1858, when he emerged professionally as a public reader. He returned to the Birmingham Town Hall on 1 and 2 April 1869 during his farewell tour to read and on 27 September 1869 to address the students of the Birmingham and Midland Institute as President.

124. Ibid.

# 55

# Proofs of *Hard Times* with Dickens' Annotations

**Dickens wrote *Hard Times* during 1854, in which he expressed his criticisms of the factory system.**

Soon after the completion of its serialisation, the story was published in one volume and these are the proofs of the printed copies returned from the publisher to Dickens and showing his corrections and annotations. As well as correcting errors, he added titles to each chapter, which did not exist in *Household Words*. *Hard Times* was dedicated to his friend, the historian Thomas Carlyle, when it was published as a book.

Dickens was motivated to write the story to improve sales of *Household Words*. *Hard Times* was the first novel that Dickens wrote specifically for *Household Words* and it featured in editions between 1 April and 12 August 1854. Its inclusion on the weekly periodical doubled its circulation. *Hard Times* was unique because it was Dickens' shortest novel, the story was not set in London, there were no illustrations and no preface. In a letter to Charles Knight, Dickens explained his objective in writing the story:

> My satire is against those who see figures and averages, and nothing else, the representatives of the wickedest and most enormous vice of this time; the men who, through long years to come, will do more to damage the really useful truths of the political economy than I could do (if I tried) in my whole life; the addled heads who would take the average of cold in the Crimea during twelve months as a reason for clothing a soldier in nankeen on a night when he would be frozen to death in fur, and who would comfort the labourer in travelling twelve miles a day to and from his work by telling him that the average distance of one inhabited place from another on the whole area of England is not more than four miles.[125]

Dickens chose to focus upon the deprivations and struggles faced by factory workers in the fictional town he called Coketown, which was believed to have been Preston, the industrialised

---

125. Pierce, op. cit., p.360.

town in north-west England. *Hard Times* was shorter than his previously written novels and underwhelmed some readers. This was primarily due to the problems of engaging his audience within the limited space for the early instalments.

The story focuses upon Stephen Blackpool, who is a poor power loom weaver employed by mill owner Josiah Bounderby. Blackpool leads a hard life working in the mill and he is mistreated by those who are rich and powerful. He is imprisoned within a miserable marriage, where he is abused by his alcoholic wife. Blackpool is unable to marry Rachel, the woman who cares for him, because he is unable to divorce his wife.

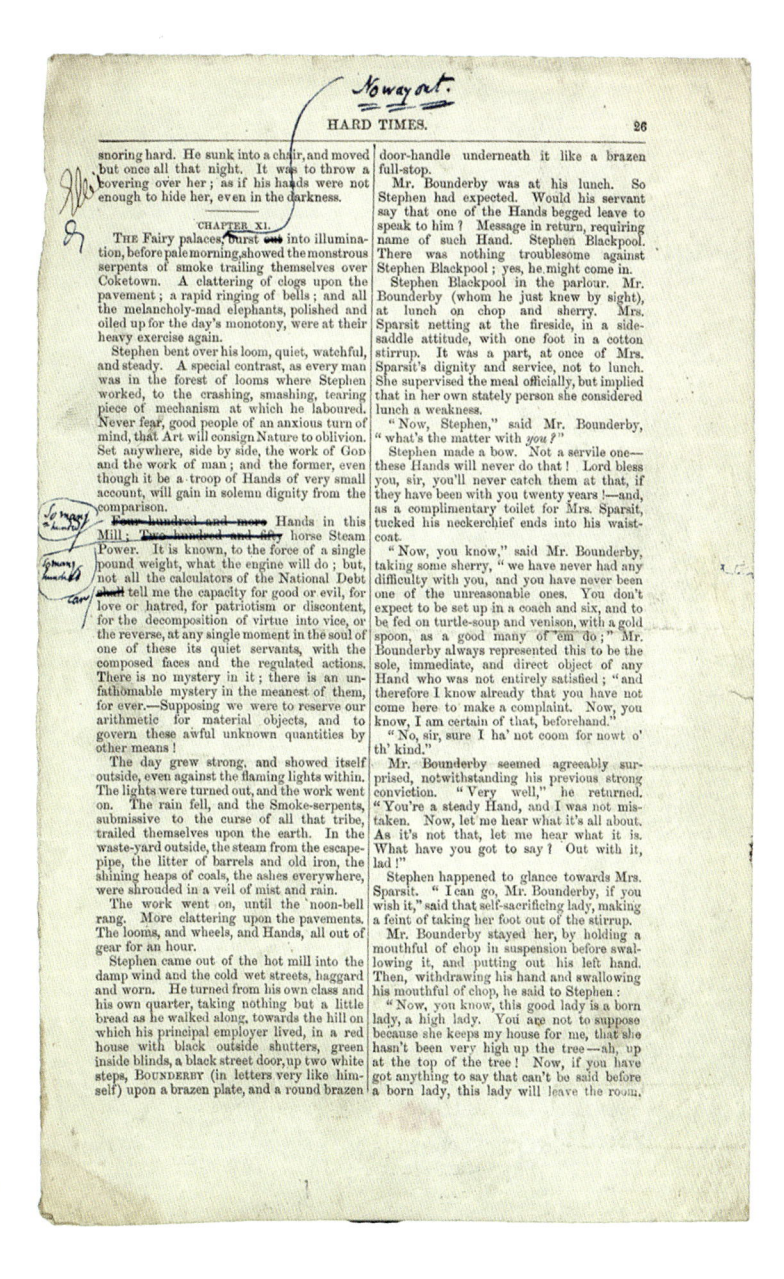

These are proofs of *Hard Times*, print copies returned from his publisher Bradbury & Evans, on which Dickens had written his amendments. (British Library)

PROOFS OF *HARD TIMES* WITH DICKENS' ANNOTATIONS

# 56

# Letter Regarding Performance of *A Christmas Carol* from Dickens to his Wife

**On 28 December 1854, Dickens gave a reading of *A Christmas Carol* for the Education Temperance Institute at St George's Hall, Bradford.**

St George's Hall was a newly built venue which opened on 29 August 1853. Dickens wrote the following letter to his wife hours before he went on stage on 28 December.

> Bradford, Yorkshire, Thursday Twenty Eighth December 1854.
>
> Dearest Catherine, We arrived here pleasantly enough, though we were nearly an hour behind time and the journey was cold. As we came northward, it snowed. A little snow is lying here now. It is a dark dingy place; but we are established in the landlady's little drawing room at the [illegible] hotel, and it is a bright neat little room. I have a comfortable small bedroom adjoining, except that it looks into what I thought yesterday afternoon was an old rabbit hutch, but which I suspect this morning to be a back street.
>
> The Hall is enormous. They expect to seat tonight, 3,700 people! I do not however, think it at all a different place. It's lighted along the upper cornice, like the Philharmonic rooms at Liverpool, and must be very fine when full. ...[126]

The doors opened at 6.30 pm and the audience entered the auditorium. Although the stalls were full, a great proportion of the galleries were unoccupied and Dickens performed to an audience of 2,500, which was less than the anticipated tickets sold, but this was still a significant number. Dickens walked on to the stage at 7 pm and the reading lasted for two and a half hours. At the beginning, he addressed the audience to welcome them and to encourage them to react in whatever manner they felt appropriate during the performance. Dickens was getting to know his audience and that he was taking them on a journey during the performance. He asked them to regard this as an intimate evening, 'to imagine this a small social party assembled to hear a

---

126. British Library/Public Domain.

Dickens wrote this letter to his wife hours before he walked on to the stage at Bradford Town Hall to give a reading of *A Christmas Carol* on 28 December 1854. (British Library)

tale told round the Christmas fire; and secondly, that if you feel disposed, as we go along, to give expression to any emotion, whether grave or gay, you will do so with perfect freedom from constraint and without the least apprehension of disturbing me. Nothing can be so delightful to me on such an occasion as the assurance that my hearers accompany me with something of the pleasure and interest, I have in conducting them.'[127]

Dickens returned to St George's Hall on 4 January 1855 to read *A Christmas Carol* for the town's Temporal Educational Institute and on 20 October 1859 to read *Little Dombey* and the Trial from *The Pickwick Papers*.

---

127. *Leeds Mercury*, 30 December 1854.

# 57

# Le Meurice Hotel, Paris

**Dickens, accompanied by his friend Wilkie Collins, made a brief trip to Paris during February 1855.**

The two authors stayed at Le Meurice Hotel on the Rue du Rivoli. Some arcades were along this affluent French road opposite Tulleries Garden during 1806 and a stretch of these were converted into Le Meurice Hotel, which opened in 1835. The entire first floor was renovated during 1855 to accommodate Queen Victoria during her state visit to Paris. Earlier during that same year, Dickens and Collins stayed at Le Meurice Hotel.

Collins, who was unwell at the time, and Dickens arrived at Boulogne on 11 February to pay a brief visit to Dickens' sons, who were being educated in the town, before proceeding to Paris. The two men arrived in Paris and at Le Meurice Hotel during the evening on 12 February. Dickens had asked his friend, Monsieur Regnier, to suggest a suitable apartment or hotel to stay during the visit. He did not want to stay at the Hotel Brighton, where he had stayed previously, because the hotel management expected the guests to dine in the hotel. Dickens wanted to stay in an hotel where he had the flexibility to explore Paris at his leisure and find appealing restaurants to dine at each day instead of being constrained to eating in the same hotel each evening. Regnier recommended Le Meurice. In a letter to his sister-in-law, Georgina Hogarth, he complimented the accommodation at the hotel and recorded his routine in Paris:

> We have a beautiful apartment, very elegantly furnished, very thickly carpeted, and as warm as any apartment in Paris can be in such weather. We are very well waited on and looked after. We breakfast at ten, read and write till two, and then I go out walking all over Paris while the invalid sits by the fire or he is deposited in a café. We dine at five, in a different restaurant every day, and at seven or so go to the theatre – sometimes to two theatres sometimes to three. We get home about twelve, light the fire, and drink lemonade, to which I add rum. We go to bed between one and two. I live in peace like an elderly gentleman, and regard myself as in a negative state of virtue and respectability.[128]

---

128. Dickens, *Letters*, Vol. 1, op. cit., pp.395–6.

A view of the Le Meurice Hotel in Paris. (Courtesy of Axou)

As Dickens walked around Paris, he was getting familiar with its streets and surroundings. Le Meurice Hotel was close to La Place de la Concorde, where executions took place using the guillotine during the French Revolution and these featured in the climax of his novel *A Tale of Two Cities*. Dickens was also becoming confident in his understanding and ability to speak the French language. Collins and Dickens originally intended on travelling to Bordeaux, but deep snow prevented them from pursuing that plan and they returned home to London.

Dickens returned to Paris later that year in October 1855 and stayed in two apartments at No. 49 Avenue des Champs-Élysées.

# 58

# No. 3 Albion Villas, Folkestone

**The first instalments of *Little Dorrit* were written in this house.**

**As he started to write *Little Dorrit* at Tavistock House in London, Dickens was restless and decided to relocate to Folkestone.**

Dickens was so impressed by the peace and tranquillity of Folkestone during a brief visit in 1852 that he returned to the Kent seaside town, spending the autumn of 1855 at No. 3, Albion Villas on Folkestone Leas. Dickens enjoyed the fishing town on the Kent coast. On 17 July, Dickens wrote to Wilkie Collins, 'we have a very pleasant little house, overlooking the sea.'[129] Dickens came to Folkestone because he was struggling to write his new novel, but it was in the attic room within this house that he wrote part of the work, which was entitled *Little Dorrit*. When he got to writing the second number, Dickens was dissatisfied with how he had begun the story and decided to abandon the previous instalment and start again from scratch. He then struggled with the third number. On 16 September, he wrote to Mr W.H. Wills, 'I am just getting to work on No. 3 of the new book, and am in a hideous state of mind belonging to that condition.'[130]

In another letter written on that same day, Dickens wrote how the solace and surroundings of Folkestone inspired his writing of *Little Dorrit*. 'How I work, how I walk, how I shut myself up, how I roll down hills and climb up cliffs; how the new story is everywhere – heaving in the sea, flying with the clouds, blowing in the wind; how I settle to nothing, and wonder (in the old way) at my incomprehensibility. I am getting on pretty well, have done the first two numbers, and just beginning the third.'[131]

Although Folkestone has transformed during the past 165 years, there are some places that were familiar to Dickens that have not changed, such as the British Lion public house, which was within walking distance of Albion Villas and frequented by Dickens. The Old High Street that leads from the harbour into the town still retains the appearance known to Dickens,

---

129. Dickens, *Letters*, Vol. 2, op. cit., p.17.

130. Dickens, *Letters*, Vol. 1, op. cit., p.402.

131. Ibid., p.403.

No. 3 Albion Villas, Folkestone. (Author's Collection)

who described it as 'a steep, crooked street, like a crippled ladder'.[132] In an article he wrote for *Household Words*, Dickens described Folkestone:

> It is a little fishing town, and they do say that the time was when it was a little smuggling town … The old little fishing and smuggling town remains … There are break-neck flights of ragged steps, connecting the principal streets by backways, which will cripple the visitor in half an hour … Our situation is delightful, our air delicious and our breezy hills and downs, carpeted with wild thyme and decorated with millions of wild flowers.[133]

---

132. Dickens, *Letters*, Vol. 2, op. cit., p.17.
133. *Household Words*, 29 September 1855.

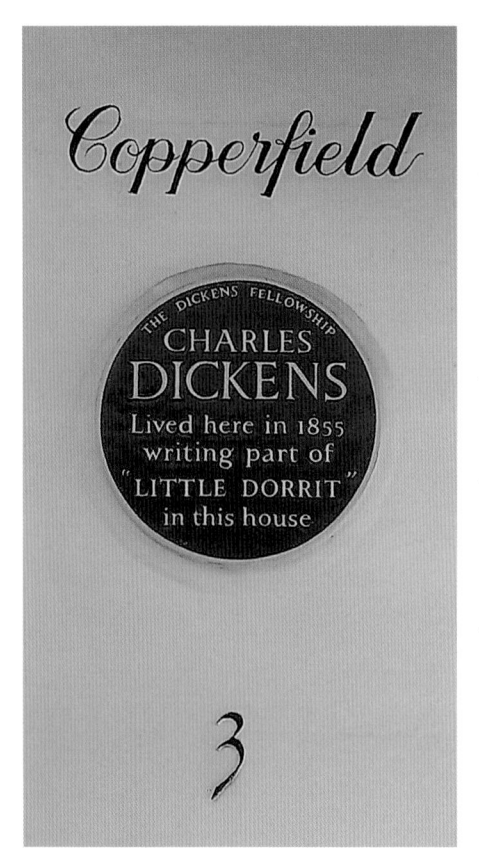

Plaque commemorating Dickens' stay at No. 3 Albion Villas, Folkestone. (Author's Collection)

When it was known that Dickens would be spending the autumn in Folkestone, he received invitations during June 1855 from two rival local groups, the Working Men's Educational Union and the Harveian Literary Institute, to read *A Christmas Carol*. Dickens was not obliged to read to both, so he accepted the invitations on the condition that he would conduct a reading where both groups could attend. The Harveian Literary Institute were reluctant to accommodate the Working Men's Educational Union, but after some persuading they conceded to Dickens' wishes. In a letter to John Forster he wrote:

> I am going to read here next Friday week. There are (as there are everywhere) a Literary Institution and a Working Man's Institution, which have not the slightest sympathy or connection. The stalls are five shillings, and I have made them fix the working men's admission at three pence, and I hope it may bring them together. The event comes off in a carpenter's shop, as the biggest place that can be got.[134]

On 5 October 1855, Dickens gave the reading in aid of the town's Mechanics' Institute. The carpenter's shop was in the Dover Road and accommodated 600 people, including the local nobility and visitors staying at the Pavilion Hotel. It was reported that: 'Dickens in his reading, drew forth much merriment and applause; his voice was clear, but not loud; altogether it was a great treat, and such an assemblage has never been seen in Folkestone at any lecture of reading.'[135]

Also in October, Dickens departed in a ferry from the harbour arm at Folkestone to Boulogne and then on to Paris, where he spent the winter. Dickens would pass through Folkestone frequently because he sent his sons to Boulogne for their education and would use the ferry to visit them. Sometimes he would stay at the Pavilion Hotel by the harbour. A section of the Pavilion Hotel stands behind the current Grand Burstin Hotel.

---

134. Dexter, op. cit., p.226.

135. *The Examiner*, 13 October, 1855.

# 59

# Original Parts of *Little Dorrit*

### Dickens novels were initially sold in instalments such as these parts, which were affordable for everybody.

The first number of *Little Dorrit* appeared on 1 December 1855 and it was serialised in nineteen parts, ending in June 1857. The story was illustrated by Hablot Knight Browne and after its completion Dickens dedicated the book to Clarkson Stanfield, the artist who painted scenery for his amateur dramatics productions.

Dickens was inspired by childhood memories of visiting his father in the Marshalsea Prison for the basis of *Little Dorrit*. Setting the story in the 1820s, he would use the novel to highlight the impact on the lives of those individuals imprisoned for debt and the injustices suffered by those who were unable to discharge the claims of their creditors or present the reasons for their predicament to the insolvent court. It was an impossible situation for many individuals trapped within the debtors' prison, because they could not work and therefore were unable to earn an income to pay off their debts and free themselves from prison.

Dickens' father spent fourteen weeks incarcerated for unpaid debts, but in *Little Dorrit* William Dorrit spends twenty-five years imprisoned in the Marshalsea Prison. Because of the years he spends within its walls he becomes known as the 'Father of the Marshalsea' and is respected by the inmates and the prison staff. Dickens may have derived the name Dorrit from another prisoner named Dorrett in the King's Bench court when his own father was paying his dues for a debt. There is also a headstone with the name Dorrett in the graveyard adjacent to Rochester Cathedral that Dickens would most likely have walked past as a boy and later as an adult. Dickens explained the vague circumstances as to the incarceration of William Dorrit:

> The affairs of his debtor were perplexed by a partnership, of which he knew no more than that he had invested money on it, by legal matters of assignment and settlement, conveyance here and conveyance there, suspicion of unlawful preference of creditors in this direction, and of mysterious spiriting away of property in that; and as nobody on the face of the earth could be more incapable of explaining any single item in the heap of

Original parts of *Little Dorrit*, which were published between 1855 and 1857. Dickens is believed to have used names on gravestones in local graveyards for names for his characters. One example can be seen in the graveyard between Rochester Cathedral and St Nicholas Church, where in the fourth grave from the cathedral can be seen the headstone for members of the Dorrett family. The spelling of the name is different, but it may have served as inspiration for *Little Dorrit*. (British Library)

confusion than the debtor himself, nothing comprehensible could be made of his case … the sharpest practitioners gave him up as a hopeless job.[136]

William Dorrit prides himself as being father of the Marshalsea, but does not make any attempt to acknowledge his failure in getting his family into such a predicament. His daughter Amy, known as Little Dorrit, is born in the prison, but his wife dies when Amy is eight years old. Dickens' story begins when she is twenty-three. Amy is devoted as she becomes the principal support to her father and her family. Her uncle, Frederick, and brother, Tip, are also imprisoned in the Marshalsea for debt. She attends upon them in the prison and earns money through working as a seamstress.

Ironically, William Dorrit spends twenty-five years of his life imprisoned unaware of an unclaimed legacy that belongs to him, which eventually results in him leaving the Marshalsea a rich man. During a tour of Italy, Dorrit dies in a palace in Rome, believing that he is in the Marshalsea.

The Crimean War was being fought while Dickens was writing *Little Dorrit*. The war was badly organised by Government departments and Dickens wanted to expose inadequacies and incompetence displayed by civil servants and government officials, focusing upon their inability to respond to crisis and disasters. He achieved this by featuring the inefficiencies of the Circumlocution Office and ineptness of its administrators within the novel. He portrayed the officers as buffoons, who requested a litany of paperwork to be completed that would be then lost in bureaucratic

---

136. Dickens, Charles, *Little Dorrit* (Bradbury & Evans, London, 1857), p.43.

chaos, with their inaction keeping good people unnecessary incarcerated in the Marshalsea. Arthur Clennam attempts to find information about William Dorrit's creditors to no avail.

European travel had widened Dickens' horizons and he would use that experience in novels such as *Little Dorrit*. The story opens in Marseilles, and the journey of the Dorrit family after they have come into legacy and travel to Italy reflects Dickens' own journey there.

Dickens explored various themes in juxtaposition within the novel. He showed acts of decency within a cruel world. Amy Dorrit is selfless, kind-hearted and caring, and places the needs of others before her own. Amy sees the good in everyone. Arthur Clennam comes from an affluent background, is comfortable with people from all parts of society and has similar caring, self-effacing characteristics as Amy. Mr Chivvy and his son, John, hold the keys to the Marshalsea but they show empathy and kindness to those who are imprisoned within its walls. Mr Pancks acts on behalf of his employer Christopher Casby to pursue and squeeze Casby's tenants for money, but he is not pitiless. He recognises that the residents of Bleeding Heart Yard are hard-working honest people and resents the hypocrisy of Casby. Pancks is a man of integrity and exposes Casby's true nature in front of his tenants in Bleeding Heart Yard before resigning from his unsavoury employment. Daniel Doyce shows gratitude to his business partner Arthur Clennam when Clennam is incarcerated in the Marshalsea prison and helps him to gain his liberty through his generosity.

Money is an important theme that is featured in *Little Dorrit*. Dickens showed the rich and poor, how people obtained money and lost money. There are examples of people who earn money through working juxtaposed with those who exploit those who work for it. Mr Plornish grafts in order to survive and feed his family, while his landlord, Christopher Casby sits back and masquerades as the benevolent, kind tenant, but in reality, he is a parasite, who employed Mr Pancks to pressurise and squeeze those hard-working, but impoverished tenants such as Plornish for the little money that they have earned through extortionate rents. Mr Merdle obtains his money through speculation and investing other people's money at great risk, where he profits. Dickens also ridiculed the snobbery associated with people of wealth such as Mr Merdle. It is probable that Dickens derived his name from the French word 'merd', which is translated into the English word for excrement. The collapse of Merdle's bank and investments has a detrimental effect upon the Dorrits' financial position, reducing them to poverty once again; and impacts upon Clennam and Doyce, for Clennam invests the company's assets in Merdle's investment, making the business insolvent and resulting in him being sent to the Marshalsea. It also affects Mr Pancks, who is also an investor. Merdle commits suicide after his financial downfall. Rigaud acquires money through sinister means. He has murdered his wife and after escaping from a Marseilles gaol, he tries to extort money through blackmail from Mrs Clennam, threatening to expose her fraud. Fanny Dorrit earns her money as a dancer in a theatre, which is frowned upon.

Imprisonment is another theme, with William Dorrit physically imprisoned within the walls of the Marshalsea, while Affery Flintwich is shackled in another way, trapped in an abusive marriage with a husband who mistreats her. Mrs Clennam is self-imprisoned in her home and by her disability, with the loss of the use of her limbs rendering her confined to her wheelchair.

# 60

# Associated Locations in *Little Dorrit*

The **Marshalsea Gate** and the southern boundary wall are the only surviving part of the Marshalsea Prison. Dickens may have used this entrance when visiting his father in 1824. He certainly described this wall in the preface of *Little Dorrit* in 1857, as mentioned previously. Amy Dorrit is born within the walls of this prison. Dickens would leave at ten o'clock when the bell was run to signal that visiting time at the Marshalsea was over and that the door would be closed and locked for the night. In *Little Dorrit*, Arthur Clennam does not heed the warnings when the bell is rung and is locked inside the Marshalsea Prison for the night.

John Chivery, the non-resident turnkey of the prison, would have been stationed at this gate. He is assisted in his duty by his son, young John, who loves and admires Amy Dorrit for many years before he summons the courage to let her know his feelings, only to be left heartbroken when she does not reciprocate. Afterwards, with tears in his eyes he imagines his tombstone in the graveyard next to this wall in the grounds of the adjacent St George the Martyr Church, with his epitaph declaring his love for Amy Dorrit.

**St George the Martyr Church, Southwark,** is situated close to the site of the Marshalsea Prison and was used by Dickens in *Little Dorrit*. After her birth in the prison, Amy Dorrit is christened in this church. When she misses the curfew and is locked out of the Marshalsea one evening, she sleeps in the church vestry using the church burial register as a pillow. Towards the end of the book, Amy marries Arthur Clennam in this church.

Although much changed since *Little Dorrit* was published, **Bleeding Heart Yard** still exists today, between Farringdon and Hatton Garden. The yard derived its name from a story about a young woman who was imprisoned in it by her father, who disapproved of her choice of suitor. She was seen singing a song with the words 'Bleeding Heart, Bleeding Heart, bleeding away' until her death. Christopher Casby is the landlord of Bleeding Heart Yard and is conceited, egotistical and gives the impression that he is a kind benefactor, but in reality he is a cruel, avaricious scrounger who profits from the misery of his poor tenants, who struggle to earn a living to pay their bills.

Dickens refers to the tenants of Bleeding Heart Yards as 'inmates', for although there are no prison walls, they are imprisoned in poverty. The plasterer Mr Plornish is one of his tenants living in the last house in Bleeding Heart Yard, with his name displayed over his gate. He is once temporarily imprisoned in the Marshalsea Prison with William Dorrit, who is able to provide some information to Arthur Clennam. Mr Plornish is a family man who struggles to make ends meet. Dickens generated Mr Plornish's name from the nickname for his youngest son, Plorn.

St George the Martyr Church in Southwark. (Courtesy of Rossographer; www.geograph.org.uk)

When the fortunes change in favour of the Dorrit family, Amy Dorrit ensures that the Plornish family have sufficient funds to open a shop and look after the childlike Maggy in Bleeding Heart Yard. At the far end of Bleeding Heart Yard is Daniel Doyce's factory. Doyce later becomes the partner of Arthur Clennam. Dickens wrote of Bleeding Heart Yard in the novel as a place where royal hunting took place during the days of William Shakespeare but that:

> No sport is left there now but for the hunters of men, Bleeding Heart Yard was to be found. A place much changed in feature and in fortune, yet with some relish of ancient greatness about it. Two or three mighty stacks of chimneys, a few large dark rooms which had escaped being walled and sub divided out of the recognition of their old proportions, gave the Yard a character. It was inhabited by poor people, who set up their rest among its faded glories, as Arabs of the desert pitch their tents among the fallen stones of the pyramids, but there was a family sentimental feeling prevalent in the Yard and it had character.[137]

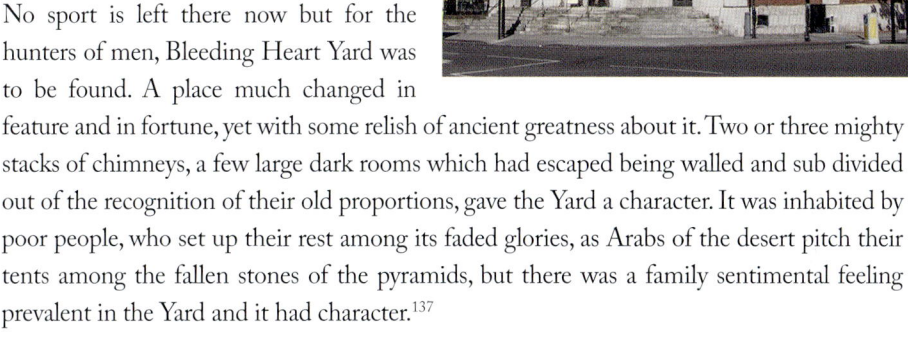

Dickens referred to **Southwark Bridge** as the 'iron-bridge' in *Little Dorrit* and it costs a penny toll to cross it. The Iron Bridge was built during 1819, but was replaced by the current construction in 1921. Amy Dorrit seeks solace and solitude walking along this bridge and on the embankment at low tide. It is where young John Chivery reveals his true feelings to Amy. Dickens wrote:

> Little Dorrit's lover very soon laid down his penny on the toll-plate of the Iron Bridge, and came upon it looking about him for the well-known and well-beloved figure … as he walked on towards the Middlesex side, he saw her standing still, looking at the water. She was absorbed in thought, and he wondered what she might be thinking about. There were the piles of city roofs and chimneys, more free from smoke than on weekdays; and there were the distant masts and steeples.[138]

---

137. Dickens, *Dorrit*, op. cit., p.97.

138. Ibid., p.157.

*Above*: Bleeding Heart Yard is situated close to Greville Street in Hatton Garden, London. (Courtesy of Marathon; www.geograph.org.uk)

*Below*: Southwark Bridge was where Amy Dorrit would often walk and where John Chivery revealed his feelings to her in *Little Dorrit*. (Courtesy of Tim Heaton; via www.geograph.org.uk)

# 61

# Gad's Hill Place, Higham, Kent

## The last residence of Charles Dickens and only property that he actually owned

Gad's Hill Place was built at Higham, near Rochester, in 1780 for a former Mayor of Rochester. Shakespeare set the scene here where Sir John Falstaff and Prince Hal rob some pilgrims travelling from London to Canterbury in *Henry IV, Part I*.

The house was known to Dickens when aged 9, who was told by his father that if he worked hard, one day he might be in a position to own such a home. That aspiration became reality in later life. During early 1856, Gad's Hill Place was on the market to be sold. He wrote in a letter to Monsieur Cerjat:

> Down at Gad's Hill near Rochester, in Kent – is a quaint little country house of Queen Anne's time. I happened to be walking past a year and a half or so ago, with my sub-editor of *Household Words*, when I said to him, 'You see that house? It has always a curious interest for me, because when I was a small boy down in these parts I thought it the most beautiful house (I suppose because of its famous old cedar-trees) ever seen. And my poor father used to bring me to look at it, and used to say that if I ever grew up to be a clever man perhaps, I might own that house or such another house. In remembrance of which, I have always in passing looked to see if it was to be sold or let, and it has never been to me like any other house, and it has never changed at all.'[139]

Dickens viewed the property, for he wrote on 13 February 1856, 'I was better pleased with Gad's Hill Place last Saturday on going down there, even than I had prepared myself to be. The country, against every disadvantage of season, is beautiful; and the house is so old fashioned, cheerful, and comfortable, that it is really pleasant to look at.'[140]

On 15 March 1856, Dickens purchased Gad's Hill Place for £1,790. He had previously leased the houses that he lived in, but this was the first and only one that he actually owned.

---

139. Dexter, op. cit., p.36.

140. Forster, Vol. 3, op. cit., p.202.

*Above left*: Charles Dickens standing at the entrance at Gad's Hill Place in a picture taken during 1865. Standing from right to left are Dickens and his daughters, Mamie and Kate. Henry Fothergill Chorley is standing left. On the steps are seated from left to right, Charles Collins (Kate's husband and Wilkie Collins' brother) and Georgina Hogarth. (Author's Collection)

*Above right*: Dickens' post box at Gad's Hill Place. (via Author)

He regarded the purchase as an investment and only intended to use it as a summer residence. Dickens commissioned various modifications to the property, including a conservatory and a false bookcase, which served as a concealed door to his study. The hall at Gad's Hill Place extended from the front of the house to the rear and on part of one of the walls, protected by glass, was the drop scene from *The Lighthouse* play painted by Sir Edwin Landseer. The modifications that Dickens made to the property quadrupled its value when it was sold after his death.

After extensive renovations were made, Dickens moved into Gad's Hill Place in June 1857 and shortly completed the last chapters of *Little Dorrit*. During the thirteen years that he lived here, Dickens wrote *A Tale of Two Cities*, *Great Expectations*, *Our Mutual Friend*, *The Uncommercial Traveller* and the beginning of *The Mystery of Edwin Drood*. Two decades before purchasing

Gad's Hill Place he described it in *A Christmas Carol* as: 'A mansion of dull red brick, with a little weathercock-surmounted cupula on the roof, and a bell hanging in it.'[141]

Sir Joseph Paxton, the architect who designed the Crystal Palace that housed the Great Exhibition, visited Dickens at Gad's Hill Place, and so did Henry Wadsworth Longfellow in 1868. Dickens and his family would perform pantomimes at Gad's Hill Place and invited neighbours to participate. On 26 December 1866, Dickens held Christmas sports in his field at Gad's Hill Place, which included a race around the field, hurdle racers, long jumps, sack races and three-legged races. Dickens marked out a course with flags, inviting the villagers from Higham, Shorne and Chalk to participate. He allowed the landlord of the Sir John Falstaff to sell alcohol at a drinking booth on his property. The event was popular, attracting between 2,000 to 3,000 spectators, including soldiers, sailors and labourers. Dickens was the judge and referee. He possessed the gravitas to control the event on his property as sports were played from 10.30 am until sunset. Mamie wrote: 'He was the last to realise, I am sure that it was his own sympathetic nature which gave him the love and honour of all classes, and that helped to make the day's sports such a great success.'[142]

The Rochester–London Road cut across land owned by Dickens. In 1859 he had a passage built beneath this road so that he could access this part of his property, known as the 'wilderness', from the lawn in front of Gad's Hill Place, as well as avoiding the muddy and busy road. The Swiss chalet gifted to Dickens by the French actor Charles Fechter was erected in the 'wilderness'. He also used this passage to cross the road to access the Sir John Falstaff public house, which was close to Gad's Hill Place and which Dickens patronised regularly and sometimes beer was delivered to him. He also used the pub as a bank when the landlord named Trood would cash Dickens' cheques. Sometimes there was not the capacity to accommodate all Dickens' guests at Gad's Hill Place and they stayed at the pub.

A post box was also installed outside Gad's Hill Place during 1859. Edmund Yates worked for the General Post Office and Dickens recommended that a post box be attached to the wall in front of Gad's Hill Place. In a letter to Yates dated 29 March 1859, Dickens wrote: 'I think that no one seeing the place can well doubt that my house at Gad's Hill is the place for the letter-box. The wall is accessible by all sorts and conditions of men, on the bold high road, and the house is the great landmark of the whole neighbourhood.'[143]

During the first three years of his ownership, Dickens used Gad's Hill Place as a summer residence, but during 1860 he decided to leave Tavistock House and use Gad's Hill Place as his permanent home, so whenever he needed to be in London, he would lease a property or use the office for *All the Year Round*.

---

141. Dickens, *Carol*, op. cit., p.45.

142. Dickens, Mamie, op. cit., p.43.

143. Dickens, Charles, *The Complete Works of Charles Dickens, Volume 38* (Charles E., Lauriat Company, Boston, 1923), p.13.

# 62

# Thomas Carlyle's Statue

**The historian known as the 'sage of Chelsea' was a good friend of Dickens.**

The statue of a seated Thomas Carlyle looking pensive stands on Chelsea Embankment, London, at the bottom of Cheyne Row, where Carlyle lived at No. 5 (Now No. 24) Cheyne Row, which Dickens visited regularly.

Dickens was introduced to Thomas Carlyle by the Whig politician Edward Stanley at a dinner party in Dover Street, London, during 1840 and this marked the beginning of a friendship that would last thirty years. Carlyle was 45 – seventeen years older than Dickens. He had written the *History of the French Revolution* in 1837, which was critically acclaimed. In a letter to his brother John, dated 17 March, Carlyle wrote of Dickens:

> Pickwick too, was at the same dinner party, though they did not seem to heed him much. He is a fine little fellow – Boz, I think. Clear blue intelligent eyes, eyebrows that he arches amazingly, large protrusive rather loose mouth, – a face of the most extreme mobility, which he shuttles about, eyebrows, eyes, mouth and all – in a very singular manner while speaking, surmount this with a loose coil of common-coloured hair, and set it on a small compact figure, very small, and dressed rather a la D'Orsay than well – this is Pickwick. For the rest a quiet, shrewd-looking, little fellow, who seems to guess pretty well what he is and what others are.[144]

Both men had been brought up from humble beginnings and they respected each other as fellow writers. Carlyle wrote:

> Since my acquaintance with him began; and on my side, I may say, every new meeting ripened it into more and more clear discernment of his rare and great worth as a brother man: a most cordial, sincere, clear-sighted, quietly decisive, just and loving man: till at length he had grown to such a recognition with me as I have rarely had for any man of my time.[145]

---

144. Teignmouth, op. cit., pp.200–1.
145. Forster, Vol. 2, op. cit., pp.514–5.

The statue of Thomas Carlyle that can be seen on Chelsea Embankment, London. (Author's Collection)

Carlyle supported Dickens' campaign to establish international copyright laws while in America, which Dickens appreciated. Dickens was a frequent visitor to Carlyle's home in Chelsea, and they also dined at Dickens' home. Carlyle was among the small circle of friends who saw Dickens give his first reading at John Forster's house and later watched him perform in his amateur dramatic productions. Carlyle believed that Dickens' 'real forte was acting, not writing'.[146]

Percy Fitzgerald compared the relationship between Dickens and Carlyle with the friendship between Dr Samuel Johnson and the actor David Garrick, for he recalled: 'Here was a quartet dinner; Forster, Dickens, Thomas Carlyle and myself! That was a privilege indeed! And a delightful meeting it was. I recall Boz "playing round" the sage as Garrick did

---

146. Frith, W.P. *My Autobiography and Reminiscences* (Harper & Brothers, New York, 1888), p.186.

Carlyle's house at 24 Cheyne Row in Chelsea, London. (Author's Collection)

around Johnson – affectionately and in high good humour and wit, and, I could well see, much pleasing the old lion.'[147]

In 1854 Dickens dedicated *Hard Times* to Carlyle and he was greatly inspired by his epic history book entitled *The French Revolution* to source factual information for his book *A Tale of Two Cities*. Dickens respected Carlyle's intellect and valued their friendship. He wrote that: 'I would always go at all times farther to see Carlyle than any man alive.'[148]

Carlyle respected Dickens' abilities as a performer. When he overheard someone comment that Dickens was a born actor, Carlyle retorted, 'Actor! Why, the man's a whole theatre.'[149] Carlyle saw his friend perform on the stage and also his readings. On 28 April 1863, Carlyle wrote:

> I had to go ... to Dickens' Readings, 8 P.M., Hanover Rooms, to the complete upsetting of my evening habitudes and spiritual composure. Dickens does it capitally, such as it is; acts better than any Macready in the world; a whole tragic, comic, heroic theatre visible, performing under one hat, and keeping us laughing – in a sorry way, some of us thought, the whole night.[150]

Dickens bequeathed his gold watch, chain and seals to John Forster and when Forster died in 1876, he left these items to Thomas Carlyle, so three great men of letters owned these items. However, within a month of possessing this legacy, Carlyle gave Dickens' items to his niece to do as she pleased with them and she gave them away.[151]

---

147. Fitzgerald, Percy, *Memories of Charles Dickens* (J.W. Arrowsmith Ltd, London, 1913), p.91
148. Forster, Vol. 2, op. cit., p.520.
149. Ward, op. cit., p.226.
150. Teignmouth, op. cit., p.287.
151. Fitzgerald, op. cit., p.99.

# 63

# Illustration Depicting Dickens' Performance in *The Frozen Deep*

## *The Frozen Deep* was performed in Dickens' home at Tavistock House.

Wilkie Collins' earlier play entitled *The Lighthouse* was originally played at Tavistock House in June 1855. During the following year Collins wrote a three-act play called *The Frozen Deep* with some collaboration from Dickens.

*The Frozen Deep* was performed privately on 6 January 1857 as an amateur production at Tavistock House with Dickens as stage manager and with members of his family, Wilkie Collins, Mark Lemon, the editor of *Punch*, and the artist Augustus Egg among the cast. The story revolved around Arctic explorers and was based on the disastrous Franklin expedition to search for the Northwest Passage. Dickens also played Richard Wardour, the principal part, for which Wilkie Collins recalled that 'he played it with a truth, vigour, and pathos never to be forgotten by those who were fortunate enough to witness the performance'.[152] The play was such a success that Dickens and the company had to repeat performances before the stage at Tavistock House was dismantled towards the end of January 1857.

When he was invited by royal command to perform in *The Frozen Deep* at Buckingham Palace, Dickens declined because he felt uncomfortable about performing at Court. Instead, Dickens suggested an alternative venue, inviting Queen Victoria and a group of her friends to see the production at a private performance of the play a week before the opening night on 4 July 1857 at the Gallery of Illustration, which was an intimate 500-seat theatre at 14 Regent Street, near Waterloo Place. Professional actresses played the female leads. Victoria enjoyed the production and praised the cast, in particular Dickens, in her journal.

Queen Victoria was so captivated by the production and cast that immediately after the performance, she sent a message to Dickens requesting him to come and see her so that she could thank him in person. Dickens still remained reticent to accept her invitation. He wrote: 'I replied that I was in my farce dress, and must beg to be excused. Whereupon she sent again, saying that the dress "would not be so ridiculous as that," and repeating the request. I sent my

---

152. Teignmouth, op. cit., p.287.

Dickens photographed with his friends and family who belonged to the original cast of *The Frozen Deep*. The charismatic Dickens is at the centre in front of the group, which includes Augustus Egg, the artist standing at the rear at the end of the row on the right. To his left stands Mark Lemon, editor of *Punch*. Seated from left to right are: Charley Dickens, Kate Dickens, Georgina Hogarth, Mamie Dickens, Wilkie Collins (with his head in his hands) and H. Hogarth. The photo was taken during 1857 and before Ellen Ternan and her family joined the company during the summer of that year. (Courtesy of The Miriam and Ira D. Wallach Division of Art, Prints and Photographs: Print Collection, The New York Public Library)

duty in reply, but again hoped her Majesty would have the kindness to excuse myself presenting myself in a costume and appearance that was not my own. I was mighty glad to think, when I awoke this morning that I had carried the point.'[153]

Hans Christian Andersen also saw the performance and wrote that: 'Dickens performed the character of Richard with affecting truth and great dramatic geniality.'[154]

Dickens then took *The Frozen Deep* on tour of principal English towns for the benefit of the family of Douglas Jerrold, who died in June 1857. The play was performed twice at the Free Trade Hall in Manchester with 3,000 people in the audience.

Ellen Ternan, together with Frances, her mother and Maria, her sister, were professional actresses cast for the performance in Manchester. Dickens' relationship with Ellen, aged 18, would develop into a romance as his marriage to Catherine broke down.

---

153. Wilson, Robert, *Life & Times of Queen Victoria, Volume Three* (Cassell & Company Limited, London, 1887), pp.381–2.

154. *Glasgow Herald*, 29 August 1860.

# 64

# Admission Ticket

**This is an admission ticket for Dickens' first public reading.**

**It was at St Martin's Hall, Long Acre, on 30 June 1857, that Dickens read for the first time to his London readers excerpts from *A Christmas Carol*.**

This first public reading in London was for the benefit of the family of his friend Douglas Jerrold, who had died earlier that month. St Martin's Hall was crammed and many admirers of Dickens' work had to be turned away. Before he began his performance, the venue management announced a further date for Dickens to read at the hall. A report in *The Times* provided an account of Dickens' performance and the reaction from his devoted audience:

> The reports respecting Mr. Dickens' command over an audience have not been in the least exaggerated. It is no such easy matter to read for upwards of two hours a book with which the listeners are acquainted, and to keep them all the while in a state of breathless interest; but this is actually done by Mr. Dickens. He does not, indeed, impersonate the various characters of his tale, except in the single case of the Miser Scrooge, whose words he speaks in senile accents. All that is spoken by the other characters he delivers, like the narrative, in his own natural voice. But though he does not act the personages, he completely enters into the spirit of the situations, and the joviality with which he describes the scenes of Christmas festivity endows his discourse with the vividness of a living picture. To transform himself into a number of successive individuals he does not attempt, but he throws himself into the atmosphere in which they all move, and compels his audience to live in it likewise. With his pathetic scenes he is more cautious than with his mirth. He would evidently avoid all imputation of maudlin sentimentality, and where he would elicit the tears of his audience he trusts to a manly, unaffected tone in the description of sorrow. But his command is equally potent over emotions of every kind, and during the whole of last evening he held the sympathies of his hearers as firmly as one might grasp a tangible object. The very aspect of that crowd, composed of the most various classes, hanging on the utterance of one man, was in itself an imposing spectacle.[155]

---

155. *The Times*, 1 July 1857.

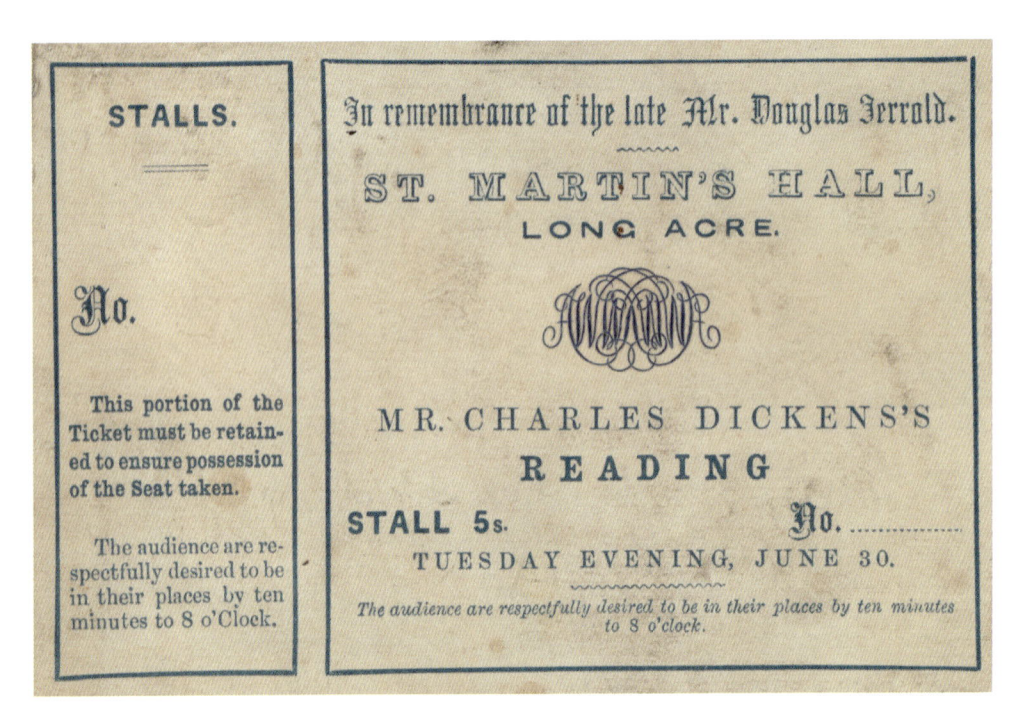

A surviving ticket for a Charles Dickens reading at St. Martin's Hall, London, on 30 June 1857. (Courtesy New York Public Library)

Initially Dickens just read the text, but in later readings he would act the parts. Dickens had the power, the gravitas and charisma to engage his audience as he brought the characters that he had created to life. It was a chance for his readers to see the spectacle of the great author reading his books. It was also an opportunity to sell more books at the venues.

Dickens demonstrated that he was a great comic performer because he was repeatedly interrupted by the laughter of the audience during the two-and-a-half-hour reading. Another reviewer said Dickens' performance 'was a treat to everyone present, and one of a very rare and memorable description'.[156]

The positive reception of the audience at St Martin's Hall inspired Dickens to give further readings and consider performing commercially where he could obtain an additional income. He continued to read during the following year for another philanthropic cause when on 22 April 1858 he carried out a reading of *A Christmas Carol* for the Hospital for Sick Children (which would later be known as the Great Ormond Street Hospital) at St Martin's Hall. Seven days later, Dickens began reading professionally for his own benefit, under the management of Arthur Smith.

---

156. *The Sun, London*, 1 July 1857.

# 65

# Dickens' Speech on Behalf of the Hospital for Sick Children

**The speech that Dickens delivered at the first fundraising dinner for the hospital, distributed at successive events and for years after his death.**

The Hospital for Sick Children was opened in February 1852 with just ten beds in a large mansion in Ormond Street in London. It was the only hospital in Britain to offer inpatient care primarily for children. Dickens was writing *Bleak House* at the time and he had used the destitution and death of the orphaned Jo to show the struggles faced by children living on the streets of London. He was one of the first celebrities to offer support and champion the need for a hospital to care for sick children.

Dickens was aware of child mortality rates in London and acknowledged that something needed to be done to mitigate against those deaths. He was a friend of Dr Charles West, who was the founder of Hospital for Sick Children at Great Ormond Street, which was also close to his home at Tavistock Square. Dickens supported West in an article entitled 'Drooping Buds', in *Household Words*, in which he highlighted that there were children's hospitals in all the major cities in Europe, but there was not a single one in Britain and that a third of the whole population perished in infancy with those deaths attributed to the poor in society. He believed that they died because of 'a want for sanitary discipline, and a want of medical knowledge'.[157]

During the first six years of its existence, the hospital admitted 47,100 outpatients; 1,860 inpatients were admitted and during that period capacity expanded from ten beds to thirty-one.[158] There was a need to raise funds to enable the hospital to continue and expand the care provided for children. There was no National Health Service until 1948, so the Children's Hospital at Ormond Street was reliant upon charity and private fundraising.

On 9 February 1858, Dickens was invited to act as chairman at the first anniversary dinner of the Hospital for Sick Children at Freemasons Hall to raise funds. After the toasts, Dickens gave a speech in which he spoke of the:

---

157. *Leicestershire Mercury*, 1 May 1852.

158. *London Daily News*, 10 February 1858.

**SPEECH OF CHARLES DICKENS, ESQ.,**

ON BEHALF OF THE

**Hospital for Sick Children,**

49, GREAT ORMOND STREET.

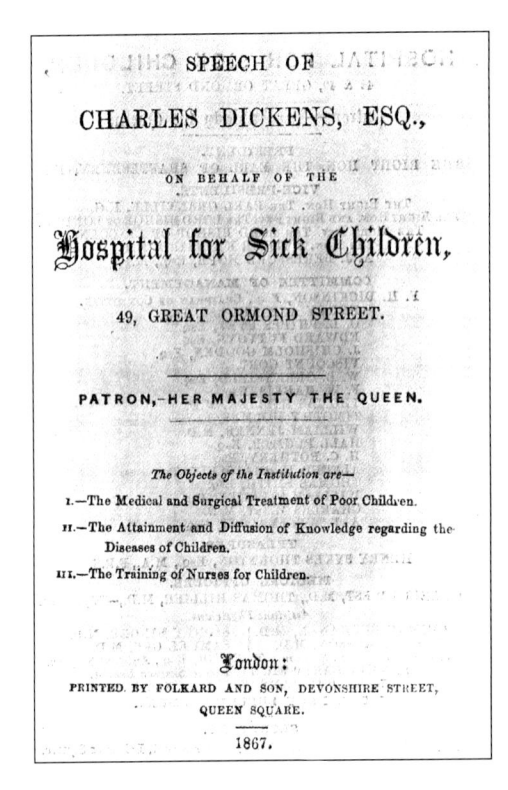

PATRON,—HER MAJESTY THE QUEEN.

*The Objects of the Institution are:—*
I.—The Medical and Surgical Treatment of Poor Children.
II.—The Attainment and Diffusion of Knowledge regarding the Diseases of Children.
III.—The Training of Nurses for Children.

London:
PRINTED BY FOLKARD AND SON, DEVONSHIRE STREET, QUEEN SQUARE.
1867.

Dickens' speech delivered in 1858 for the Hospital for Sick Children at Great Ormond Street, which was redistributed at the 1867 event. (Courtesy of the Wellcome Collection)

spoilt children of the poor in this great city, the children who are, every year, for ever and ever irrevocably spoilt out of this breathing life of ours by tens of thousands, but who may in vast numbers be preserved if you, assisting and not contravening the ways of Providence, will help to save them. The two grim nurses, Poverty and Sickness, who bring these children before you, preside over their births, rock their wretched cradles, nail down their coffins, pile up the earth above their graves. Of the annual deaths in this great town, their unnatural deaths form more than one-third.[159]

The event raised £3,000 that evening, which is worth approximately £200,000 in today's monetary value. It enabled the hospital to survive and purchase the adjoining house to expand and increase the capacity to care for more patients. Dickens also gave a public reading of *A Christmas Carol* at St Martin's Hall later during 1858 to raise further funds.

When Dickens left London to live at Gad's Hill Place, he continued to support the Hospital for Sick Children. His speech at the first anniversary dinner was printed and distributed at future fundraising dinners. Dickens continued to remind his readers of the social problem of infant mortality. We see Pip mourning at the graves of his siblings at the beginning of *Great Expectations*, and in *Our Mutual Friend*, the orphan Johnny Higden is taken to the children's hospital, 'a place where there are none but children; a place set up on purpose for sick children; where the good doctors and nurses pass their lives with children, talk to none but children, touch none but children, comfort and cure none but children'.[160] However, it was too late for Johnny because he died.

Dickens' charitable work and support helped to promote the hospital and to enable it to expand and continue to care for sick children. It still operates today and is now known as the Great Ormond Street Children's Hospital. Alongside his novels, the hospital can be counted among his lasting legacies.

---

159. *The Examiner*, 13 February 1858.

160. Dickens, Charles, *Our Mutual Friend* (Continental Press, New York, 1938), p.353.

# 66

# Publicity Photographs of Charles Dickens

**This set of photos were taken by George Herbert Watkins during a series of readings given by Dickens at St Martin's Hall in 1858.**

The success of the charitable readings brought Dickens to the realisation that he could earn large sums of money commercially for himself. He was motivated by the prospect of increasing his income very quickly. It was understandable that Dickens would go in this direction because he had a large family to support and his living expenses were high. This marked a turning point in his career, because his readings would no longer be occasional charity events but the start of a lucrative business venture of acclaimed performances that would take him around Britain and the United States of America.

It was during 1858 that Dickens' public readings of his works transformed from charitable events into a business. When Dickens read to his friends in 1844, John Forster had not been supportive of Dickens' reading for money because he believed that it would diminish his standing as an author. However, after realising the popularity of his charity readings, Dickens could see the potential to increase his income through reading professionally. He had to maintain his home at Gad's Hill Place, and when his marriage collapsed he had additional financial responsibilities to fund Catherine's London home and Ellen Ternan's home in Peckham. Large financial gains were not the only incentive. This was a vehicle for him to act and he loved performing to an audience, establishing a rapport and enjoying their instant response. On 29 April 1858 Dickens returned to St Martin's Hall to begin a run that lasted sixteen nights and ended on 22 July 1858. On the first night he read *Cricket on the Hearth*. Before the performance began, Dickens made this announcement:

> Ladies and gentleman, it may perhaps be known to you that for a few years past I have been accustomed occasionally to read some of my shorter books to various audiences in aid to a variety of good objects, and at some charge to myself both in time and money. It having at length become impossible in any reason to comply with these always

George Herbert Watkins photographed Dickens in these various poses, and many others, to promote his reading tours in 1858. (British Library)

accumulating demands, I have had definitely to choose between now and then reading on my own account, as one of my recognised occupations, or not reading at all. I have had little or no difficulty in deciding on the former course. (Cheers) The reasons that have led me to it – besides the consideration that it necessitates no departure whatever from the chosen pursuits of my life – are threefold. Firstly, I have satisfied myself that it can involve no possible compromise of the credit and independence of literature. Secondly, I have long held the opinion, and have long acted on the opinion, that in these times whatever brings a public man and his public face to face, on terms of mutual confidence and respect, is a good thing. (Cheers) Thirdly, I have had a pretty large experience of the interest my hearers are so generous as to take in these occasions, and of the delight they give to me, as a tried means of strengthening those relations, I may almost say, of personal friendship, which is my great privilege and pride, as it is my great responsibility, to hold with a multitude of persons who will never hear my voice or see my face. And thus, it is that I come, quite naturally, to be here among you, at this time. And thus, it is that I proceed to read this little book, quite as composedly as I might proceed to write it, or to publish it in any other way. (Loud cheers)[161]

Dickens also read *The Chimes* and *A Christmas Carol* during the other nights at St Martin's Hall, which were all warmly received by his attentive audiences. Dickens had created something unique where he could interact with his readers, without costumes and scenery, in which he performed a selection of characters from his novels. The *Illustrated London News* remarked that: 'Mr Dickens has invented a new medium for amusing an English audience, and merits the gratitude of an intelligent public.'[162]

Dickens then embarked on a tour of provincial towns for 125 nights beginning in Clifton in August and ending in October 1859. In Harrogate he read twice in one day. Dickens lost his voice after giving a reading during the initial stages of the tour, but he learned how to harness his vocal cords. He reduced his repertoire as the tour progressed to the popular characters, which included excerpts from *A Christmas Carol*, the trial in *The Pickwick Papers*, chapters including Mrs Gamp in *Martin Chuzzlewit* and scenes featuring Paul Dombey in *Dombey & Son*. The tour during 1858 to 1859 was a commercial enterprise where he performed for profit. In England, Dickens was earning £300 profit per week, which increased to £500 per week when he arrived in Scotland. Dickens embarked on three further reading tours where he read excerpts from his novels during 1861–63, in 1866–67 and during 1868–70. The tours would also help to increase Dickens' book sales.

---

161. *Morning Post*, 30 April 1858.

162. *The Illustrated London News*, 31 July 1858.

# 67

# The Garrick Club, London

## Dickens resigned from the Garrick Club in 1858

The Garrick Club, named after the renowned eighteenth-century actor David Garrick, was established in 1831 as a place where 'actors and men of refinement and education might meet on equal terms'.[163]

Charles Dickens was elected as a member of the Garrick Club in January 1837, but left after two years when he defended his friend William Macready after he got embroiled in an argument with a fellow member. Dickens re-joined the Garrick Club but resigned in December 1849 for reasons not ascertained. He was invited to chair the Committee of the Garrick Club in 1854 and on 22 April during that year he attended a dinner in honour of William Shakespeare, during which he delivered a speech.

During May 1858, rumours were circulating around London that implicated Dickens being involved with two unnamed women, thought to be Georgina Hogarth, his sister-in-law, and the actress Ellen Ternan. William Thackeray intervened in the gossip, championing Catherine Dickens. To protect the reputation of his friend Georgina Hogarth, when he overheard the speculation he explained that Georgina was not Dickens' mistress but it was actually a young actress. In a letter to his mother, Anne Carmichael Smyth, Thackeray described how his involvement escalated in the Garrick Club:

> Here is sad news in the literary world, Mr & Mrs Dickens – with all sorts of horrible stories buzzing about. The worst is I'm in a manner dragged into one – Last week, going into the Garrick I heard that D is separated from his wife on account of an intrigue with his sister-in-law. No says I, no such thing – it's with an actress – and the other story has not got to Dickens' ears but this has – and he fancies that I am going about abusing him! We shall never be allowed to be friends that's clear.[164]

---

163. www.garrickclub.co.uk.

164. Ray, Gordon N., *The Letters & Private Papers of William Makepeace Thackeray, Volume IV* (Harvard University Printing Office, 1946), p.86.

The Garrick Club at 15 Garrick Street, London. (Courtesy of Lonpicman)

The disagreement with Thackeray, caused by rumours that he had separated from his wife, escalated within the Garrick Club when Edmund Yates wrote an article supporting Dickens and criticising Thackeray. The article contained remarks that could have only been heard within the Garrick Club. Thackeray took offence and referred the incident to the Club's Committee, who decided to expel Yates during September 1858. Dickens thought that the treatment of Yates was too harsh, and intervened by trying to get the Committee to reverse the decision if Yates withdrew his comments and showed remorse for the offending article. Thackeray resented Dickens' interference, which caused friction between the two great authors and they did not speak for five years. The Garrick Club did not reverse its decision and Yates was expelled, while Dickens resigned in protest.

# 68

# Catherine Dickens

**Dickens separated from his wife during 1858.**

As Dickens' popularity grew, so did his work commitments, together with his celebrity status, which placed enormous strain on his marriage to Catherine, causing them to drift apart. During the twenty years that she was married to Dickens, Catherine was pregnant many times, giving birth to ten children, seven boys and three girls, as well as suffering several miscarriages. This affected her health and appearance. Catherine would suffer from depression and her sister, Georgina, and the servants would look after the children. Being relegated to the sidelines would exacerbate her anxiety. Catherine was not consulted when her husband decided to send their five sons abroad for their education and felt sadness and isolation. In 1858, Dickens used the periodical *Household Words* to announce the breakdown of his marriage.

During 1857, Dickens met Ellen Ternan and she reawakened the feelings of youthful passion that he experienced as a young man, which further worsened the situation, and his feelings were mutual. When he ordered a bracelet for his mistress, the jeweller, who regularly sold items to Dickens, mistakenly thought it was intended for his wife and delivered it to Catherine in error. Catherine was distraught, but Dickens, rather callously, insisted that she call upon the Ternan family to give the impression that there was no discord and to suppress the rumours that were beginning to surface that he was engaged in an illicit relationship with the 18-year-old actress. Dickens was concerned about the negative publicity if it was revealed to the public that despite him being an author who promoted family values and respect for women, he did not maintain those standards in his own life.

Dickens and Catherine mutually agreed to separate during 1858. He wrote on 26 May: 'Mrs Dickens and I have lived unhappily together for many years. Hardly anyone who knows us intimately can fail to have known that we are in all respects of character and temperament wonderfully unsuited for each other.'[165]

Dickens was irritated that his private life was the subject of salacious gossip and decided to address his readers directly. Despite his friends' attempt to advise him against such an action,

---

165. *Westmoreland Gazette*, 4 September 1858.

*Above left*: This image of Catherine Dickens was taken from a painting by Daniel Maclise dated 1846. (New York Public Library)

*Above right*: Catherine Dickens photographed in later years. (Author's Collection)

he issued a statement denying the rumours and it was published in *The Times* and emblazoned on the front page of *Household Words* on 12 June. The statement read:

> Some domestic trouble of mine, of long-standing, on which I will make no further remark than that it claims to be respected, as being of a sacredly private nature, has lately been brought to an arrangement, which involves no anger or ill-will of any kind, and the whole origin, progress, and surrounding circumstances of which have been, throughout, within the knowledge of my children. It is amicably composed, and its details have now but to be forgotten by those concerned in it … By some means, arising out of wickedness, or out of folly, or out of inconceivable wild chance, or out of all three, this trouble has been made the occasion of misrepresentations, most grossly false, most monstrous, and most cruel – involving, not only me, but innocent persons dear to my heart … I most solemnly declare, then – and this I do both in my own name and in my wife's name – that all the lately whispered rumours touching the trouble, at which I have glanced, are abominably false. And whosoever repeats

one of them after this denial, will lie as wilfully and as foully as it is possible for any false witness to lie, before heaven and earth.[166]

Dickens' candid announcement about the separation would impact upon the family as Catherine left Gad's Hill Place to live at 70 Gloucester Crescent, near Regents Park. The scandal revealed a darker nature to Dickens' character, because Catherine saw very little of her children, except for Charley, who lived with Catherine, and Kate, who defied her father to visit their mother. Kate would later speak to Gladys Storey for her book in 1929. 'I loved my father better than any man in the world … I loved him for his faults. My father was a wicked man – a very wicked man … This affair brought out all that was worst, all that was weakest – in him. He did not care a damn what happened to any of us. Nothing could surpass the misery and unhappiness of our home.'[167]

Dickens continued his relationship with Ellen and supported her financially while she lived in a house in Peckham. Dickens wanted to maintain the wholesome family image for the public, for if it was known that he had committed adultery and was continuing an affair with a woman half his age, he feared that his reputation would be ruined, which could potentially impact upon book sales.

The separation from his wife also affected his friendships. Thackeray became embroiled in the scandal and was no longer welcomed at his home in Tavistock Square. This caused upset within the family because the Dickens' children had a close relationship with Thackeray and his daughters. Mark Lemon, the editor of *Punch*, declined to publish the statement, which brought an end to their friendship. Elizabeth Gaskell refused to contribute to *Household Words*. The disagreement also affected his business relationship with his publisher, Bradbury & Evans, who also published *Household Words*. Dickens took complete control of *Household Words*, which he disbanded with its last issue on 28 May 1859 and replaced it with a new magazine *All the Year Round*.

Catherine became estranged from her sister, Georgina, because she remained with Dickens as his housekeeper and cared for her nieces and nephews. They were reconciled at the instigation of Kate during 1877 when Catherine was diagnosed with cancer. Catherine died in 1879 and was buried in Highgate Cemetery with Dora, her infant daughter, who died in 1851.

---

166. *Household Words*, 12 June 1858.

167. *Daily Herald*, 13 July 1939.

# 69

# Office of *All the Year Round*

## Dickens established a new magazine.

This building at No. 26 Wellington Street, London, housed the offices of Charles Dickens' weekly magazine *All the Year Round* and his private apartments from 1859 to 1870. The office was in the same street as his former office for *Household Words* and its close proximity to Charing Cross Station enabled him to commute from Higham, near Gad's Hill Place. The first edition of Dickens' new periodical *All the Year Round* was published on 30 April 1859, a month before the final edition of *Household Words*.

Dickens, as editor, and his sub-editor W.H. Willis became the sole proprietors of this publication and had total autonomy and control over its content. Although it retained the same price of a tuppence, its format changed. The leading article was replaced with an episode of serial fiction, with the author identified. Dickens dispensed with the satirical onslaughts upon politicians of the time and investigative reports in favour of short stories, which he commissioned from his peers such as Edward Bulwer-Lytton, Charles Lever and Edmund Yates. Wilkie Collins contributed with serialisations of *The Woman in White* in 1859 and *The Moonstone* in 1868. Dickens would also use the magazine as a vehicle to publish serialisations of his own work. Dickens wrote to Forster: 'I have just hit upon a name that I think really an admirable one – especially with the quotation before it, in the place where H.W. quotation stands. "The story of our lives, from year to year. – Shakespeare. ALL THE YEAR ROUND. A weekly journal conducted by Charles Dickens."'[168]

The building that contained Charles Dickens' office where he edited *All the Year Round* still stands on the corner of Wellington Street and Tavistock Street. On 21 February 1859 Dickens wrote: 'I have taken the new office, have got workmen in; have ordered the paper; settled with the printer; and am getting an immense system of advertising ready. Blow to be struck on 12th of March … Meantime I cannot please myself with the opening of my story.'[169]

Dickens was referring to his next story *A Tale of Two Cities*, which would feature in *All the Year Round* during 1859. He would also publish the serialisation of *Great Expectations* within

---

168. Forster, Vol. 3, op. cit., p.243.

169. Ibid.

This building at 26 Wellington Street, London, housed Dickens' office of where he edited the magazine *All the Year Round*. (Courtesy Stephen Richards, www.geograph.org.uk)

the magazine between 1860 and 1861. The first number of *All the Year Round*, published in 30 April 1859, was a success. Dickens was able to recover all set up expenses incurred and it still left him with £500. The Christmas pieces written by Dickens were extremely popular and boosted sales of the magazine. By the time of his death, he had sold approximately 300,000 copies.

During 1867 Dickens had to conduct a series of readings in London and instead of leasing a London residence, he installed chambers consisting of a sitting room and some bedrooms within the offices of *All the Year Round*, which he used as a base when he conducted readings and business in London. However, for the final performances of his farewell tour during 1870 he leased 5 Hyde Park Place as a London base.

Two years after his death, representatives from organisers of the World's Fair from Chicago approached the owner of the property that housed Dickens' office with a view to dismantling it, transferring it to America and displaying it at the exhibition, but the initiative failed.

# 70

# *A Tale of Two Cities*

**The first number of *A Tale of Two Cities* appeared in the first issue of *All the Year Round* on 30 April 1859.**

Published in 1859, the book was inspired by Thomas Carlyle's book *The French Revolution*. *A Tale of Two Cities* was Dickens' second attempt at writing historical fiction. Prior to writing the story, Dickens requested Carlyle send him the resource material that he used to research *The French Revolution*. Carlyle sent two cartloads of material to Gad's Hill Place, which Dickens studied.

The final number appeared in issue thirty-one on 26 November 1859. It was received well and increased sales of the new periodical and sold 35,000 back numbers. When it was later published as a book, Dickens inscribed the volume to his friend, Lord John Russell, the Liberal Prime Minister, with the words 'in remembrance of many public services and private kindnesses'.

Although he acknowledged Carlyle's book as a source for historical background, Dickens had lived in Paris, walked its streets and had developed an understanding and knowledge of the city.

First instalment of *A Tale of Two Cities* in *All the Year Round*. (University of North Texas)

# 71

# Dickens' Plaque, Campbell Square, Liverpool

**The plaque commemorates 'Charles Dickens, prolific journalist, novelist … and for one day in 1860, Liverpool Police Constable.'**

Dickens had started work on his book *The Uncommercial Traveller* in 1859. During February 1860, he visited Liverpool to conduct research for this book and was permitted to join the Liverpool Police Force as a special constable in the Old Bridewell, Campbell Street district, so that he could wander around the docks with the police and observe British and foreign seamen in their natural environment when ashore.

The streets around ports were dangerous places to wander during the night and Dickens contacted Major Greig, Head Constable of the Liverpool Police Force, to see if they could help in his research. Greig referred Dickens to Superintendent Ride, who was in command of the north division, and he arranged for Dickens to serve one night on patrol as a special constable. Dickens' experience would appear three weeks later in one of a series of articles titled *The Uncommercial Traveller*, this one relating to Mercantile Jack, which appeared as instalments in *All the Year Round*, in which Dickens wrote:

> I had entered the Liverpool Police Force, that I might have a look at various unlawful traps which are every night set for Jack. As my term of service in that distinguished corps was short, and my personal bias in the capacity of one of its members has ceased, no suspicion will attach to my evidence that it is an admirable force. Besides that, it is composed, without favour, of the best men that can be picked, it is directed by an unusual intelligence. Its organisation against fires, I take to be much better than the metropolitan system, and in all respects, it tempers its remarkable vigilance with a still more remarkable discretion.[170]

Before he started his shift, he attended police parade and took note of a photo of a suspected thief who was wanted by the police. Dickens' shift started at 10 pm, he took a lantern and

---

170. *Liverpool Daily Post*, 10 March 1860.

Plaque commemorating Charles Dickens' appointment as a special constable for one night. (Courtesy of Rodhullandemu)

accompanied the Police Superintendent with three fellow officers on patrol of the streets around the Salthouse and Albert Docks in Liverpool, including the streets called Wapping, Canning Place and Liver Street. It was along these streets that they visited places frequented by visiting sailors and encountered brothels and crimps, male and female predators who entrapped men through coercing them into crewing ships against their will. Dickens recalled:

> The night was well on into the morning, but, for miles and hours we explored a strange world, where nobody ever goes to bed, but everybody is eternally sitting up, waiting for Jack. This exploration was among a labyrinth of dismal courts and blind alleys, called Entries, kept in wonderful order by the police, and in much better order than the corporation, the want of gaslight in the most dangerous and infamous of these places being quite unworthy of so spirited a town.[171]

A plaque at the Old Bridewell, Campbell Square, on the site of the police station was unveiled in 2004 to commemorate the night Dickens served as a special constable.

---

171. Ibid.

# 72

# Dickens' Writing Desk

### Where Dickens wrote his final works.

**The desk at which Charles Dickens penned *Great Expectations*, *Our Mutual Friend* and the *Mystery of Edwin Drood*.**

Dickens used this desk and accompanying chair towards the end of his life while living at Gad's Hill Place and it was placed in various rooms that were used as his study. Dickens would work between breakfast until mid-afternoon, with a break for lunch each day at this writing desk. Among the characters that Dickens created at this desk were Pip, Abel Magwitch, Miss Havisham, Silas Wegg, Roger 'Rogue' Riderhood, Edwin Drood, Rosa Bidd and John Jasper. Mamie wrote:

> At 'Gad's Hill' he made a study from one of the large spare sleeping rooms of the house, as the windows there overlooked a beautiful and favourite view of his, His writing table was always placed near a window looking out into the open world which he loved so keenly. Afterwards he occupied for years a smaller room overlooking the back garden and a pretty meadow, but this he eventually turned into a miniature billiard room, and then established himself, finally, in the room on the right-hand side of the entrance hall facing the front garden. It is this room which Mr. Luke Fildes, the great artist and our esteemed friend, made famous in his picture 'The Empty Chair' which he sketched for 'The Graphic' after my father's death.[172]

The writing desk was passed down through the Dickens family until it was auctioned in 2004 for charity for Great Ormond Street Hospital Charitable Trust. The children's hospital was a lasting legacy from Dickens 130 years after his death, and he was still able to donate money through the sale of the writing desk. It was purchased in 2015 by the Charles Dickens Museum in London, where it is now permanently exhibited, funded by a grant from the National Heritage Memorial Fund amounting to £720,000.

---

172. Dickens, Mamie, op. cit., p.50.

*Above*: Dickens' writing desk on display at 48 Doughty Street, London. (Author's Collection)

*Right*: This drawing of Charles Dickens in his study at Gad's Hill Place, by S. Hollyer, features the writing desk that is now displayed at Dickens' former London home at Doughty Street. (Library of Congress)

# 73

# Cooling Churchyard, Kent

**The churchyard at Cooling and the surrounding marshland on the Hoo Peninsula in Kent has not changed since the days of Dickens, when it served as an inspiration for the setting of *Great Expectations*.**

During September 1860, Dickens began writing another story entitled *Great Expectations*. It was written throughout in the first person through the experience of the protagonist, Pip. The first number appeared in *All the Year Round* on 1 December 1860 and the beginning of the story was set in Cooling Churchyard. Dickens was familiar with the graves of the Comport family in the churchyard and they would represent Pip's deceased parents and siblings in the book.

Dickens as a boy would have been familiar with the St James's Church at Cooling and the desolate marshes close to the River Thames on which prison hulks were anchored. He would use the graveyard for the opening scene of *Great Expectations* where the orphaned Pip stands over the graves of his parents and the 'five little stone lozenges, each about a foot and a half long, which were arranged in a neat row beside their grave',[173] which were the graves of his infant siblings. At the very start of the novel, Dickens focuses upon the judicial system and the treatment of prisoners, for as Pip reflects upon his lost family in this churchyard, he is terrified when he is confronted by the convict Abel Magwitch, who has escaped from a hulk anchored in the Thames that incarcerated prisoners before transportation to Australia. Magwitch is famished and so desperate that he has to coerce Pip through threats of violence to bring him food and a file to remove his shackles the following day. Although Magwitch is captured and transported to Australia, he does not forget Pip's kindness and generosity displayed in this graveyard. He becomes wealthy from a sheep-farming business in Australia and sets up Pip as a gentleman, anonymously appointing the lawyer Mr Jaggers as Pip's guardian and banker. In Cooling Church there are the graves of thirteen infants from the Comport family and it is likely that they inspired Dickens.

---

173. Dickens, Charles, *Great Expectations* (Collier, New York, 1890), p.1.

Located in the churchyard of St James' Church, Cooling, are the graves of thirteen babies – a visual representation of the high infant mortality rate that once existed. (Courtesy of Paul Farmer; www.geograph.org.uk)

Looking west from St James's Church towards Gravesend, it was along this stretch of the Thames that Dickens set the scene where Pip and his friend Herbert assist Magwitch in his attempt to leave England aboard a steamer. Magwitch recognises Compeyson, the convict who was a swindler, a forger, and the man who betrayed Miss Havisham. Both men fight and fall into the river; Compeyson drowns and Magwitch is injured in the paddles of the steamer and arrested.

The serialisation of this story ended in the 3 August 1861 edition of the magazine and was published as a three-volume book. It was one of Dickens' favourite books according to his son, Henry, who wrote: '*Great Expectations* he himself regarded as one of the best of his books. Indeed, I have heard him say that, putting *Pickwick* aside as being a book by itself and quite unlike his other work, he would place *David Copperfield* first and *Great Expectations* next to it.'[174]

Dickens took pleasure in taking visitors on walks to Cooling and the churchyard when he was living at Gad's Hill Place to show where the opening scene to *Great Expectations* was set.

---

174. Dickens, Sir Henry, *The Recollections of Sir Henry Dickens, K.C.* (William Heinemann Limited, London, 1934), p.16.

# 74

# Restoration House, Rochester

**The manor house that Dickens used as Satis House, the home of Miss Havisham in *Great Expectations*.**

The name of Restoration House is derived from when Charles II stayed in this house on 28 May 1660 prior to his restoration. Dickens changed the name to Satis House and it became the home of the eccentric Miss Havisham, who he described as 'an immensely rich and grim lady who lived in a large and dismal house barricaded against robbers who led a life of seclusion.'[175]

Abuse is a common theme that resonates throughout *Great Expectations*. Pip is brought up 'by hand' by his sister through violence; his brother-in-law, Joe Gargery, is also abused in a similar manner by Mrs Gargery. She is also the victim of violent abuse because she was attacked and rendered incapacitated, disabled and trapped within her own body. Magwitch is abused, disenfranchised by society and the judicial system. Satis House symbolises the abuse suffered by Miss Havisham as a younger woman and the mental cruelty that she inflicts upon Estella to take vengeance upon that cruel treatment.

Miss Havisham has lived in self-imposed isolation after her heart was broken on her wedding day, when as she was dressing into her wedding dress, she received a letter from her lover, Compeyson, calling off the wedding. This act of betrayal broke her heart and would have a detrimental effect upon the remainder of her life, where she harbours a deep hatred of men.

The name Satis is Latin for the word 'enough', so the house was called 'enough house' because whoever possessed it should want for nothing else, they would be satisfied. Pip details his first observations of Satis House, 'we came to Miss Havisham's house, which was of old brick, and dismal, and had a great many iron bars to it. Some of the windows had been walled up; of those that remained, all the lower were rustily barred. There was a courtyard in front, and that was barred.'[176]

Inside, Pip is shown a room where the feast of the wedding is laid out, decaying as a further reminder of her tragic wedding day. Miss Havisham still wears the wedding dress that she has

---

175. Dickens, *Expectations*, op. cit., p.52.

176. Ibid., pp.55–6.

*Above and below*: Restoration House, Rochester, and the plaque that is on the wall by the entrance. (Author's Collection)

RESTORATION HOUSE, ROCHESTER

worn since the day of her wedding. Pip notes: 'I began to understand that everything in the room had stopped, like the watch and the clock, a long time ago.'[177] Here she proclaims that she will lay on that table when she dies. Miss Havisham lives in squalor and Satis House is also home to rats, mice, spiders and insects that live among the mess.

Miss Havisham lives with Estella, whom she has adopted. Estella is the daughter of Abel Magwitch, Pip's benefactor, who was brought to Miss Havisham by the lawyer Mr Jaggers when Estella was aged three. Miss Havisham's resentment towards all mankind is manifested through Estella, who she has raised to spurn affection to protect her heart against tenderness. At the same time she encourages men to love her so she can break their hearts, in the same manner that Compeyson broke Miss Havisham's heart. Estella is being used as a weapon by Miss Havisham to enact her vengeance, and although she is meant to be her guardian and foster mother, she is doing a disservice to her adopted daughter by directing her into an unhappy existence. Pip is brought by Uncle Pumblechook to Satis House to make friends with Estella, but Miss Havisham uses the situation to encourage Estella to break Pip's heart. Pip observes Miss Havisham, 'embrace her with lavish fondness, murmuring something in her ear that sounded like, break their hearts and have no mercy!'[178]

Pip mistakenly believes that Miss Havisham is his benefactor when he becomes a gentleman, which she allows him to think is the case. Miss Havisham dies a violent death when Satis House is ablaze.

The park opposite Restoration House is called the Vines, which was the priory vineyard of Rochester Cathedral but during Dickens' day it was a meadow. Dickens featured it as Monks' Vineyard in the *Mystery of Edwin Drood* and it is believed that Pip would have passed through it for his first visit with Miss Havisham in *Great Expectations*. Two days before he died, Dickens walked into Rochester and was seen leaning against a fence in the Vines looking at Restoration House.

---

177. Ibid., p.61.
178. Ibid., p.98.

# 75

# Rochester High Street

### Locations for *Great Expectations* and *The Mystery of Edwin Drood.*

**Dickens was familiar with Rochester High Street as a boy and as an adult while he was living at Gad's Hill Place. He would feature various buildings along this street in his novels.**

As previously mentioned, Dickens used Rochester High Street in *The Pickwick Papers* when Mr Pickwick stays at The Bull, and Dickens would wander along this street with his friends and make random bids in auction houses without any intention of owning the item being auctioned.

Opposite Eastgate House in Rochester High Street there is a half-timbered building that Dickens utilised as Uncle Pumblechook's premises in *Great Expectations*. Pumblechook is Joe Gargery's uncle and is a wealthy corn chandler. Dickens described Pumblechook to be 'of peppercorny and farinaceous character'.[179] Dickens also used the same building in *The Mystery of Edwin Drood* as the premises for the auctioneer and former Mayor of Cloisterham, Mr Sapsea.

The Guildhall at the western end of Rochester High Street was described by Dickens in *Great Expectations* through Pip as 'the queer place … with higher pews in it than a church'.[180] It was here that Pip was bound as a blacksmith's apprentice to Joe Gargery for twenty-five guineas. Joe is a blacksmith and his brother-in-law. Pip and Joe are both harshly treated by Pip's sister, Georgina, who brings Pip up by hand, literally, which sometimes involves violent abuse. Joe is kind, sincere and caring towards Pip and tries to protect him from his sister's rampages.

---

179. Dickens, *Expectations*, op. cit., p.54.
180. Ibid., p.108.

Building owned by Uncle Pumblechook's and Mr Sapsea in Rochester High Street. (All Author's Collection)

Plaque on Pumblechook and Sapsea's house.

180 **CHARLES DICKENS** – PLACES AND OBJECTS OF INTEREST

# 76

# Music Hall, Newcastle

The plaque on the building, which was the former Music Hall in Nelson Street, commemorates Dickens' readings in this venue during the six visits to Newcastle between 1852 and 1867.

Dickens embarked on a second reading tour beginning on 28 October 1861 in Norwich and ending in Chester on 30 January 1862. Despite grieving for the deaths of Henry Austin (his brother-in-law) and Arthur Smith (his tour manager), Dickens continued with the tour, which included the Music Hall, Newcastle.

During this second tour, Dickens gave fifty readings across Britain and admirers of his work were keen to purchase tickets to see him read his own works. Not many authors of that era would realise how popular they were in their lifetime, but Dickens could gauge this through these tours. Dickens appeared at the Music Hall on 21, 22 and 23 November 1861, where he read from *David Copperfield*, *Nicholas Nickleby*, *Dombey & Son* and *The Pickwick Papers*. On the second night, alarm was caused when his gas batten fell over. There was a fear that it would set the music hall ablaze and also cause members of the audience to be crushed as some tried to flee the venue. Dickens wrote:

> The room was tremendously crowded and my gas-apparatus fell down. There was a terrible wave among the people for an instant, and God knows what destruction of life a rush to the stairs would have caused. Fortunately, a lady in the front row of the stalls ran out towards me, exactly in a place where I knew that the whole hall could see her. So, I addressed her, laughing, and half-asked and half-ordered her to sit down again; and, in a moment it was all over. But the men in attendance had such a fearful sense of what might have happened (besides the real danger of fire), that they positively shook the boards I stood on, with their trembling, when they came up to put things right.[181]

Dickens settled the audience and continued with the reading to acclaim. After the three-night run at the Music Hall, Dickens departed Newcastle for the next destination of his tour, which

---

181. Forster, Vol. 3, op. cit., p.265.

The former Music Hall in Nelson Street, Newcastle. (via Author)

was Berwick-upon-Tweed. Dickens returned to the Music Hall on 4 March 1867 and he attracted such a large audience that there were not sufficient seats to accommodate them and many resorted to sitting in the aisles. It was reported:

> Mr. Dickens read last night in Newcastle, and giving one of the earliest and one of the latest creations of his genius, he for about two hours sustained unabated the interest of an audience who filled to overflowing the Music Hall, the passages even being occupied. His elocution and the action which formed part of that elocution, and should not, therefore, be spoken of separately, was full of pathos, humour, force, and expression – full of all those qualities, in short, which on his first appearance on the platform caused him to be singled out as being at once a leading novelist and a finished actor.[182]

Inscribed on the plaque is Dickens' opinion of the people of Newcastle, 'a finer audience there is not in England'.

---

182. *Newcastle Journal*, 5 March 1867.

# 77

# King's Arms Hotel, Berwick-upon-Tweed

A plaque commemorates Dickens' visits to Berwick-upon-Tweed in 1858 and 1861 on the wall of this hotel, where he stayed on both occasions. On 25 November 1861, Dickens read at the Assembly Room, which was part of the hotel.

Dickens was originally scheduled to give the reading at the Corn Exchange. The local newspapers advertised the event in advance that he would read here for one night only, but when Dickens inspected the venue, he thought that the acoustics within this

The King's Arms Hotel in Berwick-upon-Tweed. (Jonathan Hutchings; www.geograph.org.uk)

space were unsuitable for his voice. He wrote to Georgina Hogarth the following letter from the Kings Arm's Hotel:

> A most ridiculous room was designed for me in this odd out-of-the-way place. An immense Corn Exchange, made of glass and iron, round, dome-topped, lofty, utterly absurd for any such purpose, and full of thundering echoes, with a little lofty crow's nest of a stone gallery breast high, deep in the wall, into which it was designed to put me! I instantly struck, of course, and said I would either read in a room attached to this house [the Kings Arm's] (a very snug one, capable of holding five hundred people) or not at all. Terrified local agents glowered, but fell prostrate.[183]

Dickens read extracts from *A Christmas Carol* and the trial from *The Pickwick Papers*, however, the venue could not accommodate the large numbers that would have filled the Corn Exchange. The *Newcastle Journal* reported that:

> the room was crowded to excess, and many were compelled to leave the doors unable to gain admittance … The audience, we scarcely need say, were most highly delighted with the readings; and the description of Tiny Tim and his friends left scarcely a dry eye in the house. It is to be hoped Mr. Dickens will not be long before he returns to afford his northern friends another opportunity of hearing and admiring him.[184]

It was Arthur Smith's strategy to stop at smaller towns in between larger cities in order to pay for travel expenses and the break at Berwick-upon-Tweed was profitable.

---

183. Dickens, *Letters*, Vol. 1, op. cit., pp.188–9.
184. *Newcastle Journal*, 28 November 1861.

# 78

# Tombstone of Walter Landor Dickens, South Park Cemetery, Calcutta

### Dickens' second son died in India.

Seven boys and three girls were born to Charles and Catherine Dickens. Dora died in infancy, but the remaining nine children reached adulthood. Dickens loved his children and was a supportive father. Mamie recalled: 'I can remember with us, his own children, how kind, considerate and patient he always was. But we were never afraid to go to him in any trouble, or never had a snub from him or a cross word under any circumstances.'[185]

Walter Landor Dickens was born on 8 February 1841 and was named after his godfather, the poet and writer Walter Savage Landor. Dickens gave him the nickname 'Young Skull' and he was educated in Wimbledon, where he showed the aptitude to become an author, but Dickens instructed his tutor to deter him from that path to ensure what in his opinion would be his happiness. When Walter was aged sixteen, Baroness Angela Burdett-Coutts was influential in him becoming a cadet in the Bengal Native Infantry. In a letter to Burdett-Coutts, Dickens wrote:

> Walter has done extremely well at school; has brought home a prize in triumph; and will be eligible to go up for his India examination, soon after next Easter. Having a direct appointment, he will probably be sent out soon after he has passed, and so will fall into the strange life 'up the country' before he well knows he is alive and what life is – which indeed seems to be rather an advanced state of knowledge.[186]

Walter sailed from Southampton for India in July 1857. This was the last time that Dickens saw his son. On 7 February 1864, on his fifty-second birthday, Dickens received news that Walter had died suddenly in the officers' quarters at the hospital in Calcutta on New Year's

---

185. Dickens, Mamie, op. cit., p.14.
186. *Englishman's Overland Mail*, 22 December 1910.

The tombstone of Walter Landor Dickens in South Park Cemetery, Calcutta. (Courtesy User.Jack1956 via wikimedia.commons)

Eve 1863. He was serving as a lieutenant in the 26th Native Infantry Regiment, attached to the 42nd Royal Highlanders (The Black Watch)[187] and was aged twenty-three. Dickens wrote:

> My poor boy was on his way home from an up-country station, on sick leave. He had been very ill, but was not so at the time. He was talking to some brother-officers in the Calcutta hospital about his preparations for home, when he suddenly became excited, had a rush of blood to the mouth, and was dead.[188]

Dickens not only suffered bereavement from the deaths of Walter and Dora Dickens, but also the death of his mother Elizabeth, who died on 13 September 1863. It was a sombre time for Dickens because he also had to endure physical separation from his other son, Alfred Tennyson, who had settled in Australia, and later he was followed by his younger brother, Edward Bulwer-Lytton, in 1868.

Dickens was never able to visit Walter's grave at Bhowanipore Military Cemetery in Calcutta. The grave was lost but the tombstone is located in South Park Cemetery in the same city.

---

187. *Sheffield Independent*, 9 February 1864.

188. Dickens, *Works, Volume 38*, op. cit., p.137.

# 79

# *Our Mutual Friend*

## Dickens' penultimate and last completed novel serialised between 1864 and 1865.

**The first number appeared on 1 May 1864. Sales receipts increased as the story progressed and reached 30,000 copies, but Dickens could not maintain that demand because towards the end of the serialisation sales returned to the levels of the first instalment.**

Suicides were commonplace in Victorian London, where people in despair threw themselves into the Thames on a daily basis. Dickens would frequently see posters on the streets of London of relatives seeking the whereabouts of their loved ones. The story starts on the River Thames between London Bridge and Southwark Bridge, where Gaffer Hexam and his daughter Lizzie are in a small boat engaged in the gruesome occupation of searching and recovering dead bodies from the river.

Dickens commented upon Victorian monetary and class values in the story. Noddy Boffin is socially mobile and becomes affluent as a proprietor of a refuse collection business, which he inherits from old Mr Harmon. The rubbish is piled into heaps and his employees sift through dust heaps for valuables to sell. There were dust heaps close to York Road near King's Cross Station that Dickens would have seen. On some occasions jewellery and money that was accidently discarded was found, however, raw materials were found that could be sold on to other industries. Boffin is known as the 'golden dustman' and when he socialises with the upper classes, who have inherited money, he is regarded as new money. Bella Wilfer desires money and cannot borrow, plead or steal it, but vows to attain it through marriage. Charley Hexam, brother

The first eight issues of *Our Mutual Friend*. (University of North Texas)

of Lizzie, rises from poverty through education, but when he has risen in status, he attempts to remove himself from his past and his sister Lizzie in a brutal and cruel way.

**Silas Wegg** is a ballad seller with a wooden leg. The illiterate Boffin believes him to be a literary man and hires him to teach him to read, even though Wegg's reading ability is limited.

**Roger 'Rogue' Riderhood** is the partner of Gaffer Hexam, but when Riderhood is convicted of theft, he is spurned by Hexam. Riderhood takes revenge by framing Hexam for the murder of John Harmon, with the hope of receiving the reward offered by Boffin. Riderhood becomes the deputy lock keeper at Plashwater Weir Mill and is an accomplice to Bradley Headstone's assault upon Eugene Wrayburn. Riderhood attempts to extort money from Headstone and both men drown in a fight in the Thames.

Silas Wegg. (Author's Collection)

Roger 'Rogue' Riderhood. (Author's Collection)

# 80

# Dickens' Swiss Chalet

### Gift from the actor Charles Fechter.

**The chalet once stood in Dickens' garden at Gad's Hill Place and is now in the garden of Eastgate House in Rochester. The author used it as a summer study from 1865 until his death in 1870.**

The two-storey, prefabricated Swiss chalet was given to Dickens by his close friend, the actor Charles Fechter, towards the end of 1864. It arrived from Paris in ninety-four pieces and had to be assembled. Mamie wrote:

> One very severe Christmas, when the snow was so deep as to make out-door amusement for our guests impossible, my father suggested that he and the inhabitants of the 'bachelors' cottage' should pass the time in unpacking the French chalet, which had been sent to him by Mr Fechter, and reached Higham Station in a large number of packing cases. Unpacking these and fitting the pieces together gave them interesting employment, and some topics of conversation for our luncheon party.[189]

Dickens decided that it should be constructed in his garden at Gad's Hill Place on the north side of the London – Rochester Road, known as the 'wilderness', which meant that he had to use the underground passage to access it. On 7 January 1865 Dickens reported to Forster, 'the chalet is going on excellently, though the ornamental part is more slowly put together than the substantial. It will really be a pretty thing; and in the summer (supposing it not to be blown away in the spring), the upper room will make a charming study. It is much higher than we supposed.'[190]

The Swiss chalet was erected in the annex to Gad's Hill Place so that Dickens could see the Thames from the first floor. It became Dickens' favourite place to work; a peaceful sanctuary where he could write and a private space to rehearse his readings. He wrote to Fechter on 22 May 1868:

---

189. Dickens, Mamie, op. cit., p.36.
190. Forster, Vol. 3, op. cit., p.111.

Dickens' Swiss chalet displayed in the garden of Eastgate House, Rochester, Kent. (Courtesy of Ethan Doyle White)

> I have put five mirrors in the Chalet where I write and they reflect and refract, in all kinds of ways, the leaves that are quivering at the windows, and the great fields of waving corn, and the sail dotted river. My room is up among the branches of the trees and the birds and the butterflies fly in and out, and the green branches shout in at the open windows, and the lights and shadows of the clouds come and go with the rest of the company. The scent of the flowers, and indeed of everything that is growing for miles and miles, is most delicious.[191]

Dickens wrote his last words in the upper room of this chalet on the day before he died, where he was working on *The Mystery of Edwin Drood* and a letter to his friend Charles Kent. After Dickens' death, his family presented the Swiss chalet to Lord Darnley and it was erected in Cobham Park. It was moved to Eastgate Gardens, Rochester, in 1960.

---

191. Dickens, *Works, Volume 38*, op. cit., p.294.

# 81

# Engraving Depicting the Staplehurst Railway Accident

### Dickens was involved in the train accident at Staplehurst.

During the spring 1865, Dickens felt overworked and fatigued, so towards the end of May he went on a short holiday to France with Ellen Ternan and her mother, Frances. Dickens kept his relationship with the young actress secret, but it risked being revealed when the party returned to England as they were involved in a railway accident at Staplehurst.

On 9 June, they had arrived from Boulogne at Folkestone at 2.30 pm and then embarked on a train to London. At 3.13 pm the train passed over a viaduct between Headcorn and Staplehurst in Kent where a length of track had been removed during engineering works. The engine was derailed and the train broke in two, with eight of the carriages plunging into the stream. One hundred and ten passengers were aboard the train; ten of them were killed and fifty-two injured. Dickens was unhurt but helped those that had been injured, and some victims died as he was attending to them. Before leaving the scene, Dickens returned to his carriage to retrieve the manuscript of the latest instalment of *Our Mutual Friend*.

Dickens was reluctant to take part in the inquest or say anything publicly about the tragedy. He also had good reason for keeping a low profile because he did not want the press to discover his intimate relationship with Ellen. Dickens was shaken by the accident and as a consequence the sixteenth instalment of *Our Mutual Friend* was two and a half pages shorter.

Although he was uninjured, the accident traumatised Dickens and he would never fully recover. After the crash he was reluctant to travel on trains and in horse carriages. On 26 August 1868, he wrote to Cerjat:

My escape in the Staplehurst accident of three years ago is not to be obliterated from my nervous system. To this hour I have sudden vague rushes of terror, even when riding in a hansom cab, which are perfectly unreasonable but quite surmountable. I used to make nothing of driving a pair of horses habitually through the most crowded parts of London. I cannot now drive with comfort to myself, on the country roads here; and I doubt, I could

A depiction of the scene at the Staplehurst train crash. (Author's Collection)

ride at all in the saddle. My reading secretary and companion knows so well when one of these odd momentary seizures comes upon me in a railway carriage, that he instantly produces a dram of brandy, which rallies the blood to the heart and generally prevails.[192]

Despite his concerns about travelling by train, it did not stop Dickens using the railways to travel around Britain during his final reading tour of Britain.

---

192. Dickens, *Letters*, Vol. 2, op. cit., p.364.

# 82

# St George's Hall, Liverpool

## Venue where Dickens performed during the two English reading tours from 1866 to 1867.

**Dickens performed *The Frozen Deep* and gave readings on numerous occasions in Liverpool. Those readings initially took place at the Philharmonic Hall. During his later years he preferred to perform at St George's Hall, which is opposite Lime Street Station.**

Dickens gave a reading in the small concert room at St George's Hall during the evenings of 11 and 13 April 1866 and on the following afternoon of 14 April. During the first night he read *Doctor Marigold* and extracts from *Nicholas Nickleby* at Mr Squeers' school. Dickens read *David Copperfield* and the trial from *The Pickwick Papers* on 13 April, and he read extracts from *Dombey & Son* on 14 April.

On arrival at St George's Hall, Dickens personally supervised the arranging of the screen, battens and reading table before each performance. The venue was full to capacity and one man was so desperate to buy three stalls tickets that he placed an advertisement in a local morning paper offering to pay double the price, but he had no takers. Dickens wrote to Mamie about the audience interaction and popularity of his tour in Liverpool:

> The police reported officially that three thousand people were turned away from the hall last night. I doubt if they were so numerous as that, but they carried in the outer doors and pitched into Dolby with great vigour. I need not add that every corner of the place was crammed. They were a very fine audience, and took enthusiastically every point in Copperfield and 'The Trial.' They made the reading a quarter of an hour longer than usual.[193]

Dickens was referring to George Dolby, who was the theatre manager employed by Chapman & Hall to look after him during the reading tour. Dolby wrote that:

> It was well known with what care Mr. Dickens prepared his books, and the same system was carried out in the preparation of his Readings. He had a singular habit, too, of

---

193. Dickens, *Works, Volume 38*, op. cit., p.175.

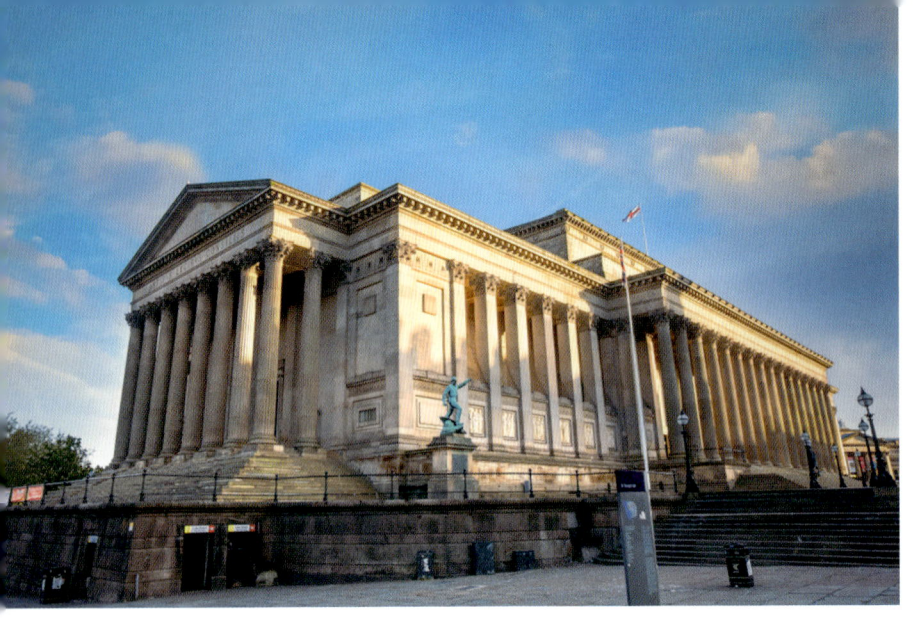

St George's Hall in Liverpool, which was constructed in 1854. (Cowardlion/Shutterstock)

regarding his own books as the production of someone else, and would almost refer to them as such. Chief among his favourites was '*David Copperfield*,' so that it is not a matter of surprise that, when he presented it to the public as a Reading, he should throw into it all the colour, light, and shade of which his artistic nature was capable, until the word-painting made such a picture as has never been surpassed.[194]

A Liverpool reporter wrote of Dickens' performance:

Mr. Dickens last night gave a reading to a crowded audience in the small concert room at St George's Hall. Some years ago, Mr Dickens paid a visit to this town in the character of a 'reader' – only less distinguished as a reader than as a novelist – and at the Philharmonic Hall charmed large audiences by his splendid elocutionary abilities. Time has considerably altered his personal appearance, but it has not diminished one jot the dramatic force and truth by which in a marked degree his readings are distinguished. There are the same freshness and vigour of delivery, and the same happy power of treating both the humorous and the pathetic pages of his subject. Few of our celebrated novelists could vocally do justice to their own works, but Mr. Dickens has that rare faculty of bringing out into a new light and investing with a new interest points which the most careful of his readers have overlooked, and well-conned passages acquire a new meaning and a greater force when heard from his lips.[195]

Dickens returned to Liverpool on 8 November 1867 and on the following day he departed aboard the *Cuba* for his second and final tour of America. On the completion of his series of farewell readings, a banquet was held in Dickens' honour at St George's Hall, Liverpool, on 10 April 1869, which was attended by 600 guests, including fellow author Anthony Trollope and 500 spectators.

---

194. Dolby, op. cit., pp.19–20.

195. *Liverpool Mercury*, 12 April 1866.

# 83

# Door to Dickens' Room at the Parker House, Boston

## Dickens used this hotel as his home base during his 1867–68 American Tour

**In 1867, Dickens was offered the opportunity to return to the United States of America to embark on a reading tour. His family tried to persuade him not to consider these proposals, but after consideration he decided to accept.**

Dickens sailed from Liverpool on 9 November 1867 aboard the Cunard ship *Cuba*, arriving in Boston ten days later. This was his second visit to Boston and he found the city comparable to Edinburgh, Leeds and Preston in Britain. He was fond of Boston and it was a place where he felt comfortable because many of his American literary friends lived here. Dickens stayed at the Parker House ('House' was a common name for hotels at the time), which stood on the corner of School and Tremont Streets. During his first American visit twenty-five years earlier he had stayed at another hotel, the Tremont House; the Parker House had not yet been built at the time. The Parker House was around the corner from Tremont Temple, the venue where Dickens performed his readings in Boston. When he arrived on 19 November, Dickens received a warm reception in the Parker House from eminent Bostonians. He rented a suite in the hotel for five months during 1867–68, using it as a base for his tour. Dickens wrote from the Parker House on 21 November 1867:

> This is an immense hotel, with all manner of white marble public passages and public rooms. I live in a corner high up, and have a hot and cold bath in my bedroom (communicating with the sitting room), and comforts not in existence when I was here before. The cost of living here is enormous, but happily we can afford it.[196]

The room used by Dickens was saved and honoured for years, but the entire hotel was demolished, rebuilt, and modernised during 1925–27, so there is no remnant of his actual room. One of the demolition men saved the 8ft-tall wooden door to Dickens' suite and since 2015 this has been

---

196. Dickens, *Letters*, Vol. 2, op. cit., p.305.

*Above*: Dickens Door & Historical Gallery at Omni Parker House today. (Courtesy of the Omni Parker House)

*Left*: Parker House photographed during 1866, eleven years after it was constructed and one year before Dickens arrived for his American tour. The hotel is the 2nd building from the left. (Robert N. Dennis Collection)

on display in the historical gallery of the Omni Parker House, which is on the site of the original hotel. There is a small conference room named after Dickens on the mezzanine level that contains the original mantelpiece from Dickens' room. It is in the approximate location of the bedroom suite Dickens rented in the former incarnation of the hotel.

Ten days were allocated for him to rest in the hotel before the first reading, but Dickens became restless and prepared for the readings instead. He was feeling anxious to begin the tour and was yearning to return home at the onset. He wrote to his daughter from the Parker House: 'my anxiety to get to work is greater than I can express, because time seems to be making no movement towards home until I shall be reading hard. Then I shall be able to count and count and count the upward steps to May.'[197]

Dickens' Mantelpiece at the Omni Parker House today. (Courtesy of the Omni Parker House)

Dickens declined the multitude of invitations to breakfast, lunch, dinner and various social functions that he received from eminent Bostonians and only spent time with selected individuals. During his residence at the Parker House, he dined with fellow American authors Ralph Waldo Emerson, Henry Wadsworth Longfellow and Oliver Wendell Holmes. On Thanksgiving Day, Dickens visited Longfellow's home in General George Washington's headquarters during the siege of Boston during the American War of Independence. Dickens was aware of the tragedy that occurred in this house as this was where Longfellow's wife died in a fire.

After conducting readings in New York, Philadelphia and Washington DC, Dickens returned to the Parker House on 22 February 1868. The intention was for Dickens to perform eight readings in Boston, but President Johnson's impeachment affected sales of the first four nights and it was decided to abandon the other four in order to allow Dickens to rest in the hotel and try to recover from fatigue and influenza.

---

197. Kitton, *Life*, op. cit., p.353.

# 84

# Dickens' Mirror at the Parker House, Boston

### Dickens used this mirror to rehearse his readings.

**Down the hall and around the corner from the Dickens Conference Room, at Parker House, hanging near the elevators, is the large mirror in front of which Dickens used to practise his animated talks.**

Tour manager George Dolby decided that Dickens should be shielded from the public while in Boston. Dickens wrote that 'the less I am exhibited for nothing the better', so access to him was restricted. Dickens isolated himself in this hotel so that he could devote time to preparing for his readings. He would only leave it to go for his daily 8-mile walk. Dickens wanted to ensure that his audience received value for money when they bought a ticket for his readings. He told a journalist from the *New York Tribune*:

> I am come here to read. The people expect me to do my best, and how can I do it if I am all the time on the go? My time is not my own when I am preparing to read any more than it is when I am writing a novel and I can as well do one as the other without concentrating all my powers on it until it is done. [198]

Part of Dickens' preparation involved a read through and an enactment of each character in front of a mirror. He would rehearse the entire reading, investing all his energy into each part, and this is the actual mirror that he used when he stayed at the Parker House, which can be viewed by guests at the Omni Parker House. In this mirror he would be able to see his facial mannerisms and adapt his voice according to each character. The audience was not just listening to Dickens reading the story, but seeing him physically transform into the characters that he had created. The journalist from the *New York Tribune* also commented, presumably from the interview with Dickens, that, 'indeed the public has but little idea of the cost – in downright hard work of mind, and body, and voice – at which these readings are

---

198.  *Stirling Observer*, 19 December 1867.

Dickens' Mirror in the Omni Parker House today. (Courtesy of the Omni Parker House)

produced. Although Mr Dickens has read, now, nearly five hundred times, I am assured, on the best authority, that he never attempts a new part in public until he has spent at least two months over it in study.'[199]

---

199. Ibid.

# 85

# Tremont Temple, Boston

**Dickens opened his second American tour with four readings at the Tremont Temple in Boston. The first performance took place on 2 December 1867 with *A Christmas Carol* and the trial in *The Pickwick Papers*.**

Tremont Temple was originally a theatre built in 1827 and was one of the largest halls in Boston. Although the premises were bought by the Free Church Baptists in 1843, it was also used as a venue for public events, such as the readings given by Dickens, and had a capacity of 2,000. The seats were arranged on a raised floor that would enable everyone in the house to be able to view the stage, not only to be able to hear the readings, but also to see Dickens' facial effects as he performed each character, which was an integral part of the performance.

Eight thousand tickets for Dickens' first four readings at Tremont Temple in Boston were sold within twelve hours of release to the public on 18 November 1867. It was reported that an African-American purchased the first ticket. He had stood at the offices of Ticknor and Fields, Dickens' American publisher, at No. 124 Tremont Street, from midnight for seven hours before it opened in the bitter cold in his determination to see Dickens read.[200] George Dolby estimated that the queue to purchase tickets was half a mile long. The Boston Police Force were called to ensure the safety of the large crowds that were queuing. Such was the demand that some of those tickets were resold at double the face value by ticket speculators, known nowadays as touts. Dickens was reluctant to add more dates to the tour and many people without tickets arrived at the venue in the hope of purchasing one. Distinguished American figures from literature and science were in the audience, including Henry Wadsworth Longfellow, Ralph Waldo Emerson, Louis Agassiz, Whittier, Lowell and Oliver Wendell Holmes, as well as the Governor of Massachusetts.

Despite the 8 pm start time for the performance, the audience was not settled until 8.15 pm, when Dickens entered the stage. *The Express* reported: 'Mr. Dickens appeared unaccompanied on the platform. He was greeted with the clapping of hands, vociferous cheers, and shouts of "Welcome," and other enthusiastic manifestations of warm appreciation. The welcome was a

---

200. *Stirling Observer*, 19 December 1867.

Still standing today, Tremont Temple, at 88 Tremont Street Boston, was the venue where Dickens began his second American tour on 2 December 1867. This view of the building was taken c.1900. (Library of Congress)

most cordial one, and it came from the elite in the city and vicinity. Mr. Dickens bowed his acknowledgements modestly.'[201]

A reviewer from the *New York Tribune* in the audience wrote:

> But at last he comes! He enters, holding the book in both his hands; comes up the steps with a quick, sprinting walk, and, standing at his velvet desk, proceeds to work, like a man of business. He is dressed with perfect neatness and simplicity, not a trace of the old foppery – the autumn's flower of all the youthful dandyism – is seen in the button-hole in the shape of white carnation, and a pink rosebud on his shirt front. There nothing more pretending than a plain gold stud. He has, to be sure, considerable watch-chain, and on his finger a diamond ring –but nothing is noticeable in his dress. He stands there a quiet gentleman, plain Charles Dickens, and that name is grace and ornament enough.[202]

---

201. *The Express*, London, 14 December 1867.

202. *Stirling Observer*, 19 December 1867.

A drawing of Charles Dickens as he appeared while reading in Boston during 1867, sketched by Charles A. Barry. (Library of Congress)

On the day after the first night, he was jubilant at the response, for he wrote: 'Most magnificent reception last night, and most signal and complete success.'[203] John Whittier, the American poet and abolitionist, was among the audience and wrote: 'My eyes ached all next day from the intensity of my gazing. I do not think his voice naturally particularly fine, but he uses it with great effect. He has wonderful dramatic power … I like him better than any public reader I have ever before heard.'[204]

Dickens returned to Tremont Temple to give further readings in Boston in January and in April 1868. For most of the tour Dickens had been suffering from catarrh and by the time he reached Boston for his final readings, his condition grew worse. Despite his friends advising him not to perform, Dickens carried on. George Dolby attentively sat by the stage to keep an eye on Dickens as he read. The last reading in Boston took place on 8 April.

---

203. Dickens, *Letters*, Vol. 2, op. cit., p.310.

204. Wagenknecht, Edward. *John Greenleaf Whittier: A Portrait in Paradox*. (New York: Oxford University Press, 1967), p.108.

# 86
# Publicity Photographs of Dickens

## Photographed in New York during 1867

**The energy Dickens invested in the performance of each reading took its toll upon his health, which is evident in his appearance in these American publicity photos.**

They were taken during December 1867 in New York during his last tour of America. The routine of travelling, rehearsals and performing consumed Dickens' energy. The experience would exhaust him and severely impact upon his health, contributing to his premature death two and a half years later. The original intention was for Dickens to conduct eighty readings across America and Canada, but this plan had to be modified and restricted to the east coast, including Boston, New York, Baltimore, Philadelphia and Washington. He would perform four readings each week on Mondays, Tuesdays, Thursdays and Fridays, leaving Wednesday, Saturday and Sunday for rest. Dickens wanted to limit the amount of travelling, but instead read in these specific cities and try to get the people to go to him, rather than him travelling to them.

Tickets for the four scheduled performances at the Steinway Hall in New York sold out within a few hours of release. Two thousand people had formed a queue at the box office, three-quarters of a mile long, in the snow from 2 am. To prevent people buying large numbers of tickets and selling them on for a profit above face value, they were restricted to four only for each reading per person. There were also fraudulent attempts to profit from Dickens' tour when one individual in New York printed fake tickets but his attempts to sell them were thwarted.

Dickens had a setback when he arrived in New York because he was afflicted with influenza and suffered severely from catarrh, which he would not recover from until he returned to England. On the first night at the Steinway Hall on 9 December 1867 he read *A Christmas Carol* and the trial scene from *The Pickwick Papers*. A reviewer from the *New York Herald* noticed from Dickens' voice that he might have been ailing, for he wrote:

> In the outset his voice appeared a little weak and husky, but after a few lines had been recited ... the reader began to warm up to his work and the house began to realise that the first comedian of the present generation was before them, acting the various characters

*Above left*: A photograph taken of Dickens in 1867 during his stay in New York. (New York Public Library)

*Above right*: Another of the promotional images of Charles Dickens. (Library of Congress)

of one of the prettiest of the domestic dramas of Dickens, just as Dickens himself would wish it to be done.[205]

The first night was deemed a triumph and Dickens began to get into his stride for the second night, when he read a condensed version of *David Copperfield* and Bob Sawyer's party from *The Pickwick Papers*. A greater rapport was established between Dickens and his audience, for which he was energised by their positive response. A reviewer from the *New York Times* wrote: 'Everyone was bent on the reader's expressive face and the contagion of his mood seemed to pass directly to every individual in the room like a subtle magnetic influence. Mr. Dickens appeared to feel the sympathy of his audience and to be inspired by it. His manner was exceedingly animated and effective, and he really seemed to enjoy the reading quite as much as those who listened to him.'[206]

Tickets for further readings in New York were sold, during which a fight took place when some people, including speculators, attempted to jump the queue. Dickens was exhausted by the routine of travelling between cities and performing. He wrote to Mamie, that 'it likewise happens, not seldom, that I am so dead beat when I come off stage, that they lay me down on a sofa after I have been washed and dressed, and I lie there extremely faint for a quarter of an hour. In that time, I rally and come right.'[207] Despite feeling under par, he continued his tour with four readings each week.

---

205. *Cambridge Chronicle & Journal*, 28 December 1867.

206. Ibid.

207. Dickens, Mamie, op. cit., pp.98–9.

# 87

# The White House, Washington DC

## Dickens' success as an author led him to the seat of American government.

**Dickens met President John Tyler in 1842 and President Andrew Johnson in 1868.**

During his first visit to America in 1842, Dickens arrived in Washington DC on 9 March and visited the White House during the following morning. President John Tyler was astonished at the youthful age of Dickens and was expecting to meet someone older. Dickens wrote that 'the President's mansion is more like an English clubhouse, both within and without, than any other kind of establishment which I can compare it'.[208] Dickens was given an audience with President Tyler. He was ushered into his office:

> where, at a business-like table covered with papers, sat the President himself. He looked somewhat worn and anxious, and well he might; being at war with everybody – but the expression of his face was mild and pleasant, and his manner was remarkably unaffected, gentlemanly and agreeable. I thought that in his whole carriage and demeanour, he became his station singularly well.[209]

During his second and final tour of America, President Andrew Johnson and his family attended all Dickens' public readings in Washington, purchasing a row of seats for each night, together with Congressmen and ambassadors. President Johnson invited him to the White House for a private audience on 7 February 1868, which was his fifty-sixth birthday. Dickens wrote that: 'I have just seen the President … He is a man with a remarkable face, indicating courage, watchfulness and certainly strength of purpose.'[210] Their meeting was cordial, but Dickens reported that 'each of us looked at the other very hard.'[211]

---

208. Dickens, *American Notes*, op. cit., pp.83–4.
209. Ibid., p.84.
210. Forster, Vol. 3, op. cit., p.423.
211. Ibid., pp.423–4.

The White House in 1846, four years after Dickens' first visit. (Library of Congress)

President Johnson was in awe of Dickens, which rendered him lost for words. George Dolby accompanied Dickens to the White House and wrote: 'We most cordially received by the President who seemed to be impressed by the presence of his distinguished visitor, and for some moments sat looking at him, uncertain how to commence a conversation. He warmed up, however, in congratulatory expressions as to the effect of the Readings had produced on him. This gave Mr. Dickens the opportunity of saying a few kindly words to his distinguished host.'[212]

Dickens returned home from New York on the ship *Russia* on 19 April 1868, arriving in Liverpool. Despite his ill health and exhaustion, Dickens' last tour of America was a triumphant and a financial success. He had earnt £19,000 for six months' work, but he missed companionship with Ellen Ternan.

---

212. Dolby, op. cit., p.236.

# 88

# Caricature of Dickens Astride the English Channel

**This image appeared on the cover of *L'Eclipse*, the French magazine, on 14 June 1868.**

Andre Gill, the French caricaturist, shows Dickens standing triumphantly across the English Channel, from London to Paris, holding a selection of his books. It emphasised Dickens' influence and popularity in both Britain and France as he is depicted as a literary colossal.

Dickens was most probably the first international celebrity. His novels were translated in French and his work was widely read and very popular in France. He was the favourite author of the renowned French writer Jules Verne, who was inspired by Dickens' work. Verne wrote: 'I don't know more than a hundred words of English, and so have had to read him in translation, but I declare to you sir, that I have read the whole of Dickens ten times over. I love him immensely, and in my forthcoming novel, *P'tit Bohomme*, the proof of this is given and acknowledgement of my debt is made.'[213] The French composer Claude Debussy dedicated a humorous piano composition *Hommage à S. Pickwick Esq. P.P.M.P.C.* (no. 9 of *Préludes*, $2^{ème}$ *Livre*) forty-three years after Dickens' death during 1913.

Dickens visited France regularly throughout his life and sent his sons to a school in Boulogne for their education. He could speak French fluently and could write in the language. In several of his novels there exist French influences. *A Tale of Two Cities* focuses upon the character Sydney Carton in London and Paris during the French Revolution. In *Bleak House*, Dickens created the French character Hortense, who was the servant to Lady Dedlock and played a prominent role in the plot. Dickens begins *Little Dorrit* in Marseille and features the Frenchman Rigaud, alias Lagnier or Bladois, who was a former prisoner convicted of killing his wife.

---

213. *Toronto Saturday Night*, 17 March 1894.

This caricature of Dickens drawn for *L'Eclipse* celebrated the British author's appeal and popularity with the French nation. (via Author)

# 89

# Charles Dickens' Travelling Cutlery Kit

**The travelling cutlery kit owned by Dickens was used during his Second American tour.**

As a child, when his family endured hard times and money was scarce, he experienced hunger, so food became a focal theme in his novels. Dinner was also important when Dickens socialised, either when he was entertaining in his home or eating with friends in a pub.

Food was prominent in Dickens' novels and in *Oliver Twist* he focused upon child hunger, epitomised in Oliver's much-quoted plea, 'Please sir, can I have some more.' He used food to highlight the injustices between the rich and the poor, the well fed and the impoverished, with those members of the board of the workhouse overindulging in an abundance of food, while those under their care were being neglected and close to starvation. Dickens presented the same argument in *Nicholas Nickleby*, where Wackford Squeers ate 'a plate of hot toast, and a cold round of beef,'[214] while the students under his care were given watered-down, lukewarm milk to sustain them throughout the day. Dickens believed that everyone had the right to be fed properly, irrespective of their status in society.

In *A Christmas Carol* he showed how parents struggled to feed their children and could only afford a goose for Christmas dinner. Dickens wrote: 'there never was such a goose. Bob said he didn't believe there ever was such a goose cooked. In tenderness and flavour, size and cheapness were the themes of universal admiration. Eked out by apple sauce and mashed potatoes, it was a sufficient dinner for the whole family.'[215] Scrooge's journey of redemption involves food, for when he realises the hardships that Bob Cratchit endures, he sends his family a turkey as a gift for Christmas dinner, which they cannot afford.

The Pickwick Club are frequently seen being entertained at a sumptuous dinner table, while Sam Weller comments 'that poverty and oysters always seem to go together … the poorer the place is, the greater call there seems to be for oysters'.[216]

---

214. Dickens, *Nickleby*, op. cit., p.25

215. Dickens, *Carol*, op. cit., p.86.

216. Dickens, *Pickwick*, op. cit., p.317.

Dickens' travelling cutlery kit. (Library of Congress)

In *Great Expectations*, Pip steals a pork pie from his sister and brother-in-law in order to feed Abel Magwitch, the starved, escaped convict, while Miss Havisham's putrid wedding cake, concealed beneath a bed of cobwebs, represents her decaying life, devoured, eaten by mice from within.

As an adult, dinner was important for socialising as Dickens invited many of his famous friends to dine in his home. During the months that he lived in London, Dickens enjoyed embarking on walks or on horseback to Hampstead Heath where he would enjoy lunch in pubs such as Jack Straw's Castle and the Spaniard's Inn. John Forster mentioned that his first visit to Jack Straw's Castle was while Dickens was living at Doughty Street when they went for a walk over Hampstead Heath and enjoyed a 'red-hot chop for dinner, and a glass of good wine'[217] at the public house. Dickens visited the inn while he was writing *The Old Curiosity Shop* and read an instalment to friends in the inn. Dickens referred to visiting the inn in 1844 with the artist Maclise: 'Stanfield and Mac have come in, and we are going to Hampstead for dinner … We shall stroll leisurely up, to give you time to join us, and dinner will be on the table at Jack Straw's at four.'[218]

The travelling cutlery kit owned by Dickens, marked with his initials, was used by him during his second American tour of 1867–68. It contained a steel spoon, knife and corkscrew that unfolded from the ivory-covered case.

---

217. Forster, Vol. 1, op. cit., p.133.

218. Matz, B.W., *Dickensian Inns and Taverns* (Cecil Palmer, London, 1922), pp.162–3.

# 90

# Dickens' Wooden Walking Stick

**This wooden walking stick with carved ivory head was used by Dickens during his second tour to America (1867–68) and at Gad's Hill Place for the remainder of his life.**

Dickens' ownership of the walking stick is authenticated by accompanying notes from his sister-in-law, Georgina Hogarth, to whom Dickens left his personal possessions.

Throughout his life Dickens was an ardent walker and enjoyed covering long distances as part of his daily routine, wherever he was living. His daughter, Mamie, recalled that: 'walking, was perhaps, his chiefest pleasure, and the country lanes and city streets alike found him a close observer of their beauties and interests. He was a rapid walker, his usual pace four miles an hour, and to keep up with him required energy and activity similar to his own.'[219]

Dickens would use walking for contemplation and sometimes when friends and family joined him on such walks he would not speak. His son, Henry Fielding, recalled: 'often did I accompany him in these walks, but rarely did any conversation pass between us, for I knew his mind was at work.'[220]

While staying in Broadstairs on 19 August 1845, Dickens wrote to John Forster: 'Everything here at Broadstairs is the same as of old. I have walked 20 miles a day since I came down.'[221] After Dickens moved to Gad's Hill Place, he was regularly seen walking with a vigorous stride by the locals, usually with Georgina Hogarth or with his dogs. He discovered that 'the seven miles between Maidstone and Rochester is one of the most beautiful walks in England'.[222] Dickens would walk 20 miles from Gad's Hill Place, near Rochester, to London at a brisk pace. Anyone who accompanied him found it difficult to keep up with his strides. His friend, Mary Boyle, who joined him on various walks, remembered: 'He walked at his usual swinging rate, and we had proudly kept up with him. Only five minutes was allowed

---

219. Dickens, Mamie, op. cit., p.71.

220. Dickens, Sir Henry, *Recollections*, op. cit., p.32.

221. Forster, Vol. 2, op. cit., p.133.

222. Dexter, op. cit., p.38.

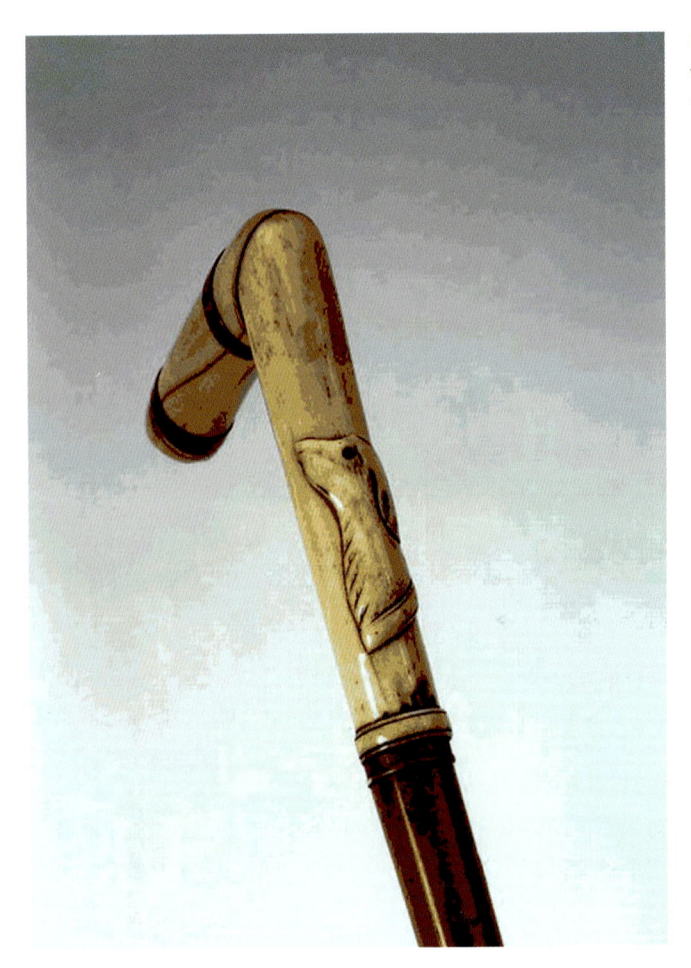

Dickens' wooden walking stick, which he used from 1867 to 1870. (Library of Congress)

for refreshment, as he called it, otherwise rest, between reaching the goal and arriving at home. How pleased his fellow pedestrians were to receive the following tribute: "Well done! ten miles in two hours and a half."'[223]

He used this stick during his second American tour in 1867–68. On Thanksgiving Day, Dickens walked 4 miles from the Parker House in Boston to Longfellow's house at Cambridge, a suburb of the city. When he departed New York to return home Dickens was reported to have used his cane and placed his hat upon it as he waved goodbye.

During February 1865 Dickens suffered from frostbite in his foot due to walking for hours in the snow. He developed an infection and he would suffer intermittently with this condition for the remaining five years of his life.

---

223. Courtenay, op. cit., pp.239–40.

# 91

# Programme of Dickens' Farewell Readings, St James's Hall

A combination of failing health and the desire to devote more time to writing new stories were the reasons for Dickens to retire from giving readings. A series of 'farewell readings' took place between 1868 and 1870.

While he was touring in America, Dickens agreed with Messrs Chappell to conduct a series of readings in a tour of Britain in the autumn of 1868. Dickens gave five readings at St James's Hall during October to December and this programme announced those dates and the excerpts that he would read. During the performances at the same venue in January 1869 Dickens would depart from usually reading only comic pieces in public and gave a recital of the murder scene from *Oliver Twist*.

Dickens wanted to offer something different to his audience by reading the scene of Bill Sikes' murder of Nancy as part of his repertoire. He was concerned how his audience would react to this darker subject matter and deliberated as to whether he should include it during this tour. Dickens pondered: 'I cannot make up my mind, however, whether to do it or not. I have no doubt that I could perfectly petrify an audience by carrying out the notion I have of the way of rendering it. But whether the impression would not be so horrible as to keep them away another time, is what I cannot satisfy myself upon.'[224]

As a precaution he tested this part of the reading with a small private audience at St James's Hall in London on 18 November 1868. The audience reacted positively and the scene was included in the readings, which proved extremely popular. The audience was enthralled with Dickens' emotive and emotionally charged performance. They were totally absorbed with his delivery. Dickens wrote to Percy Fitzgerald that: 'when the murder was done in London, the people were frozen while it went on, but came to life when it was over and rose to boiling point.'[225]

---

224. Forster, Vol. 3, op. cit., p.448.

225. Fitzgerald, op. cit., p.62.

## ST. JAMES'S HALL.

# MR. CHARLES DICKENS'S
## Farewell Readings.

MESSRS. CHAPPELL & Co. beg to announce that, knowing it to be the determination of Mr. DICKENS finally to retire from Public Reading soon after his return from America, they entered into arrangements with him while he was still in the United States, for a final

### FAREWELL SERIES OF READINGS
in this Country.

The First Course in London will commence in ST. JAMES'S HALL,
ON
### TUESDAY EVENING NEXT, OCTOBER 6th, 1868,
When he will read his
" Doctor Marigold," and "The Trial from Pickwick,"

AND WILL BE CONTINUED AS FOLLOWS, VIZ.:

### TUESDAY, OCTOBER 20th, 1868,
" David Copperfield," and " Mrs. Gamp."

### TUESDAY, NOVEMBER 3rd, 1868,
" Nicholas Nickleby" and " Boots at the Holly Tree Inn."

### TUESDAY, NOVEMBER 17th, 1868,
" The Story of Little Dombey and Mr. Bob Sawyer's Party."

### TUESDAY, DECEMBER 1st, 1868,
" Christmas Carol" and " Mr. Chops the Dwarf."

It is scarcely necessary for Messrs. CHAPPELL and Co. to add that any announcement made in connexion with these FAREWELL READINGS will be strictly adhered to, and considered final: and that on no consideration whatever will Mr. DICKENS be induced to appoint an extra night in any place in which he shall have been once announced to read for the last time.

*Prices of Admission:*
Sofa Stalls, (of which there will be a limited number only), 7s.   Stalls, 5s.   Balcony, 3s.
Admission,   -   ONE SHILLING.
Tickets may be procured at CHAPPELL and Co.'s, 50, New Bond Street, and at AUSTIN'S, 28, Piccadilly.

PRINTED BY J. MILES AND CO., WARDOUR STREET, OXFORD STREET,—W.

Programme of Charles Dickens' Farewell Readings, St James's Hall. (Courtesy New York Public Library)

A reporter from *The Globe* reported:

> As the tale of horror progressed, countenances became more and more fixed, and people listened with a sort of scared curiosity which was all the more remarkable, as people must have known what was coming as well as Mr Dickens himself … At the scene where the murder is actually committed, some ladies covered their faces with their hands, as if they would shut their eyes to horrors addressed to the imagination only.[226]

The murder scene from *Oliver Twist* was favourably received by the audience, which was mesmerized by Dickens' gravitas and charisma. Some women were so overwhelmed by Dickens' performance of this scene that they fainted and had to be carried from the auditorium. However, the passion and energy that Dickens exerted into this part of his performance caused him to feel tremendously exhausted. His health was failing and he was suffering from insomnia. To ensure that he was rested, he would spend the day before reading lying on a sofa. A doctor named Carr Beard accompanied Dickens while on the tour to monitor his health and his pulse. George Dolby recalled:

> If other proof were wanting as to the immense strain on Mr. Dickens' nervous system during the delivery of the Readings, it would have been sufficient to observe the changes in his pulse. It was curious to note the different effects of the different Readings. The ordinary state of Mr. Dickens' pulse was 72. *David Copperfield* brought it up to 96; *Doctor Marigold*, 99; the first night of the murder (during the last Readings), it was 112; and the second, 118; *Nicholas Nickleby* brought it to 112; and *Dombey* to 114. On one occasion it rose to 124. At the last Reading of all, when he went on the platform for the *Christmas Carol*, his pulse marked 108, and at the conclusion of the Reading it had risen to 110. He, himself, was astounded at the high state of his pulse after the last *Copperfield* Reading and explained it by the emotion he felt by parting (for the last time), with the Reading which he liked better almost than any of the others, and which had done so much to popularize the whole series. Although his pulse frequently ran as high during many other readings, the after effects were not so serious as when he left the platform on the termination of the 'Murder' Reading. On these occasions, he would have to be supported to his retiring-room and laid on a sofa for fully ten minutes, before he could speak a rational or consecutive sentence.[227]

After his recovery, Dickens would drink a wine glass full of brandy diluted with water before completing the reading. Dickens placed all his emotions and used his body as a conduit to project and bring alive the characters so loved by his readers. He placed himself under enormous pressure to deliver the consummate performance that his audience deserved, but it caused him stress and anxiety. He would conduct four readings a week during 1869 and the physical strain that these performances had upon Dickens' health probably caused his premature death.

---

226. *Fife Herald*, 14 January 1869.
227. Dolby, op. cit., pp.443–4.

# 92

# Dickens' Last Reading

### The final reading took place on 15 March 1870 at St James's Hall, London.

Despite his failing health, Dickens resumed the final twelve readings from the series of Farewell Readings at St James's Hall from 11 January 1870 until the middle of March. Three of those readings took place during the daytime, so that members of the theatrical profession who normally worked during the evenings would have a chance to see Dickens read for the last time. He was also working on *The Mystery of Edwin Drood* and *All the Year Round*. Dickens was warmly received by his audience, but he felt sadness that this phase of his career was coming to an end.

Dickens was in poor health, for during the second night of the readings his pulse had increased from 72 to 118. After reading the murder scene from *Oliver Twist* it had risen further to 120 and he had to lie on a sofa for ten minutes to recover during the interval. It also affected his speech. His son, Charles Dickens Junior, recalled that during one of these final readings he was unable to pronounce the word Pickwick.

The final reading took place at St James's Hall at 8 pm on 15 March 1870. On this final phase of the tour, he read the trial from *The Pickwick Papers* and *The Christmas Carol*. According to George Dolby: 'Mr. Dickens walked on to the platform, book in hand, but evidently much agitated. He was thinking, I dare say, that this was to be the very last time he would address an audience in this capacity.'[228] Dickens received a standing ovation and cheers for several minutes before he began reading from *A Christmas Carol*, standing beside the red velvet reading desk that he used during his American tour and farewell tour of Britain.

After completing reading from *The Pickwick Papers*, Dickens responded to several curtain calls before the moment he dreaded, addressing the audience with these final words:

> Ladies and gentlemen, – it would be worse than idle, it would be hypocritical and unfeeling, if I were to disguise that I close this episode in my life with feelings of very considerable pain. For some 15 years, in this hall and in many kindred places, I have had

---

228. Dolby, op. cit., p.447.

Charles Dickens' last reading. (New York Public Library)

the honour of presenting my own cherished ideas before you for your recognition, and, in closely observing your reception of them, have enjoyed an amount of artistic delight and enjoyment which, perhaps, it is given to few men to know. In this task and in every other I have ever undertaken as a faithful servant of the public, always imbued with a sense of duty to them, and always striving to do his best, I have been uniformly cheered by the readiest response, the most generous sympathy, and the most stimulating support. Nevertheless, I have thought it well at the full dead tide of your favour to retire upon those older associations between us which date from much further back than these, and henceforth to devote myself exclusively in the art that first brought us together. Ladies and gentlemen, in but two short weeks from this time I hope that you may enter, in your own homes, on the new series of readings at which my assistance will be indispensable, but from these garish lights I vanish now for evermore with one heartfelt, grateful, respectful and affectionate farewell.[229]

Mamie was in the audience and recorded the audience's response. 'There was a dead silence as my father turned away, much moved; and then came from the audience such a burst and tumult of cheers and applause as were almost too much to bear, mixed as they were with personal love and affection for the man before them.'[230]

His friend, Charles Kent, observed that 'the manly, cordial voice only faltered once at the very last, the mournful modulation of it in the utterance of the words. As he moved from the platform after the utterance of the last words of the address, and, with his head drooping in emotion, passed behind the screen on the way to his retiring-room, a cordial hand (my own!) was placed for one moment with a sympathetic grasp upon his shoulder.'[231]

Dolby stated that Dickens left the stage with a 'mournful gait, and tears rolling down his cheeks'.[232] This final performance marked the end of an era. Apart from the charitable readings for charity between 1854 and 1858, Dickens performed 423 readings for commercial benefit from the first one at St Martin's Hall on 29 April 1858 to this last reading at St James's Hall on 15 March 1870. He earned a total of £45,000 from the readings. Dickens' last public speech was when he attended the Royal Academy Banquet on 30 April 1870, where he paid tribute to the artist Daniel Maclise who had recently died. Although he felt sorrow that his reading tours had concluded, he felt relief that he had time to rest and devote time to writing.

229. *The Times*, 10 June 1870.
230. Dickens, Mamie, op. cit., p.105.
231. Teignmouth, op. cit., p.302.
232. Dolby, op. cit., p.450.

# 93

# *The Mystery of Edwin Drood* Locations

**The first instalment of *The Mystery of Edwin Drood* appeared in April 1870. Dickens had only written six parts before his untimely death.**

Dickens first ventured into detective fiction with *Bleak House*, but after admiring Wilkie Collins' novel *The Moonstone* in 1868, he decided to return to the genre with *The Mystery of Edwin Drood*. The premise for the book revolved around the disappearance of Edwin Drood one Christmas Eve. The other characters are left with the question of his whereabouts and to consider if a murder has been committed.

Dickens sold 50,000 copies of the first number of *The Mystery of Edwin Drood* and demonstrated that he maintained his popularity. Henry Wadsworth Longfellow affirmed it as 'certainly one of the most beautiful works, if not the most beautiful of all'.[233] The story dealt with opium addiction and Rochester featured predominantly as Cloisterham. It is surmised that Dickens derived the name Drood from Mr Trood, the landlord of the Falstaff Inn close to Gad's Hill Place.

**Eastgate House** is an Elizabethan dwelling that dates from 1591, which is inscribed on one of the beams inside the building. It was called Westgate House by Dickens in *The Pickwick Papers* and in *The Mystery of Edwin Drood* he named it the Nuns' House, a school for young ladies run by Miss Twinkleton and where Rosa Bud was educated. Eastgate House was an actual school for ladies during Dickens' lifetime and later became the headquarters of the Rochester Men's Institute.

On the corner of the High Street and Boley Hill can be seen **Jasper's Gatehouse** and Mr Topes' House. It is surmised that Mr Topes was based on William Mile, Chief Head Verger of Rochester Cathedral, who held that office for thirty-five years. Dickens described these two buildings as one in *The Mystery of Edwin Drood*, linked by a connecting door. He described it as 'an old stone gatehouse crossing the Close with an arched thoroughfare

---

233. Anonymous, *Bookman*, op. cit., p.17.

*Above and left*: Eastgate House and its plaque. (Author's Collection)

**220 CHARLES DICKENS** – PLACES AND OBJECTS OF INTEREST

Jasper's Gatehouse and Mr Topes' House. (Author's Collection)

passing beneath it'.[234] The cathedral choirmaster, Mr Jasper, lived in the lodgings above the gatehouse, while Mr Topes, the chief verger, lived next door. The gatehouse was built around 1550 and led to the cathedral precincts.

Dickens had intended to write twelve instalments of *The Mystery of Edwin Drood*, but he had only written six prior to his death, without leaving a plan or synopsis for the entire plot. Therefore, the ending of Dickens' final novel would never be known and would eternally remain a mystery.

---

234. Ibid., p.162.

# 94

# Queen Victoria Monument & Buckingham Palace

### Dickens met Queen Victoria.

**Queen Victoria received Dickens for a private audience at Buckingham Palace on 9 March 1870. The monarch regarded him as one of her favourite novelists alongside Sir Walter Scott and George Eliot.**

The first instalments of Dickens' *Oliver Twist* were published in 1837 during the year Victoria ascended the throne and it was through reading this serial that she became more aware of the deprivations of the poor in the realm over which she reigned. Victoria was an avid reader of Dickens' work and she mentioned reading his novels in her journal several times. Ever since those early days of her reign she expressed a desire to make the acquaintance of the renowned novelist, but Dickens was wary of patronage and was reluctant to meet his sovereign. He performed before the Queen on 16 May 1851 at Devonshire House, where he acted in a play written by Edward Bulwer-Lytton. As previously mentioned, he performed in *The Frozen Deep* at a private performance on 4 July 1857 at the Gallery of Illustration and declined to meet her after the show.

Determined to meet the author whom she admired, Victoria made another attempt the following year, when she requested to hear Dickens read *A Christmas Carol*. Dickens wrote: 'I was put into a state of perplexity.'[235] Dickens responded to Colonel Phipps at Buckingham Palace with the words: 'I should assure him of my desire to meet any wish of her Majesty, and should express my hope that she would indulge me by making one of some audience or other, for I thought an audience necessary to the effect; Thus, it stands, but it bothers me.'[236] Victoria did not get the opportunity to hear Dickens read *A Christmas Carol*.

Dickens eventually met Queen Victoria in 1870 at Buckingham Palace. On his last American tour, he had acquired some photographs of American Civil War battlefields. Victoria had a strong interest in this subject and was keen to see the images. On hearing of

---

235. Wilson, op. cit., p.382.

236. Ibid., p.382.

The imposing Queen Victoria Monument, which stands in front of Buckingham Palace in London. (Shutterstock)

her interest from Arthur Helps, Clerk of the Privy Council, Dickens immediately sent the photographs to Buckingham Palace. Victoria then invited Dickens to the palace so that she could thank him in person.

The meeting took place on 9 March 1870. Victoria wrote: 'I saw Mr Helps this evening at half past six, who brought and introduced Mr Dickens, the celebrated author. He is very agreeable, with a pleasant voice and manner. He talked of his latest works, of America, – the strangeness of the people there, – of the division of classes in England, which he hoped would get better in time. He felt sure that it would come gradually.'[237]

John Forster wrote a more detailed account of his meeting with Queen Victoria:

> The Queen's kindness left a strong impression on Dickens. Upon Her Majesty expressing regret not to have heard his readings. Dickens intimated that they had become now a thing of the past, while he acknowledged gratefully Her Majesty's compliment to regard to them. She spoke to him of the impression made upon her by his acting in the *Frozen Deep*, and, on his stating, in reply to her inquiry, that the little play had not been very successful on the public stage, said this did not surprise her, since it no longer had the advantage of his performance in it.[238]

---

237. Buckle, George Earle, *The Letters of Queen Victoria, A selection of from Her Majesty's correspondence between the years 1862 and 1878, Volume 2* (John Murray, London 1926), p.9.

238. Wilson, op. cit., p.383.

Victoria requested from Dickens some of his current writings to be sent to Buckingham Palace so that she could read them that afternoon but he suggested instead that he would send her a bound copy. Dickens wanted to delay sending her some writings of *The Mystery of Edwin Drood* to allow time for them to be bound. The audience ended when Queen Victoria presented Dickens with a copy of her book *Leaves from the Journal of Our Life in the Highlands, from 1848 to 1861* with an autographed dedication: 'To Charles Dickens, the humblest of writers would be ashamed to offer it to one of the greatest.'[239]

The Queen's journal was published in January 1868, receiving positive reviews, however, at the time Dickens was not enamoured by Her Majesties' literary endeavours when he rebuked his sub-editor William Will's praise of the work in *All the Year Round*, writing to him in February 1868: 'I would not have had that reference made to the Queen's preposterous book (I have read it) for any money.'[240] Two years later, Dickens accepted the gift with grace and was genuinely pleased to have received it.

Dickens expected the audience with Queen Victoria to last fifteen minutes and had arranged to meet George Dolby at Burlington Arcade to dine at the Blue Posts in Cork Street immediately afterwards. However, he spent ninety minutes with the sovereign. When he arrived an hour late for his appointment, Dolby recalled that Dickens 'was radiant with smiles'[241] as he disembarked from his Brougham Coach and instructed his servant to drive to his home at Hyde Park Place, which once stood opposite Marble Arch, and give the book that Queen Victoria had presented to him to his daughter.

The Queen was interested to know whether there was American support for the Fenian Brotherhood, who were championing for an independent Ireland, and the American perception of the British monarchy. Dickens assured Her Majesty that there was little support for Irish independence and that there was respect for her as sovereign. They also discussed national education and the cost of bread and meat.

The Queen offered Dickens a baronetcy in recognition for his literary achievements, but he declined the honour. Dickens did send Victoria a bound copy of his current writings, which she received and sent an acknowledgement from Balmoral Castle in a letter dated on the day of his death. When Dickens died on 9 June 1870, Victoria wrote that: 'he is a very great loss. He had a large, loving mind and the strongest sympathy with the poorer classes. He felt sure that a better feeling, and much greater union would take place in time. And I pray earnestly it may!'[242]

---

239. Wilson, Robert, op. cit., p.383.

240. The Royal Collection, www.royal.uk

241. Dolby, op. cit., p.455.

242. Buckle, op. cit., p.21.

# 95

# Charles Dickens' Court Suit

## This is the only surviving item of clothing that belonged to Dickens.

**Shortly after his audience with Queen Victoria, Dickens and his daughter were invited to attend a levee (a royal reception) in the drawing room of St James's Palace, where they were received by Edward, Prince of Wales, on 6 April 1870. This was the suit that he wore for that event.**

This suit revealed that Dickens was 5ft 9in tall and was slim with a 34in waist. Dickens was unaccustomed to wearing such clothing and regarded it as 'Fancy Dress', but the design of the suit complied with Court protocol. C. Smith & Sons Limited, Piccadilly, handstitched the suit, which has a black silk lining with gilt buttons, and Dickens wore a cocked hat and a sword with it. The trousers were made from the same material with a concealed pocket for Dickens' watch. George Dolby recalled:

> We got a good deal of fun out of the 'make-up,' in which Dickens heartily joined, but the climax was his utter bewilderment on the subject of the cocked hat. Fancy Dickens in a cocked hat! 'What an earth am I to do with it?' he asked in a woebegone manner.[243]

Edward, Prince of Wales, was keen to meet Dickens, as was the Belgian King Leopold II, who was in attendance. At the levee, the Prince of Wales and the Belgian King had accepted an invitation to dinner from Dickens' friend Lord Houghton, and Dickens was also invited. This dinner took place two weeks prior to his death. Dickens' problem with his foot reappeared and it was doubtful whether he would attend, but he persevered. Dolby confirmed that 'the Prince got a very agreeable impression of Dickens and Dickens liked the Prince, who expressed at parting a hearty wish for his speedy and complete recovery'.[244]

---

243. Dolby, op. cit., p.459.

244. Ibid., p.460.

The Court suit worn by Dickens was dark and sombre, totally opposite to the flamboyant, stylish, colourful suits and waistcoats that he normally wore. The suit was later owned by the Hungarian Countess Wenckheim, Jeanne-Marie Dickens, the widow of Dickens' great-great-grandson Christopher. This unique piece of clothing was presented to the Charles Dickens House Museum at Doughty Street, London, in 2015, where it is on display.

The woollen court suit that was worn by Charles Dickens when he met Edward, Prince of Wales, at St James' Palace on 6 April 1870. (Author's Collection)

226 CHARLES DICKENS – PLACES AND OBJECTS OF INTEREST

# 96

# Dickens' Couch

**Dickens died on this couch on 9 June 1870.**

**Dickens spent 8 June 1870 writing the last page of the sixth number of *The Mystery of Edwin Drood* in the Swiss chalet at Gad's Hill Place. The last words that he wrote for this unfinished novel related to Rochester, the town that he adored. 'A brilliant morning shines on the old city. Its antiquities and ruins are surpassingly beautiful, with the lusty ivy gleaming in the sun, and the rich trees waving in the balmy air.'**[245]

Dickens went to the house for lunch, followed by smoking a cigar in the conservatory, but against his normal routine he returned to the Swiss chalet to continue to work throughout the afternoon. Dinner was planned for six o'clock and before it was served, he wrote some letters, including one to Charles Kent, his friend, with whom he was arranging an appointment to see in London during the following day. The contents of that letter were as follows and were most likely the last words that Dickens ever wrote:

> My dear Kent, Tomorrow is a very bad day for me to make a call, as in addition to my usual office business. I have a mass of accounts to settle. But I hope I may be ready for you at 3 o'clock. If I can't be, why then I shan't be. You must really get rid of these opal enjoyments. They are too overpowering: 'Those violent delights have violent ends.' I think it was a father of your Church who made the wise remark to a young gentleman who got up early (or stayed out late) at Verona? Ever affectionately, Charles Dickens.[246]

When dinner began, he started to become incoherent in his speech. Georgina Hogarth saw that he was in a distressed state and Dickens told her that he had been feeling unwell for an hour. Georgina wanted to send for a doctor, but he insisted that they should continue with the dinner. Dickens was suffering from a stroke and at 6.10 pm, he collapsed. Georgina prevented him from falling. She encouraged him to go to his bedroom while she called for a doctor. Georgina said,

---

245. Dickens, Charles, *The Mystery of Edwin Drood* (Chapman & Hall, London, 1870), p.189.
246. *The Times*, 17 June 1870.

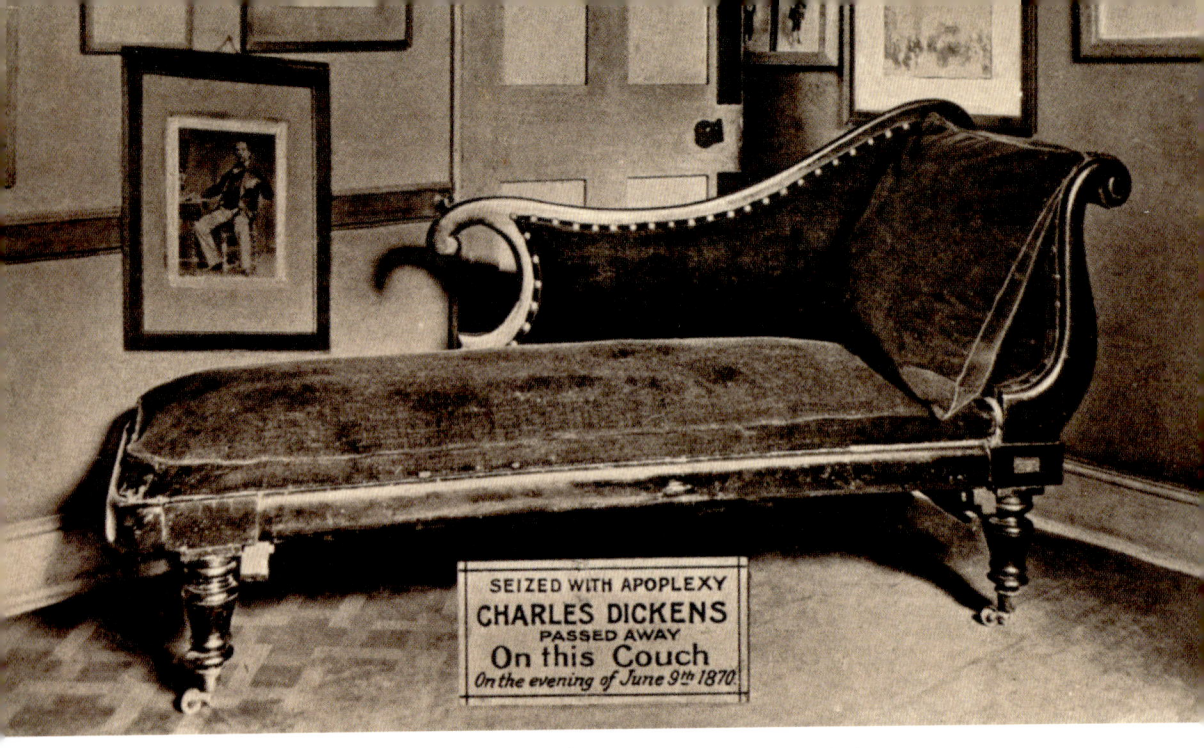

The couch on which Dickens died was donated to the Charles Dickens Birthplace Museum at Portsmouth in 1909 by his sister-in-law, Georgina Hogarth. (Author's Collection)

'Come and lie down,' and he responded, 'Yes, on the ground.'[247] These words were the very last words spoken by Dickens as Georgina lowered him to the floor of the dining room. The servants brought this couch and they struggled to get him on it. Dr Stephen Steele, a local surgeon from Strood, was summoned immediately and found Dickens in a critical state. He attended upon him through the night and Dr Russell Reynolds, a physician from London, arrived the following day. His two daughters and medical attendant Frank Beard arrived later that night, followed by his eldest son, Charles, during the next morning. Mamie recalled:

> All through the night we watched him – my sister on one side of the couch, my aunt on the other, and I keeping hot bricks to the feet which nothing could warm, hoping and praying that he might open his eyes and look at us, and know us once again. But he never moved, never opened his eyes, never showed any sign of consciousness through all the long night.[248]

Dickens had experienced an effusion on the brain, a haemorrhage. The pupil of his right eye was dilated, his pupil in the left eye contracted, his breathing affected and his limbs became flaccid an hour before his demise. He survived for twenty-four hours, but there was no improvement in his condition. He did not open his eyes and he remained unconscious. At 6.10 pm on 9 June 1870, Dickens gave a sigh followed by a tear running down his cheek before dying on this couch. He was aged fifty-eight years and four months.

---

247. Dickens, *Works, Volume 38*, op. cit., p.364.
248. Dickens, Mamie, op. cit., p.123.

# 97

# Drawing Depicting Dickens in Death by Millais

### The death of Dickens.

**Dickens' body was transferred from the couch to a bed that was placed in the dining room, where he could rest before the funeral. On 10 June, the day after Dickens' death, the artists John Millais and Thomas Woolner visited his family at Gad's Hill Place to offer condolences and support. Woolner took a cast of Dickens' head, which was modelled as a bust. Millais drew a sketch of Dickens in death.**

Dickens had been critical of a Millais painting entitled *Christ in the House of his Parents*, which was exhibited at the Royal Academy in 1850, denouncing the work in *Household Words* as 'mean, odious and revolting'.[249] However, Dickens met Millais at a dinner party at Wilkie Collins' home on 29 January 1855 and they became friends. Millais held Dickens in high esteem and when Dickens was searching for an artist to illustrate *The Mystery of Edwin Drood* they spent a lot of time discussing the project in London. When Millais was due to go to Gad's Hill Place to begin illustrating the novel, he read in the newspaper an announcement that Dickens had died. Millais wrote: 'The death of Dickens had an extraordinary effect upon me. It seemed as though the cup of happiness had been dashed from my lips.'[250]

Millais made a pencil drawing depicting Dickens on his death bed. According to his son, Millais intended to leave the outline drawing as a sketch but Dickens appeared so calm and beautiful that he decided he wanted to capture that state of tranquillity in a completed portrait. Millais presented the portrait to Dickens' daughter Kate, who was extremely grateful in the following thank you letter:

> My Dear Mr Millais, C has just brought down your drawing. It is quite impossible to describe the effect it has had upon us. No one but yourself, I think, could have

---

249. Millais, John Guille, *The Life & Letters of Sir John Everett Millais, Volume I* (Frederick A. Stokes Company, New York, 1899), p.75.

250. Teignmouth, op. cit., pp.302–3.

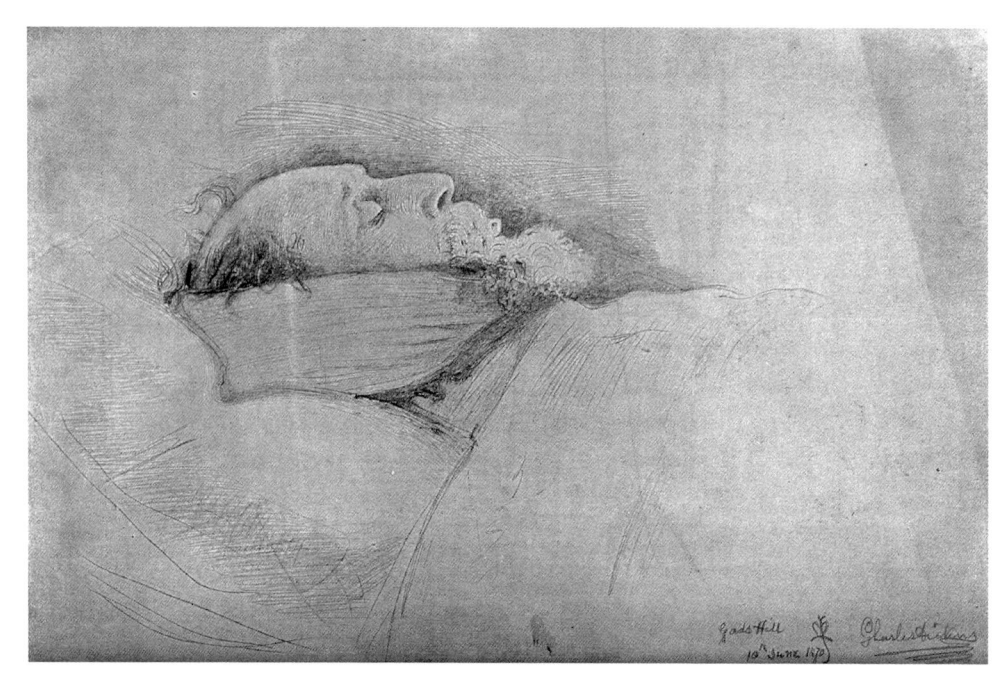

Charles Dickens on his deathbed, by John Millais, 1870. (Courtesy of the Wellcome Collection)

so perfectly understood the beauty and pathos of his dear face as it lay on that little bed in the dining-room, and no one but a man with genius bright as his own could have so reproduced that face as to make us feel now, when we look at it, that he is still with us in the house. Thank you, dear Mr Millais, for giving it to me. There is nothing in the world I have, or can ever have, that I shall value half as much. I think you know this, although I can find so few words to tell you how grateful I am. Yours most sincerely, Katie.[251]

---

251. Millais, op. cit., pp.30–3.

# 98

# Tablet indicating Dickens' wish to be buried in Rochester

## As a boy, Dickens would sit in the grounds of Rochester Castle and read. During his adult life he would frequently wander around the surrounding precincts.

**Dickens had expressed a wish to be buried in Rochester Castle moat, which formed part of the graveyard of St Nicolas Church, adjacent to Rochester Cathedral. The cathedral is the second oldest in England and was built around 604. A tablet can be seen on the graveyard wall that crosses the moat that notes Dickens' intended place of burial.**

Conscious of his desire to be buried close to Gad's Hill Place, Dickens' family made arrangements for his remains to be interred in the churchyard of St Peter and St Paul at Shorne. His daughter, Mamie, confirmed that his favourite walk from Gad's Hill Place was to the village at Shorne and that he had expressed a wish to be buried in its churchyard.[252] However, Dickens wanted to be buried at Rochester Cathedral according to John Forster, who confirmed that 'he had a notion that when he died, he should like to lie in the little graveyard belonging to the Cathedral at the foot of the castle wall'.[253]

Despite there being an Order of Council that forbade further internments in this small churchyard, the Dean and Chapter of Rochester Cathedral was considering how to facilitate the burial of Dickens within the cathedral but events were moving fast in London. Contrary to his wishes, *The Times* recommended that Dickens should be buried at Westminster Abbey, expressing the general feeling on behalf of the general public that it would be a fitting burial place for the popular author. John Forster and Charley Dickens approached Arthur Penrhyn Stanley, the Dean of Westminster, who showed an immediate interest and offered the abbey as a place of interment.

Although Dickens expressed his wish to be buried at Rochester Cathedral to John Forster, when his will was scrutinised, the author did not confirm a specific place of burial, however he did explicitly stipulate that he did not want any pomp or show at the funeral. The executors

---

252. Dickens, Mamie, op. cit., p.10.

253. Forster, Vol. 3, op. cit., p.540.

*Above and opposite*: The graveyard and plaque in the moat at Rochester Castle where Dickens wanted to be interred. (Author's Collection)

of his will thought that they could use their discretion to concur with the national mood of burying Dickens in Westminster Abbey, providing that they could comply with his wish for privacy and ensure that his burial was done privately and in secret. His will stipulated that: 'I emphatically direct that I be buried in an inexpensive, unostentatious, and strictly private manner.'[254]

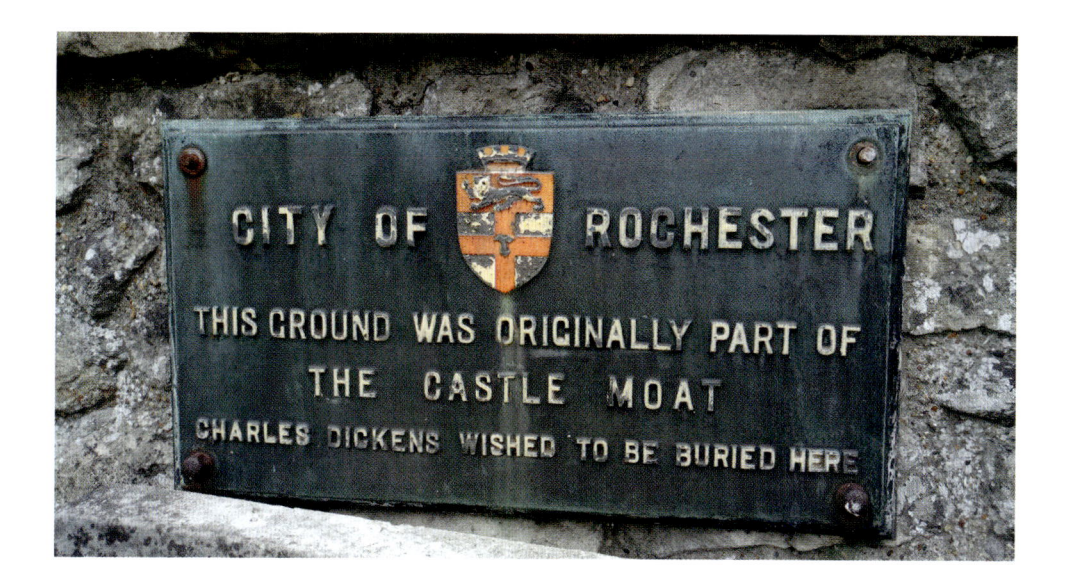

The executors agreed to the proposition on the proviso that the burial should take place privately and with no previous announcement in accordance with his wishes. During the day of Dickens' funeral at Westminster Abbey on 14 June 1870, the bell of Rochester Cathedral was tolled at one o'clock as a mark of respect. According to *The Times*, the Dean and Chapter Rochester Cathedral had made plans to receive Dickens' remains within Rochester Cathedral. It was reported that 'a vault had been prepared in St Mary's Chapel, Rochester Cathedral – a beautiful chapel near the entrance to the choir … for the internment of the deceased, and vault was rapidly constructed. Yesterday a number of men were engaged in filling up the vault with earth, and restoring the pavement, while the bell was tolling for the funeral.'[255] The construction firm Foord & Sons dug the grave and invoiced Rochester Cathedral.

During the early hours of the morning on 14 June, Dickens' remains were placed on a hearse at Gad's Hill Place and taken to Higham Station on the Chatham to London railway line, before people had risen from their beds. His coffin was loaded on to a special train and transported to Charing Cross Station, London. This was the last journey he made from Rochester, the town that he loved.

A plaque was placed upon the wall of the graveyard between Rochester Castle and the cathedral indicating that this is where Dickens wished to be buried.

---

254. Dickens, *Works, Volume 38*, op. cit., pp.365–6.
255. *The Times*, 15 June 1870.

# 99

# Dickens' Grave

**Dickens was buried in Westminster Abbey.**

**During the evening 13 June 1870, the Dean of Westminster had selected from the few unoccupied spaces within the south transept, known as Poets' Corner, a place for the burial of Dickens and the grave was dug by the Clerk of Works during that night. The Dean and canons were the only people who knew that the eminent author would be interred within the abbey.**

Dickens' remains arrived promptly at 9 am on 14 June at Charing Cross Station. Within minutes the hearse and the sombre cavalcade of mourners passed down Whitehall as it was conveyed to Westminster Abbey. Passers-by walking along Whitehall were unaware that the hearse contained the remains of Dickens. The hearse, followed by three mourning coaches, entered Dean's Yard at Westminster Abbey and the coffin, which was plain and made from solid oak, was carried through the cloisters to the door of the nave. It was received by the Dean and five canons and Dickens was interred in Poets' Corner at 9.30 am in the presence of his family and close friends, John Forster and Wilkie Collins. *The Times* reported:

> The service was most impressively read by the Dean, all but the Lesson, which was read by the Senior Canon. There was no anthem, no chanted psalm, no hymn, not even an intoned response of 'Amen;' but the organ played at intervals during the mournful ceremony. The earth was cast into the grave by the Clerk of the Works; the service ended, the mourners – 14 in number, with perhaps as many more strangers who accidently chanced to be present – gathered round the grave to take a last look at the coffin which held the great novelist's remains, and to place wreaths of immortelles and other flowers upon the coffin-lid, and the service was at an end.[256]

This article in *The Times* confirmed fourteen mourners, but only listed thirteen, which included Dickens' children, Georgina Hogarth and Forster and Collins. Catherine, his estranged wife, had received a letter of condolence from Queen Victoria but did not attend the funeral.

---

256. *The Times*, 15 June 1870.

Dickens' grave in Westminster Abbey immediately after the wreath laying by Prince Charles and Camilla, Duchess of Cornwall, during the 200th centenary commemoration of his birth in 2012. (Courtesy of User Jack 1956)

Dickens' insistence of a private funeral enabled his partner, Ellen Ternan, to be the fourteenth mourner to attend. Dickens' son, Henry, recalled:

> The funeral was one of the most solemn and impressive occasions at which I have ever been present. Except ourselves and the officiating clergy and the answering choir there was not a soul in that vast and imposing building (except one man who we heard afterwards had somehow found his way in). That was sufficiently impressive in itself, but it became far more so, as we stood in the dim light of Poet's Corner, in which not a sound was heard but the reverberation of the clergyman's voice intoning,

with touching emphasis, the beautiful words of the Burial Service, which seemed to fill the surrounding space.[257]

The death of Dickens shocked the nation and both rich and poor felt his loss. The grave was left open for the following three days, allowing hundreds of admirers of Dickens to pay their respects. Among them was Percy Fitzgerald, a contributor to *Household Words*, who recorded in his diary on 14 June 1870:

> Just come from Westminster Abbey, leaving outside a sultry, hot, fiercely-glowing day – and walked into the great cool vault, across under the stained-glass window to where was a crowd, and found forms tied together to make a fence, with a black cloth fringe: down below – not very low – the oak coffin in panels – handsome – and a well-cut, bold inscription. How it affected me looking down on that bright name, Charles Dickens. To think that he was lying there looking up. A wreath of white roses over his feet, a great bank of ferns at his head, rows of white and red roses down the side.[258]

The open grave was filled with flowers and when it was closed on the 17 June 1870, many were placed on the grave. Dickens decreed in his will 'that my name be inscribed in plain English letters on my tomb … I rest my claims to the remembrance of my country upon my published works …'[259] Dickens' grave is marked by a simple black stone on which the following words are inscribed: 'CHARLES DICKENS, BORN 7TH FEBRUARY 1812, DIED 9TH JUNE 1870'.

To the north of Dickens' grave lie the remains of Rudyard Kipling and the ashes of Thomas Hardy. Richard Cumberland, dramatist and friend of Dr Samuel Johnson, is buried south of his grave. To the west of Dickens' grave lies the composer George Frederick Handel, while on the east is Richard Brinsley Sheridan. Thackeray's bust overlooks Dickens' grave.

The Dickens Fellowship was established in 1902 for those who admired his work and to promote the social causes that he championed. Annually on the anniversary of his death on 9 June, it remembers Dickens by laying a wreath upon his grave in Westminster Abbey.

---

257. Dickens, Sir Henry, *Recollections*, op. cit., p.88.

258. Fitzgerald, op. cit., p.82.

259. www.westminsterabbey.org.

# 100

# Statue of Charles Dickens, Portsmouth

**First life-sized statue of Dickens in Britain.**

**Contrary to Dickens' wishes, a bronze statue depicting him sitting on a stack of books that he had written was unveiled at Guildhall Square, Portsmouth, during February 2014.**

Dickens objected to posthumous honours and monuments, which was demonstrated when Thomas Fairbairn asked for his assistance in establishing a memorial to Ralph Brooke in Westminster Abbey. Dickens responded on 24 June 1868:

> I am very strongly impelled to comply with any request of yours. But these posthumous honours of committee, subscriptions, and Westminster abbey are so profoundly unsatisfactory in my eyes that – plainly – I would rather have nothing to do with them in any case … I hope you will believe in the possession of mine until I am quietly buried without any memorial but such as I have set up in my lifetime.[260]

Dickens stipulated in his will that there was to be no monument to be erected in his honour. He also added that: 'I rest my claim to the remembrance of my country upon my printed works.'[261] Some Dickens' admirers believe that his wishes were not granted according to his will, but others have argued that his comment had been taken out of context. They argue that he could not possibly have known that his books would remain popular nearly 150 years after his death, and that modern admirers would want to commemorate his life and legacy. Dickens is an important literary figure, whose books defined an era in British history that shone a light upon the plight of the poor, the impoverished and the downtrodden, and contained themes that are relevant today. Although there are statues commemorating Dickens across the world including Philadelphia in the USA, as previously mentioned, and in Sydney, Australia, where two of his sons emigrated, this is the first statue dedicated to him in Britain.

---

260. Forster, Vol. 3, op. cit., p.487.

261. *The Times*, 6 September 1920.

In 2012, Dickens' great-great grandsons, Ian and Gerald Dickens, wearing top hats, walked 75 miles from London to Portsmouth in the footsteps of Nicholas Nickleby and Smike to raise £3,000 for the funding of the statue. It was unveiled 202 years after his birth in Portsmouth, his birthplace, in the presence of approximately forty of his descendants.

The statue of Charles Dickens in Portsmouth. (Courtesy of Tim Spriddell)